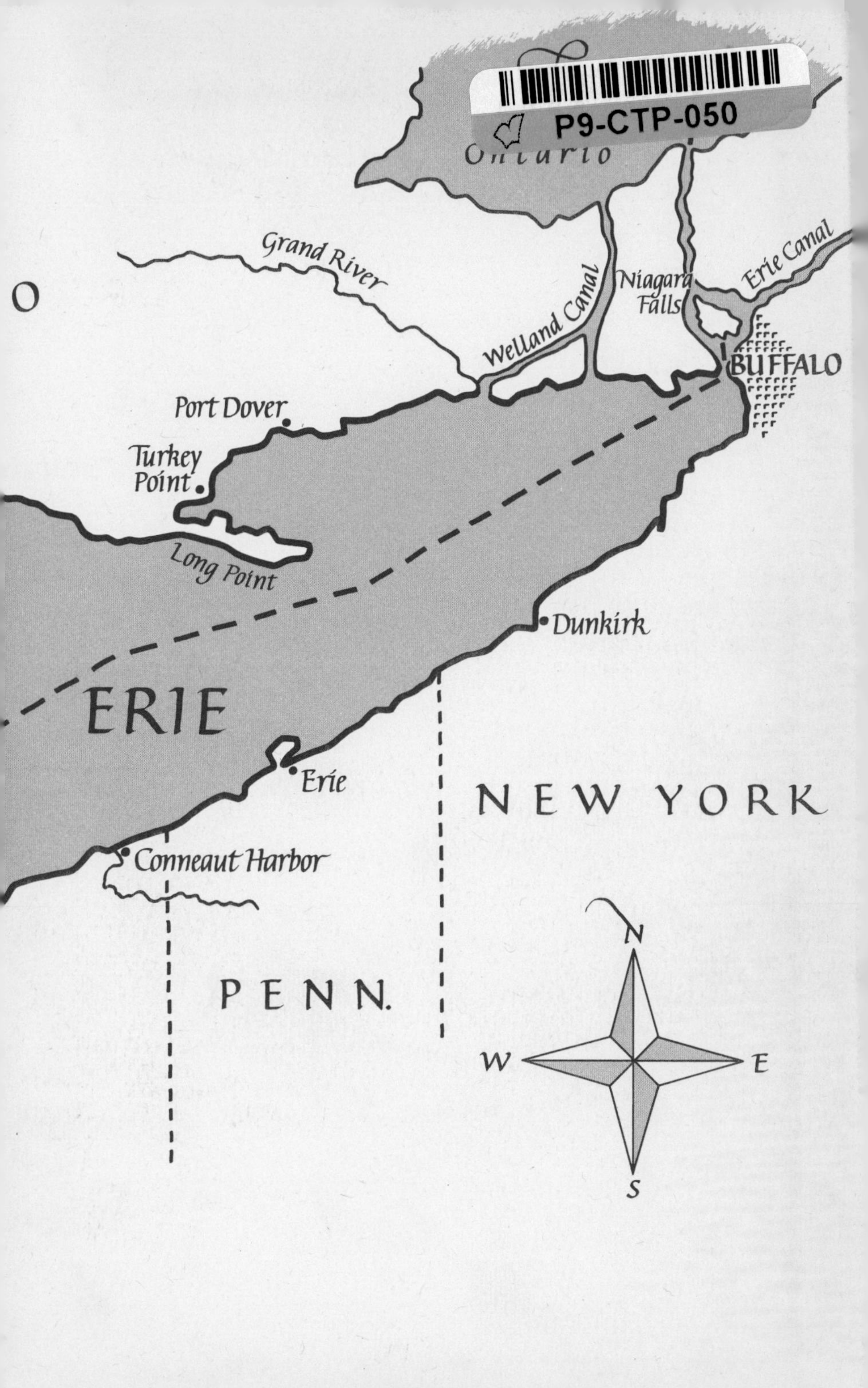

Ontario
O
Grand River
Welland Canal
Niagara Falls
Erie Canal
BUFFALO
Port Dover
Turkey Point
Long Point
Dunkirk
ERIE
Erie
NEW YORK
Conneaut Harbor
PENN.
N
W
E
S

P9-CTP-050

The Silent Syndicate

The Chairman: You have never had any publicity in the past?
Mr. Dalitz: No, sir. —*Kefauver Committee, 1951*

THE SILENT SYNDICATE

by Hank Messick

THE MACMILLAN COMPANY, NEW YORK
COLLIER-MACMILLAN LTD., LONDON

CARNEGIE LIBRARY
LIVINGSTONE COLLEGE
SALISBURY, N. C. 28144

Copyright © 1967 by Hank Messick

All rights reserved. No part of this book may be reproduced or transmitted in any form or by any means, electronic or mechanical, including photocopying, recording or by any information storage and retrieval system, without permission in writing from the Publisher.

Library of Congress Catalog Card Number: 66-17904

First Printing

The Macmillan Company, New York
Collier-Macmillan Canada Ltd., Toronto, Ontario

Printed in the United States of America

364.1
1563

ACKNOWLEDGMENTS

THE OPPORTUNITY TO COLLECT and coordinate the intelligence data upon which this study is based was unique, and I would thank Dr. Paul Ylvisaker and the Ford Foundation for making it possible. Cooperating in the project were Dr. Philip Davidson, president of the University of Louisville, and Colonel David A. McCandless of the Southern Police Institute.

My search for data took me from Pelee Island in Lake Erie to San Juan, from Washington to Los Angeles, from Cleveland to Tucson, from New York to Miami, from Detroit to the Bahamas. There were also stops along the way.

I regret I cannot be too specific about individuals or even agencies, but collectively I would like to thank the intelligence divisions of the Treasury Department. Their help was essential.

My thanks go also to Virgil Peterson of the Chicago Crime Commission and Daniel Sullivan of the Miami Crime Commission. Aid was also provided by the police departments of New York City, Detroit, Tucson, and Los Angeles. The files of the Dayton *Daily News,* the Detroit *Free-Press,* the Philadelphia *Call-Bulletin,* the Cincinnati *Enquirer,* the Kentucky *Post & Times-Star,* the Louisville *Courier-Journal,* the New York *Times,* and the Tucson *Star,* were helpful.

Special thanks are due Forrest Allen of the Cleveland *Press,*

63103

and to his editors. I would also thank Mrs. Barbara Pickett at the Louisville Free Public Library, and Miss Elizabeth Fudold of the Justice Department Library in Washington. The staff in the Diplomatic, Legal, and Fiscal Section of the National Archives was of great assistance. I owe a special debt to Mrs. Jeanette Lee who managed to translate my tape-recorded notes, some of which were not recorded under ideal conditions.

Then finally, I would thank my chief file clerk—who also serves as critic and wife.

HANK MESSICK

May 10, 1966

PROLOGUE

JONAS T. HAGGLOVE shivered as the CG-106 headed out into the open waters of Lake Erie from its home base at the Lorain Coast Guard Station. It was March 6, 1930, and the air was cold.

Three hours of cruising northeast by east brought the boat off Avon Point. Hagglove changed course to east. Soon the Terminal Tower of Cleveland was visible off starboard. Again the commanding officer of the CG-106 shivered. Darkness was approaching. It was getting colder.

He turned to sweep the port side with his glasses—and forgot the cold. Two miles away, almost due north, a boat rode at anchor. What was it doing? Waiting for night, perhaps? Waiting to slip into Cleveland harbor with a cargo of Canadian booze?

The operations of a mysterious rum-running fleet on Lake Erie had become the talk of the Coast Guard. No one knew who commanded it, but several boat seizures on the water and murders on land had left no doubt the operation was large and well-organized. It had to be well financed too, for its protection, on land at least, was so good a landing of illicit booze at the foot of Ninth Street in downtown Cleveland was entirely possible. Was this boat planning to discharge its cargo there? There was an easy way to get the answer.

Hagglove barked an order. His six-man crew obeyed and the CG-106 turned north. Instantly the mysterious boat came to life, went into motion. Within seconds it was headed north by west at full speed.

There could be no doubt the boat was a rummy. The CG-106 gave chase. Minute by minute the distance between the boats shortened. Soon the rummy was within range. The one-pound cannon was prepared for action. Five blanks were fired at short intervals. It was the signal to heave to. The rummy ignored the signal.

"Try a solid shot," ordered Hagglove. A small geyser fifty yards in front of the rummy was an unmistakable signal as the shot fell where aimed. The rummy was not impressed.

"Keep firing," ordered Hagglove. His men obeyed, testing their skill by dropping solid shot fore and aft, port and starboard of the rummy. "Still it continued," Hagglove said later in his official report.

The Coast Guard boat closed to within one-half mile and a new weapon was put into action. Tracer bullets were sent glowing through the darkness, carrying their deadly message across the rummy's bow. This was more spectacular than the results achieved by the cannon, but just as unproductive. Hagglove was becoming exasperated.

"Fire at the boat," he ordered.

Again the fiery path cut through the night. It reached the rummy, then splattered in all directions. The bullets were ricocheting.

The surprised Hagglove ordered a series of short bursts. The bullets glanced in turn off the pilot house, off the cabin, off the sides of the boat. The one-pound was loaded with solid shot and fired. The shot glanced off as well.

"We'll board them," Hagglove decided. "Stand by."

The CG-106 ran alongside the rummy and the searchlight was turned on. At a range of twenty-five feet, the machine gun was fired again. Every bullet hit the pilot house and burned away into the darkness.

During the chase the sea had become rough. Waves were breaking over both boats and ice was forming on the decks. It was almost impossible to stand. Yet the crew of the CG-106 stood and waited, poised to board, as Hagglove tried to close the gap.

The rummy had been unable to outrun its pursuer, but it could swing out of the way to thwart a boarding attempt. It could do more than that.

"Look out," came a shout. "He's going to ram us."

The rummy had pulled out to avoid the CG-106, then suddenly cut back sharply and darted forward. Quickly the CG-106 met the threat by swinging around. Within seconds the boats were abreast of each other and almost touching.

It was the opportunity Hagglove had been seeking, but one look changed his mind. The hatches on the rummy were bolted down. The door to the pilot house was closed and, presumably, bolted from the inside. His men could get aboard all right, but could they get into the boat? And if they couldn't, would they be able to get off? The rummy might head for Canada taking the coastguardmen with him, marooned on an icy deck.

"I wouldn't even be able to fire at the boat with them on board," Hagglove realized.

But the thought generated another one. He ordered Joe Franklin to man the one-pounder. The cannon was trained on the pilot house at point blank range.

"Heave to or we'll sink you," shouted Hagglove.

The rummy ignored the warning. Reluctant to take life, Hagglove tried to bluff. A blank shot was fired. It made no apparent impression. There was no choice. Solid shot was loaded.

"Fire," said the commander of the CG-106.

The shot passed through the pilot house narrowly missing the man at the wheel. The rummy shook from the impact. But it did not stop.

The end seemed inevitable, but when Hagglove ordered another shot it was discovered that only two shells remained. As wild as conditions had become on Lake Erie, anything might happen. The commander decided he'd better save his ammunition for an emergency.

The search for solid shot uncovered a few rounds of armor-piercing ammunition. The crew of the CG-106 prepared to try again. The boat was allowed to drop astern where a square shot at the pilot house could be obtained. Using rifles, the crewmen began firing the armor-piercing bullets into the pilot house.

Suddenly the rummy began to run in circles. The bullets had found a target. A flashlight signaled from the door of the pilot house.

"Cease firing," said Hagglove wearily.

The rummy stopped. After some difficulty because of the rough sea and the ice that now covered every surface exposed to the waves, three coastguardmen were put aboard. Promptly they reported the boat was the *Sambo-G,* and it was loaded with liquor.

The *Sambo-G's* crew consisted of two men. One was wounded and the other drunk. The drunk had a broken arm, but he began to fight. The boarding party restrained him temporarily, then transferred him across the icy decks to the CG-106. Because of his heavily bandaged arm, he could not be handcuffed. He was put in the galley and a member of the crew, John Witkowski, was left to guard him. The moment Witkowski turned his head, the prisoner took the lid-lifter from the stove and tried to brain Witkowski. The coastguardman jumped aside, and the iron lid-lifter hit the stove and broke.

Meanwhile, the rest of the crew were having problems. They attempted to bring the wounded man aboard, but the decks had become too slippery. The wounded man, who said his name was Fred Hentrie of Detroit, asked to be left aboard the *Sambo-G.* Later it was discovered he had two bullet wounds in the small of the back. He had been hit as he stood at the wheel. Asked why he didn't stop sooner, he snarled: "I wouldn't have stopped at all if I hadn't been hit."

Two hours had passed since the sighting of the *Sambo-G,* but the end was not yet. The bilge of the captured rummy was full of gasoline fumes. To start the motor was to risk an explosion. To get the prize back to port it would be necessary to tow it.

A line was passed from boat to boat and the rummy was taken in tow. Hagglove headed for Cleveland harbor, the closest port. He made 200 yards before the tow parted.

The seas were too high for the course to Cleveland. Patiently the coastguardmen ran out another line, brought their boat close to the drifting *Sambo-G* and tossed the line aboard. The new course was south by west, and the speed was moderate. By running with the seas, it was possible to arrive off Avon Point some three hours later, and there to change course for Lorain. The voyage ended at 1:45 A.M. Hentrie was immediately taken to a hospital.

Examination revealed the *Sambo-G* was a sixty-five-foot tug with a fourteen-foot beam. Armor plate one-fourth of an inch thick covered the pilot house, the engine room, the gasoline tanks. The boat was equipped with a 300-horsepower motor. Its cargo consisted of 540 cases of Peter Pan Canadian whiskey and 1,000 cases of Canadian ale and beer.

This answered some of the questions but not all. Years passed before it was learned that the *Sambo-G* was the pride of the rum-runners' fleet. It had been built to order in Canada and had made only one "pass" before being captured. The armor had been designed to protect the boat from hijackers—generally speaking a worse menace on land and sea than law-enforcement agents.

But the crew of the CG-106 had more immediate things to think about. They learned that after their prize was taken to Cleveland for safekeeping, the cargo was stolen. Four coastguardmen were ultimately fired. The booze, none the worse for the short detour, went on to its original destination.

The crew could also ponder the fate of Hentrie, their wounded prisoner. After two bullets were cut from his back at St. Joseph Hospital in Lorain, his recovery was swifter than expected.

There were plans to question him about his employers, but Hentrie didn't wait. By March 13 he felt well enough to make an exit through the hospital window.

Investigation disclosed that while the prisoner was performing rope tricks with a twisted sheet, the man assigned to guard him was enjoying a late snack down the hall. A friendly nurse had arranged things. Investigators also learned that a car had been waiting on the street outside the hospital, its motor running. Hentrie, still unquestioned, got into the car and vanished.

The crew might well guess that powerful forces were silently at work behind the scenes. That seemed obvious. But what it couldn't know was that while the *Sambo-G* had made its last voyage as a rummy, the Cleveland Syndicate which owned it was just finishing its shakedown cruise.

More than thirty-five years later, the syndicate was still sailing smoothly—and silently—along. But the voyage had not been uneventful.

CHAPTER ONE

We are all pots and our bottoms are all sooty.
Mark Hanna

THE ROAD to Cleveland for Samuel A. "Sambo" Tucker began in Central Europe in 1348. The Black Death swept eastward across the Continent, killing millions and driving the survivors almost insane with fear. A scapegoat was wanted, and, as usual, one was found in the Jews.

Faster than the plague swept the rumor—the Jews had poisoned the wells. The population rose in fury and the Jews fled eastward for their lives. They found sanctuary in Poland where, centuries before, others of their faith had found safety from persecutions arising out of the religious hysteria that inspired the Crusades.

Milton Steinberg in *The Making of the Modern Jew* noted that "so large was the migration that even today almost half of the fifteen or sixteen million Jews of the world live in Eastern Europe, and the vast majority of American Jews are of East European descent."

"Thus it comes to pass," continued Steinberg, "that Jews in Magyar Hungary, Latin Roumania, and Slavic Russia or Poland generally carry distinctly Teutonic family names. This is the reason they speak Yiddish, a dialect of old German corrupted by Hebrew and the idioms of the land of their residence."

Tucker's ancestors were welcomed in Poland by Casimir the Great, busy trying to build a nation. He gave them "the right of being judged according to their own laws." Rumor had it that Casimir was influenced by a Jewish mistress, the daughter of a tailor. Estherka lived in the royal palace and bore the king four children. The two daughters were brought up in the Jewish religion, the two sons were educated as Christians.

The position of Jews who moved on into Lithuania was even more favorable. A Jewish historian, S. M. Dubnow, has noted that "medieval culture had not yet taken hold of the inhabitants of the wooded banks of the Nieman, and the Jews were able to settle there without having to face violence and persecution."

In 1386, a royal marriage made Lithuania part of Poland, and a degree of relative stability was achieved. Slightly more than four centuries passed before the Partition. In three bites, Poland was devoured by its more powerful neighbors and by 1795 many hundreds of thousands of Jews found themselves residents of Russia. Among them were the ancestors of Tucker and such individuals as Maier Suchowljansky who, as Meyer Lansky, was to become an overlord of the Eastern Syndicate and a business associate of Tucker in some joint ventures.

A country which a generation before had ordered all Jews expelled "as enemies of Christ," now wondered what to do with those it had acquired by conquest. The system known as "the Pale of Settlement" was devised. Jews were confined by law to rural areas along the frontier. They were not permitted to enter the interior of Russia—to do so was to go "beyond the Pale."

The grandfathers of Tucker, of Lansky, of Moe Dalitz and Louis Buchalter were dealt an economic blow in 1807 by Alexander I. In a decree effective January 1, 1807, he ordered that "no one among the Jews in any village or hamlet shall be permitted to hold any leases on land, to keep taverns, saloons, or inns, whether under his own name or under a strange name, or to sell wine in them, or even to live in them under any pretext whatever, except when passing through."

Dubnow noted that this order "eliminated from the economic life of the Jew an occupation which, though far from distinguished, had yet afforded a livelihood to almost one-half of the whole Jewish population of Russia."

The keeping of inns, the selling of liquor had been the one occupation permitted Jews. Now they were to be restricted to agriculture. But before the decree could be fully enforced, Napoleon marched on Moscow and Alexander found himself occupied with other matters.

In the decades that followed, as "good" Russian rulers were followed by crazy ones, the Jew's fortunes waxed and waned. It was an old story, of course, and over the centuries he had learned the tricks of survival. He had learned the value of wealth very early. As Steinberg put it:

> Other groups during the Middle Ages might find wealth desirable. It was not a condition for their being. Only with Jews was money indispensable for survival, only to them was ready cash as necessary as food or air. For, when the monarch called, there must be gold forthcoming. If the noble threatened, there must be a handsome gift. Even when the Mob growled, without silver there would be no way of bribing public officials to extend protection. Money then was a prime prerequisite in Jewish life. Without it, the Jew was defenseless. . . .

And Russia in the nineteenth century was just as backward, just as greedy, just as corrupt as a western European nation in the Middle Ages. The grandparents of Tucker and Louis Rothkopf had every opportunity to learn the superiority of the bribe to the bullet—and it was a lesson they handed on.

Conditions went from worse to terrible with the accession to the throne in 1881 of Alexander III. Aware that the great mass of the Russian people lived in misery, unable or unwilling to do anything constructive to correct conditions but needing as always a scapegoat to blame, the government turned on the Jews with renewed vigor. And, as sometimes happens when a majority is given official encouragement, many individual Russians sought diversion from their woes by persecuting the minority. The humblest serf could feel superior to a Jew—the untouchable caste of Russia.

Even a secret organization, a Ku Klux Klan of the steppes, came into being. Called "The Sacred League," it had as its official objective the defense of the Tsar, but in actual practice it seemed more concerned with pogroms against the Jews.

And thus it was that the final trek in the long road to Cleveland began. Thousands upon thousands of Jews, convinced at last that life in Russia was impossible, resumed the ancient quest for a promised land. More than 8,000 came to the United States in 1881, more than 17,000 in 1882. By 1889, the yearly total had reached 31,889.

Two new restrictions speeded the exodus. Russia imposed a severe fine for evasion of military service, and, at the same time denied to most Jews the right to an education.

Traditionally, Jews had not been eager to fight for nations that only, at best, tolerated them, and this reluctance was not lessened by policy which barred them from officer rank. But the Jew had always sought an education—it was essential to his identity as an individual and as a Jew.

America offered free schooling without compulsory military service. In 1891, more than 100,000 Jews came to take advantage of it. The accession of Nicholas II to the throne in 1894, brought new acts of terror and swelled the flood of emigrants. Persecution reached new extremes—as did conscription—during the Russo-Japanese War, and more than 125,000 additional Jews fled to the United States.

The parents of Samuel Tucker came during that period, bringing with them their son, born July 11, 1897, in that part of Russia known before and later as Lithuania. On October 18, 1912, Louis Tucker took the oath of allegiance and he, his wife Jennie and their children became citizens of the United States of America.

More than a million Russian Jews in that period did the same thing. The great majority struggled through the early period of adjustment and achieved respectability through legitimate channels. A small minority were forced to watch their children take short cuts to reach the same objective.

New York was for the Russian Jew, as for refugees from other nations, the immediate goal in the United States. But there were other ports of debarkation. Moe Dalitz' parents got off the boat at Boston, and it was there the "first among equals" of the

Cleveland Syndicate was born on December 24, 1899. The parents moved on to Michigan. Moe was a grown man before he reached Cleveland.

Many families headed for Cleveland immediately. It was there on September 3, 1903, that Louis Rothkopf was born. It was there on September 19, 1896, Morris Kleinman was born.

The city at the mouth of the Cuyahoga River was a magnet for people of many nationalities. They came in waves, each settling in a slum area known loosely as the Woodland district and moving out to better areas as they could afford it—the Jews, the Italians, and the Negroes.

Wellington G. Fordyce, writing in the *Quarterly* of the Ohio State Archaeological and Historical Society, commented in 1936 on the results:

> In 1917, over one-half of the children in the public schools spoke a language other than English. In 1923, only 35.4% of the children in the public schools were of unmixed white American parentage. In 1924, Cleveland had 100,000 unnaturalized aliens which represented 50% of the foreign-born residents of voting age. In 1923, Cleveland had the eighth largest Jewish population of any city in the world and stood fourth in the United States.

In 1940, it was found that the foreign-born in Cuyahoga County (Cleveland) were 222,978, out of a total population of 1,217,250. F. Leslie Speir, in a history of Cleveland prepared for the Cleveland public schools, said there were 80,000 Jews in the city in 1940, most of them descendants of Russian immigrants.

As with other immigrants in other cities, the parents of Tucker, Kleinman, and Rothkopf had to struggle to adjust to not only a new land but a new way of life. True, as Fordyce noted, the "anti-Semitic feeling of old Russia" was strong in Cleveland—but hostility was so familiar as to be almost welcome. It was the new freedom that had to be tested before it could be trusted.

Life in Russia, however terrifying, had at least been organized. There were rules, restrictions, and authorities to enforce an autocratic will. In America, a citizen was supposed to make his own way. The children of some immigrants accepted the challenge joyously—and became wealthy. The more cautious parents sought guidance from a "boss."

Newspapers quoted a Russian immigrant of the period who, when asked about the American form of government, replied: "Mark Hanna is king."

As boss of Cleveland and as maker of Presidents, Mark Hanna not only helped the newly arrived immigrant, but, by introducing the concept of the businessman-in-politics, he smoothed the path to prosperity for their children. The Cleveland Syndicate would owe much to him.

2.

That Russian immigrant might have been vague about the political structure of his new country, but he was aware of the economic realities. In June, 1896, according to William Allen White, 8,000 men in Cleveland were on Hanna's payroll—"on the docks, and in the mines, and at furnaces, and at desks, and on street cars."

Hanna had as little consideration for people en masse as Ivan the Terrible. As White put it, "Hanna believed in every man for himself and the devil take the hindermost. Little social altruism tinged the simplicity of his creed. To him failures in life were failures. He did not mince matters, nor go into heredity nor environment in locating the blame for their condition."

Members of the Cleveland Syndicate were to adopt a similar pragmatic approach to life. At an impressionable age they were but following an old American custom of emulating the local hero. To the children of Russian immigrants, Hanna was more real than Washington or Lincoln.

Born September 24, 1837, at New Lisbon, Ohio, Hanna came to Cleveland with his parents in 1852. Ironically, for a man who was to champion the cause of Big Business, he failed in his first venture. The grocery store left to him by his father went bankrupt, and the young man was forced to turn to his father-in-law for help.

Daniel P. Rhodes, a coal and iron merchant considered one of Cleveland's most successful businessmen, had opposed the marriage of his daughter to Hanna. But what Hanna wanted, Hanna got. And with his foot in the door of a successful enterprise, he soon took over from his father-in-law and became known as "the Lord of the Great Lakes."

As Matthew Josephson noted in *The Politicos,* Hanna's wealth was not pyramided upon a single conquered industry. He was a great merchant, whose fleets transported every year an increasing tonnage of coal and iron ore along the shores of the Great Lakes. He was president of a large bank, and thus on intimate terms with Middle Western capitalists. His street railways led him to give strict regard to local politics. His opera house made him welcome in the cultural circles of the city.

Like the European Jew of the Middle Ages, Hanna wanted money. But money was not needed to buy security. As Josephson put it:

"He wanted power, and only money was the symbol of power in his world . . . 'instinct' told him that the easy way to make money was through the seizure, and protection by law, of natural resources, railways, public utility corporations. Law-made wealth was easy and sure."

The children of immigrants who called Hanna "King" were to find other easy ways to wealth in which "protection by law" was equally essential.

In quest of power, Hanna created "the businessman in politics," according to White. "In 1880 he learned that politics, properly controlled, prospered every business that he touched. So he set out to make a brand of politics as profitable as his mines, his ships, his railways, and his banks."

Led by Hanna, businessmen for the first time moved to control the machinery of national politics, and Hanna selected William McKinley as the man he would push upward through Ohio politics into the White House.

The problem was not only to make McKinley a success, but to be able to control him. A businessman had to be sure of a return on his investment. Opportunity came during McKinley's first term as Governor. The future President had piled up a heavy load of debts. He was seriously considering a return to private law practice as the only way of paying them. But Hanna came to the rescue. Calling upon a group of wealthy men, such as Andrew Carnegie, Henry Frick, Charles Taft, and John Hay, Hanna formed a fund to which all subscribed. The necessary $130,000 was raised, the governor's debts were paid, his career restored. Hanna and his friends had saved a valuable freighter from shipwreck. Now they had firm control of the pilot house.

William Allen White, that old newspaperman and sometimes reluctant Republican, noted that out of the principles and practices of the political machine Hanna built, "the Ohio Gang grew." It was the Ohio Gang, headed by Harry Daugherty, which put Warren G. Harding in the White House, and, in a few short months almost stole the country blind. The coup made inevitable the failure of the "Noble Experiment" that was Prohibition, and enabled some first-generation Americans to form the Cleveland Syndicate.

Daugherty was given a personal lesson in corrupt politics in 1897. It came after Hanna had installed McKinley in the White House and, by pulling some strings, got himself appointed to the United States Senate to fill a vacancy he had created. But next year it was necessary to be elected if he was to keep his seat. In those days state legislatures elected United States Senators so Hanna went back to Ohio to arrange it.

Ralph G. Martin in *The Bosses* has described the arrangements:

> Some state legislators were found intoxicated, some drugged, some got threats of assassination and asked for bodyguards, some were put under lock and key by their candidates to keep them away from the persuasion of the opposition to switch their votes. One Hanna legislator was kidnapped and locked in the opposition headquarters until he was recaptured

by Hanna's men and locked in his room. Armed guards were everywhere.

Hanna won, of course, but the stink reached Washington. The Senate launched an investigation when a state representative said he was given a $1,750 bribe to vote for Hanna. There was plenty of evidence to back up the charge, for the telephone line to Hanna's hotel suite had been tapped and various conversations overheard.

Among the witnesses called was Daugherty. A quarter of a century later his conduct as Attorney General was to be the subject of a Senate investigation. But, in 1898, he refused to answer most of the questions about Hanna on the grounds to do so would be self-incrimination. And—since Hanna was in reality a "national boss" of the party in power—the charges against him were dismissed on grounds of insufficient evidence.

Six years later Hanna was re-elected. He personally managed the campaign which swept his state ticket to victory with him. Elected Lieutenant-Governor on Hanna's ticket was Warren Gamaliel Harding, at Daugherty's prodding taking his first step toward the White House.

Hanna might have been there ahead of Harding had not typhoid fever intervened. Following the assassination of McKinley, a Hanna-for-President boom was started by men who shared Hanna's distaste for "that damned cowboy," Theodore Roosevelt. But Hanna became ill and died on February 15, 1904.

The "King" was dead, but his principles remained to guide other men in search of money and power.

3.

Back when Mark Hanna was fighting Reform Mayor Tom Johnson for control of Cleveland's streetcar system, he found it necessary to have editorial backing. Newspapermen being what they were, Hanna decided he'd better have his own newspaper if he was to dictate editorial policy. So he got two—the *Leader*, a morning paper, and the afternoon *News*.

Following Hanna's death, the newspapers were managed by a son, Daniel R. Hanna, Sr. Competition developed between the *News* and the *Leader* on the one side, and the Cleveland *Plain Dealer* and the *Press* on the other. Hanna acted in the family tradition. He brought Arthur B. "Mickey" McBride from Chicago in 1913 to be head of the *News'* circulation department.

McBride was twenty-seven years old, but he had made a name for himself in Chicago circulation wars. His problem in Cleveland was basically simple. As he later told the Kefauver Committee: "They were chasing our boys [newsboys] off the corners." To stop this chasing, McBride recruited a group of toughs who were later to prove their quality as members of the Mayfield Road Mob.

It was the Mayfield Road Mob which became the Mafia division of the Cleveland Syndicate. Various of its members were junior partners in syndicate ventures ranging from rum-running to steel companies. Most of them were youths when McBride assembled them. Upon graduation from his school, they were ready for Prohibition's opportunities.

The Italians followed the Jews, settling in the Woodland district even as the Jews had done. But as economic conditions improved they too began moving toward the suburbs.

Alfred "Big Al" Polizzi, who was brought from Sicily when he was nine years old, lived in the Woodland district. His father was a blacksmith. When Polizzi went to work for Mickey McBride, he sold newspapers on the corner of Ninth and Woodland. Later, after many Italians moved to an area centering around Mayfield Road from East 119 to East 125, Polizzi was recognized as head of the Mayfield Road Mob.

The exodus from the Woodland district is shown in figures prepared by the Cleveland Metropolitan Housing Authority. In 1910, according to the study, there were 10,688 Italians in Cleveland, of whom 211 or 2 per cent lived in the Woodland district. By 1920 the total had reached 18,398, of which 2,736, or 14.9 per cent, lived in the district. By 1930, however, only

9.6 per cent of the 23,526 Italians in Cleveland lived in the Woodland district.

Actually, the district was a melting pot. Many Negroes, seeking better economic conditions than they had found in the South, lived there, as well as some of the less-prosperous Jews who had been unable to follow their neighbors to 105 Street north of Superior Avenue. The Housing Authority's study showed that of 998 murders in Cleveland from 1918 to 1930, 213 occurred in the Woodland district. Of 373 houses of prostitution found in eight undercover surveys, 98, or 26 per cent, were in this district.

The "Sugar War" of the Prohibition era was responsible, as will be seen, for much of the violence in the area. But it was there in 1913 McBride drew his recruits and formed some lasting associations. Polizzi, for example, was later to team with McBride to build much of Coral Gables, Florida.

Fred Angersola, a lifeguard with Polizzi at Luna Park in 1917, was another future member of the Mayfield Road Mob trained by McBride. He became a delivery man, a tough assignment in a circulation war. His brother John, who was to rank high in the syndicate, was working as a building cleaner when he met McBride in 1918. McBride was so impressed, he said, he retained the youth to clean for him.

The two Angersolas, and a third brother, George, called themselves "King" by the time they invested their bootleg profits in Miami Beach real estate.

Another man who was to become important to the syndicate was Morris "Mushy" Wexler. He worked for McBride first as a newsboy and later as the driver of a wagon. When he quit the newspaper business, he went into a related field—the wire service. With his brother-in-law, Sam "Gameboy" Miller, he developed Empire News which became the Ohio division of the Cleveland-based Continental Press. A co-owner of Continental was Mickey McBride.

Gameboy Miller soon left the wire service to Mushy and went

on to become a "casino troubleshooter" for the Cleveland Syndicate. His assignments ranged from the Lookout House near Covington, Kentucky, to the Island Club at Miami Beach. Wexler was also to venture into other fields. He developed the Theatrical Grill on Vincent Street into "the" place to eat in Cleveland. It became the social headquarters of the syndicate. Many were the deals hatched there. The Hollenden Hotel, where the syndicate had many of its business offices, was just next door, and the Ninth-Chester Building housing the wire-service office was a hundred feet away.

McBride, when confronted by the Kefauver Committee with various examples of associations born in those not-so-innocent days before World War I, commented: "Life is just a game of chance."

But coincidence could not explain the fact that McBride became co-owner of Continental Press, that vast organization which took over the job of supplying race information to the nation's bookies when Moses Annenberg went to prison in 1940. His associate in Continental was none other than James Ragen who, back in 1913, had been circulation manager of the Hanna newspaper, the *Leader*.

The long association of Ragen and McBride ended in August, 1946, when Ragen was murdered on the streets of Chicago during the famous "Wire-Service War." McBride emerged as sole owner of Continental Press, and peace returned to the troubled "industry."

A rival circulation manager in 1913 was Thomas Jefferson McGinty. He recruited the strong-arm boys for the Cleveland *Plain Dealer* to oppose the forces of Ragen and McBride. Advising him as attorney for the circulation department was Samuel T. Haas.

McGinty came to represent a third force in the Cleveland underworld—the Irish. The youngest of the eight children of John and Bridget McGinty, Tom was born in Cleveland in 1892. He was to become in time the highest-ranking non-Jewish member of the Cleveland Syndicate, and for that distinction he could give much credit to Sam Haas.

"A fabulous, elusive figure" was the description applied to Haas by a Kefauver Committee investigator. He was to remain the man in the background, the man with a thousand hidden interests and as many connections. Much of his power stemmed from the fact that his father, Adolph Haas, had been chief political lieutenant of Mark Hanna in Cleveland. The son acquired both the necessary knowledge and the necessary contacts.

Haas was indicted in 1916, along with Fred McClure, an ex-circulation manager of the *Plain Dealer*. The case concerned a car-theft ring which allegedly used a place called Chardon Farms to hide the cars. McClure was sent to prison, but the charge against Haas was dismissed on a pretrial motion.

Also suspected in the auto-theft case was E. P. Strong, another mysterious character who was to serve as a front for Haas and for the syndicate in various race track investments. Strong also provided a link between Cleveland and New York gangsters that proved invaluable when the National Syndicate was organized.

So powerful had Haas become by 1919, he was able to beat the rap when indicted on an arson charge growing out of the investigation of affairs at Chardon Farms. Tried in Cleveland Police Court, he was convicted, but the Ohio Supreme Court set aside the one-to-twenty-year sentence and ordered a new trial. Instead, the case was dismissed. A disbarment proceeding was brought and the evidence that had been the basis of the conviction was again presented. The charges were dismissed. Haas, moving to consolidate his position, sued the Cleveland *Press* for libel and collected a $500 judgment.

The day was to come when some would say—but not very loudly—that Haas was the "quiet brain" behind the Cleveland Syndicate. In any case, he was to be associated over the years with many of its members in many of its deals. As it grew powerful, Haas grew prosperous.

Many others who were to play active roles in the years ahead were recruited by McBride, Ragen, and McGinty to fight for the right to sell newspapers that cost a half cent per copy to produce. It was thus—contrary to the legend that gangs and gangsters were products of Prohibition—many of the principals of the syndicate-to-be were assembled and trained in violence years before the National Thirst. Some of the men who would command were still in their teens, but the troops were ready.

Mark Hanna had introduced the concept of the businessman-in-politics. Soon his spiritual heirs would recapture the White House and in their greed make a farce of Prohibition, thus providing the Mob with a bankroll. But, before the Cleveland Syndicate could put down roots, something else would be needed. The concept of the gangster-in-business would have to be established if bootleg profits were not to blow away as easily as they had been obtained.

The Great Depression provided individual investment opportunities around the country. Situations varied, but in general, cash was needed and only the bootlegger had it.

In Cleveland, two brothers who liked to play with railroads helped give the syndicate a chance to dig in.

4.

Back in 1916 when Sam Haas was worrying about automobiles and Mushy Wexler was driving a wagon, the Van Sweringen boys were wondering about a railroad. Oris and Mantis Van Sweringen did not get beyond the eighth grade in school, but by the time Oris, the elder, was twenty-one, they were in the real estate business. They constructed the Cleveland suburb known as Shaker Heights on a plateau east of the city. It was a good location. Later, many of Cleveland's richest gangsters moved there.

But for the suburbs to grow, better transportation links with the downtown area than either wagons or the autos of the era were needed. Railroads—a rapid transit system—seemed the answer. Ready at hand was the Nickel Plate Railroad. Connecting Buffalo and Chicago, it ran right through Shaker Heights.

The boys managed to buy a controlling interest in the Nickel Plate, rebuilt it and began to make money. Real estate became incidental as their ambitions grew. By 1920 they were ready to expand.

The country returned to "normalcy" and the wild boom that gave the twenties its name carried the Van Sweringens along. They were too busy acquiring railroads to have time for courtship or marriage. The House of Morgan, rulers of the financial world, took an interest in them and helped them along with loans and advice.

By 1930, the "twin-bed boys" as some called them—they still shared the same room—bossed a railroad system reaching from the Atlantic to Chicago. They were moving in on the Missouri-Pacific, and a transcontinental system was but a merger away.

A giant holding company, the Allegheny Corporation, had been created to support the tower of blocks the boys had built. When it collapsed, the entire structure came tumbling down.

Tumbling along with the railroads was much of Cleveland's financial world. For, as a "mere detail" of their campaign of conquest, they had rebuilt downtown Cleveland. Subsidiary companies had put millions (at least on paper) into such projects as office buildings, a hotel, and the Terminal Tower. The Tower, hailed as the tallest building in the country west of New York, became a city landmark, but the Van Sweringens didn't even bother to attend the formal dinner celebrating its opening.

To finance their local projects the boys had involved their local companies in debts to local banks. Among the two most deeply involved were the largest, Union Trust and Guardian Trust. Came the crash of 1929, and to save their railroads the brothers had to borrow $40 million from the House of Morgan. All the collateral having market value which had been pledged to the Cleveland banks was released to serve the Morgan loan.

Immediately the two largest banks in Cleveland closed their doors. The Depression came to Cleveland. Within a few months people having any great amount of ready cash had a buyer's market with which to work. They could set their own prices.

The gangster-in-business became a reality as the sons of immigrants whose ancestors fled before the Black Death began to achieve security at last.

CHAPTER TWO

Good God! How the money rolls in!
Jesse W. Smith

IT IS EASY to look back today and say Prohibition was doomed from the beginning. After all, as every gambler, dope peddler, and pimp will tell us, "You can't legislate morals." But, contrary to some legends of the day, National Prohibition did not slip up on anyone. It followed a long, democratic trail. At many places along that trail, public opinion could have established roadblocks. Had there been basic opposition to the idea, roadblocks would have been set up.

One thing is certain, however. After the arrival in Washington early in 1921 of the Ohio Gang, Prohibition was doomed. The sight of the White House bootlegger, Elias H. Mortimer, personally catering to the wants of President Harding was bad enough. But the activity just beneath the surface was worse. The very machinery of government was used to corrupt the laws instead of enforcing them.

Harding, in a gesture to Prohibition forces who were politically powerful if amazingly naïve, appointed an honest Quaker, David Blair, Commissioner of Internal Revenue. But there was delay in confirming the appointment, so Millard West served as acting commissioner. West had been introduced to Harding by Representative John Langley of Kentucky. Within a short time West released 4,000 cases of bonded whiskey to Langley, who sold it for $100,000. In the first scandal of the administration, West and Langley were indicted.

Key to the scandal, as to many of those that followed, was an instrument in writing known as the "Permit for Withdrawal."

It enabled the lucky owner to withdraw from bonded warehouses the whiskey—or alcohol—stored there. Medicinal uses were cited as reasons for withdrawing the whiskey. The alcohol was supposed to be used in the manufacture of everything from antifreeze to hair tonic.

It was the presence in the warehouses of hundreds of thousands of gallons of whiskey and alcohol that gave the Ohio Gang its opportunity. And when it opened the tap, the "inevitable" did happen. The "stuff" on hand was consumed in the first stage. Home-brew was featured in the second stage, but finally the big syndicates got organized and the third stage—rumrunning—began. A fourth stage, the illegal maunfacture of alcohol on a massive scale, was started just before Prohibition ended and continued for years. It continues today as gangsters take advantage of the high tax on legitimate whiskey to produce a cheaper product.

When Blair was finally given the job he had been promised, he acquired as his Prohibition commissioner a member of the Ohio Gang. Harry Daugherty, the new Attorney General of the United States, foisted a protégé named Roy Haynes off on Blair. Among other favorites installed in key spots was William J. Burns, "the world's greatest detective," who became head of the Bureau of Investigation, later better known as the F.B.I. An "unofficial assistant" to Burns, was Jesse W. Smith from Daugherty's home town of Washington Court House.

The unofficial headquarters of many high officials of government became "the Little Green House on K Street." As Frederick Lewis Allen in his *The Lords of Creation* put it:

> Senators, Congressmen and Cabinet members dropped in to have a drink from supplies obligingly furnished by Government officials who diverted confiscated wet goods thither, and to play in the sky-limit poker game. . . . The Ohio Gang traded in liquor withdrawal permits, protection to bootleggers, appointments to office, illegal concessions, immunity from prosecution, pardons, paroles, privileges and general graft. . . . The Little Green House slumbered not nor slept. It was open for business by day and for pleasure mingled with business

by night. Greeks came bearing gifts. Also Italians, Armenians, Jews, Germans, Swedes, and native-born Americans—all the internationale of bootleggery.

One of the men who transacted business with Jess Smith was George Remus who in a few short months won the title, "King of the Bootleggers." Realizing early the potential, Remus sold his law books in Chicago and moved to Cincinnati, Ohio, the geographical center of the distilling industry of Ohio, Kentucky, and Indiana. In a little more than two years he sold $70 million worth of whiskey. In 1924 he told a Senate investigating committee how he did it:

"Well, I would organize drug companies and wholesale drug companies and obtain B permits. That gave you the privilege of withdrawing alcoholic liquors from distilleries or bonded warehouses pursuant to the Volstead law, as it is prescribed. It is, of course, upon those withdrawals (permits) being issued, legally issued, the liquor would be sold. For those institutions [the drug companies] I paid $50,000 to $325,000 for each one of them."

He also found it convenient to buy the distilleries and warehouses better to withdraw liquor in railroad-car lots. Eventually he owned seven distilleries that he could remember, and "possibly more."

Both the essential withdrawal permits and the freedom from federal interference had to be purchased. Remus told the Senate committee that he did business with Jess Smith, meeting him the first time in New York. He paid Smith $50,000 at that first meeting, he testified, and more than $200,000 at later meetings. In addition to the permits, he was to receive "immunity from prosecution and/or conviction." This meant, he explained, that if the worst happened and prosecution could not be avoided, there would be "no ultimate conviction."

Firm in the belief this bargain would be enforced, Remus continued to pay Smith even after he had been convicted. Smith assured him, he said, that "General" Daugherty would arrange to have the charges dismissed on appeal. There would be "no ultimate conviction."

Remus had more than a passing influence. To carry out his operations on such a huge scale, it was also necessary to bribe local officials. He estimated he spent $20 million for "protection." In spending it, he corrupted the officials of the Cincinnati-Newport-Covington area to the extent that, years later, the Cleveland Syndicate was able to move in and set up the largest illegal gambling operation in the country. Not only had the officials been taught to hold out their hands, but the public had come to accept such gestures as natural and normal.

While Remus was rather unique, Abraham Auerbach was rather typical of the operators the Ohio Gang encouraged. With his brother, Louis, Abe Auerbach came to the United States about 1900. They worked as laborers in New York for several years, arriving in Cleveland in 1906. After learning how to use scissors as skillfully as they had used shovels, they opened barber shops in the Woodland district. Hard and honest toil brought rewards. By 1912, Abraham bought a furniture store and Louis began to manufacture hair tonic.

Abraham became, in the words of his attorney, "the patron saint of the Woodland District." He was always willing to sell a newly married couple secondhand furniture on credit. But it was Louis who provided the road to wealth with his well-named Million Dollar Hair Tonic and Love Me, Dearie brand of toilet water. Both contained alcohol.

In September, 1922, the first giant alcohol diversion conspiracy of the Prohibition era broke open. Charged with having withdrawn nearly $1 million worth of alcohol from storage, ostensibly to make hair tonic, and diverting it to bootleggers were Louis and Abraham Auerbach.

The Auerbachs pleaded guilty, and later testified against various high-ranking officials who were implicated in the scandal. Among them were the Attorney General of Ohio, the Ohio prohibition director, and a federal prohibition agent.

While serving time in Atlanta, Abraham decided to learn to write. Eventually, President Calvin Coolidge commuted part of his sentence. Abraham returned to Cleveland where in 1932 he was convicted of murdering Sam and Rose Grossman in their speakeasy. Grossman had ranked second only to "Big Joe" Lonardo during the home-brew phase of Prohibition. A year later Auerbach, at work in the Ohio Penitentiary barber shop, cut his own throat with a razor.

Another man who would become more immediately useful to the syndicate was Jacob Stein. But before that happened, Stein would become a reluctant witness and by his testimony expose the extent of the Ohio Gang's corruption. Stein became involved with that fantastic fraud, Gaston B. Means.

Elmer L. Irey, for many years chief of the Treasury Department's enforcement agencies, has told how Prohibition Commissioner Haynes informed his boss, Blair, that he had found "the greatest agent in the world." But Blair rebelled when Means was named. Blair was from North Carolina, Means' home state. He knew the man.

So did Bureau of Investigation Chief Burns know the man, and he gave him the run of the Justice Department. Back during World War I, Means had worked for Burns' private detective agency. Neither man had illusions about the other.

Jacob Stein, a disbarred New York attorney with a record of liquor-law violations, met Means on November 13, 1922, at the Vanderbilt Hotel in New York. The introduction came after a Bertram Weil presented Stein to Samuel Schmidt of Chicago.

"Mr. Schmidt asked me," Stein said in a sworn statement which is now part of the National Archives, "whether I could possibly get the police connection of New York City who were giving protection to the boats bringing liquor in, and stated that if I could get that connection he had the proper Federal connection."

Schmidt then took him to the hotel where he met Elmer Jarnecke, Means' assistant. After some questions about the police "connection," Jarnecke introduced him to Means who

> stated that I could assure my people that he could provide the Federal protection so that liquor could be brought into New York City. . . .

At that time, I asked Mr. Means who he was and in what capacity he was connected with the Government. He then showed me his badge and also his identification card, and in addition thereto he showed me about seven or eight different letters purporting to be signed by Attorney General Daugherty and by William J. Burns, giving him full authority to take charge of any and all papers in any Federal District Attorney's office and any and all papers in the Prohibition Department and also giving him authority to take those papers, cause an investigation of any cases pending, and present any and all matters that he may deem desirable to the grand jury for indictments. . . .

Stein said he became convinced Means had the power he claimed, and an agreement was reached:

"He told me he knew the police were getting $7.00 per case for every case that was brought in from the three-mile limit, and he wanted in addition thereto $7.00 per case in order to give them Federal protection, and that if the deal was consummated, I was to get for my interest $1.00 per case."

After some discussion "of bringing whiskey up from Savannah, Georgia," the meeting adjourned. Stein quoted Means as saying at the time that his connections in Savannah "were Goldstein & Goldstein." Be that as it may, there is also on record an affidavit from Willie Haar, head of the famous "Haar Ring" of Savannah, which tells of two $5,000 payments made in Savannah to Means. The money was, allegedly, to prevent prosecution for income-tax evasion, growing out of the "Haar Ring's" tremendous profits from rum-running.

Stein next met Means on November 20, 1922, in New York, and was informed, he said, that Means no longer desired the "police connection."

Means said he had been promised [Stein continued] by Mr. William J. Burns that within a day or two thereafter there would be established a department to be known as the Prohibition Unit of the Department of Justice and that he would have full charge of said Department and that he would

> then be in a position to release liquor from any bonded warehouse or distillery in this country, and that he desired me, if possible, to line up for him various distilleries who were desirous of releasing liquor.
>
> He stated that the price for releasing liquor would be $200 per barrel, and that I was to receive my share from the distilleries, or from anybody who desired to release liquor, as this $200 was to be divided in four equal ways: $50 going to William J. Burns; $50 going to the Attorney General; $50 to the Republican Campaign Committee; and $50 was his share. He also stated that the price on case goods would be $20 per case. He stated to me that in removing liquor from these different warehouses or distilleries, that if the parties desired to have the liquor removed by Government trucks, it would cost them $50 per barrel, and Government trucks would deliver the liquor to its permanent destination.

The facts as outlined here by Stein were confirmed, and largely on the basis of Stein's testimony, Means was later convicted. The real question arising is to what degree was Means lying about details when he talked to Stein? That Means was an accomplished liar, there can be no doubt. But there can be no doubt either that Burns made Means a Bureau of Investigation agent, and then, when objections were raised, made him a secret agent paid from funds for which Burns did not have to account. Both Means and Jess Smith had complete freedom within the Justice Department, and both collected from bootleggers and any other crook who wanted to buy privileges. If Means did not always deliver the privileges he promised, his failure to do so was exactly in line with the ethical code then in vogue in Washington from the President on down. Men who did not hesitate to cheat the country would have felt no remorse at cheating other crooks.

Stein testified he did become a field man as proposed by Means, and he arranged deals all about the country. One such involved the distillery at Meadville, Pennsylvania. As Stein told it:

There was to be an alleged violation by the distillery, and Mr. Means, acting in the capacity bestowed upon him by the Department of Justice, was to seize the distillery, remove the gaugers therefrom, and place Department of Justice men in charge. He was then to get a chemical analysis of the whiskey in the distillery which would state that the whiskey was unfit for medicinal purposes and would have to be destroyed. Instead of destroying the whiskey, the whiskey was to be removed and in six months thereafter an order entered—the whiskey was destroyed as per order. He was to receive the sum of $200 per barrel, and as a deposit he, Means, was to receive $60,000 from these bankers who, to the best of my recollection, never paid this money over but did put up the $25,000 deposit with the owners of the Meadville Distillery as evidence of good faith in purchasing the said distillery.

Means and Stein went to Cleveland to make some arrangements and it was there the only instance of Means returning money to a dissatisfied customer was recorded. As Stein put it:

> Mr. Means became intoxicated one evening at the Statler Hotel and returned $5,000 to Mr. Al Levy, whose office is in the Knickerbocker Building at 42nd and Broadway, New York City. The money belonged to Sam Cohen of Cincinnati. This Sam Cohen went to Louisville with Mr. Means and they stopped at the Seelbach Hotel. Mr. Means obtained, I believe, about $15,000 from a party in Louisville whose name I cannot, offhand, recall.

The return of the $5,000, Stein added, came at a party at the Statler. Means extracted sixty-five $1,000 bills from a money belt and counted off five for Levy. The act so impressed Cohen, he took Means to Louisville to find another sucker who more than made up the loss.

The last act Stein performed as Means' field agent, according to his statement, was to take his boss to Pittsburgh and spread the word that 3,000 cases of Overholt whiskey had been seized by the government at Erie, Pennsylvania. Anyone desiring to buy at $55 a case could make arrangements by contacting Means at the Penn Hotel. But they were to select one man to act for all of them and handle the cash.

On March 1, 1923, Stein was scheduled to return to New York to do more advance work. Before he left, in a rare display of trust, "Means told me there was no such thing as the liquor, but that when this man came up there he and Jarnecke would frame a holdup job, and take the said $165,000, which this party was supposed to have on his person."

By March 1, 1923, the temperature had begun to climb in Washington. Steam was beginning to escape through a crack in Teapot Dome. Jess Smith, official collector for the Ohio Gang, had killed himself. Smith had shared a house in Washington with Attorney General Daugherty, and rumors were flying. Under the circumstances, there had to be an end to Means' freewheeling activity. On June 28, 1923, Stein was appointed an official Department of Justice investigator and assigned to investigate Means. His period of employment ran to March 15, 1924, at which time he was told by Hiram C. Todd, special assistant to the Attorney General and an honest man, that "You will be a witness for the government" in the case against Means.

Means was convicted in July, 1924, and went to prison, but both he and Stein were to be heard from again. Stein was to reappear as an important figure in a joint liquor venture of the Eastern and Cleveland syndicates. Means got out of prison in time to write a best seller, *The Strange Death of President Harding.* It was his thesis that Mrs. Harding murdered her husband in a partly successful effort to protect his reputation from the scandals she knew were about to break.

Perhaps a final footnote will serve to sum up the Ohio Gang. According to Samuel Adams' book, *The Incredible Era,* "a damaging financial exposure" was narrowly avoided following Harding's death. "Ungerleider & Company, the Cleveland brokerage house which had established a successful Washington branch," had an account—Adams said—showing President Harding owed them $180,000. "He had been speculating under an 'account' name."

The problem of collecting was referred to Newton D. Baker, former mayor of Cleveland, former Secretary of War under Wilson, and Ungerleider's counsel. A compromise was worked out with Harding's estate and the account settled for $30,000.

Samuel Ungerleider, head of the firm, was also associated with Edward P. Strong, Sam Haas' sponsor in Cleveland. Another who dealt with Ungerleider, according to his testimony, was George Remus of Cincinnati, King of the Bootleggers.

2.

If it could be said the Ohio Gang took over the national government, it was equally true the Cleveland Gang took over the Ohio government at the same time. Harry L. Davis, who had been mayor of Cleveland and would be again, was elected governor in a Republican landslide.

The son of Welsh parents, Davis was born in 1878 in a Cleveland suburb. His father worked in the steel mills of Newburgh, and at the age of thirteen Harry took a job beside him. Home study and night school gave him an education, and he turned to insurance for a career. In 1909 when Mark Hanna's old foe, Mayor Tom Johnson was defeated, Davis was elected city treasurer on the Republican ticket. In 1913 he opposed Democratic Mayor Newton D. Baker, and lost by a narrow margin, but won recognition from fellow Republicans.

By 1915 Davis was ready to try again, this time with the full support of Maurice Maschke, for many years the Republican "boss." It was a bitter campaign, with the European war a decisive factor for many of Cleveland's newly naturalized citizens. Davis won, defeating Baker's handpicked candidate. Baker, meanwhile, had become Woodrow Wilson's Secretary of War.

Two more terms followed the first. Cleveland achieved a reputation as a "safe" city for gangsters and national publicity as such in the "Nicky" Arnstein case.

New York City in 1918 became aware that messenger boys delivering securities to brokerage houses and banks were being slugged and robbed. The securities usually consisted of highly negotiable Liberty Bonds, and the total value of those taken after eighteen months was almost $5 million. Police claimed the robberies were masterminded by one man, and evidence pointed to Arnold Rothstein.

As in so many cases involving the mysterious Rothstein, the situation became confused. The blame was shifted to one Jules W. Arndt Stein, the husband of Broadway comedy star Fanny Brice. She called her husband "Nicky," and reporters heard the last name as one word instead of two, so it was as Nicky Arnstein that the "fall guy" for Rothstein fled New York.

He went to Cleveland where, according to New York officials, "influential politicians in Cleveland were closely connected with confederates of Arnstein in the disposal of upward of $2 million worth of stolen securities."

One of the confederates proved to be E. P. Strong, that associate of Sam Haas. In a deposition taken in federal court in New York, Strong admitted he knew "Cheeks" Ginsberg of Cleveland and had represented Ginsberg in the sale of $25,000 in Liberty Bonds. Police said the bonds were stolen from Richard C. Whitney in New York. Strong also admitted giving money to Mortimer Bernstein, another bond thief.

Arnstein upon reaching Cleveland sent word to New York officials and to Rothstein that he would not surrender unless bond was arranged in advance. Strong said he told Miss Brice —who, in the meantime, made famous the song, "My Man"—that he would put up the $60,000 bail for Nicky if she would keep it quiet.

William J. Fallon, "the Great Mouthpiece" and Rothstein's lawyer, represented Strong at the New York hearing. Later, when Arnstein did surrender, Fallon defended him in the first of two trials. On the second attempt, Arnstein was convicted and sentenced to prison. Most of the bonds were not recovered, but in years to come they turned up in such places as England, Scotland, Canada, and Cuba as payment for bootleg whiskey.

Sam Haas, associate of T. J. McGinty, and later counsel for

the syndicate, was also mentioned in the stolen bonds case. But New York officials reserved most of their ire for their counterparts in Cleveland. The charge was made repeatedly that the search for Arnstein was hampered because of "interference by Cleveland officials."

The national publicity the Arnstein case received did not harm Mayor Davis. Nor did the discovery by his political foes of Executive Order No. 73 do immediate damage. The order provided simply that the city safety director was to be advised in advance of plans by the police vice squad to conduct any raid.

On January 14, 1921, Davis became governor. His major achievement was the creation of a state prohibition enforcement agency. Mention has already been made of the Auerbach case in which state officials were implicated. It was an interesting four years, but toward the end the Harding scandals cast dark shadows and Davis was defeated in a bid for re-election.

Meanwhile, the quality of government Cleveland was receiving on the local level had not improved much. Nor was it to improve for several years. Republican administration or Democratic—it did not seem to matter. Corruption was commonplace. Run-of-the-mill hoodlums supported one party or the other and lost with their candidates. This was not the case with the professionals who were to build a syndicate.

There was no abatement of the syndicate's activities during the mayoral administrations of either Fred Koehler or Ray T. Miller. Koehler, who also served at intervals as sheriff and police chief, left $450,000 in government bonds when he died. It was found in a strongbox. Years later the Kefauver Committee asked Sam Haas why Koehler remembered him in his will with a $5,000 bequest. "He was a very close dear friend of mine, sir," was the reply.

Miller was a more modern type of politician. He worked his way through Notre Dame, where he played football with Knute Rockne. Later, his brother, Don Miller, was to become one of Rockne's fabled "Four Horsemen." Ray was not that good, but he liked action. After college he joined the army, chased Pancho

Villa along the Mexican border, then went to France as a captain. Returning a war hero, he practiced law, entered politics, and after two terms as county prosecutor was elected mayor in 1931. He served one term.

In later years, Miller became a power behind the scenes in the Democratic organization. His brother, the ex-Horseman, became United States Attorney, and the two were politically active during the golden years of the syndicate's expansion.

Miller's defeat in 1933 was at the hands of ex-Governor Davis, back for his fourth term as mayor. He tried for a fifth term and failed. Conditions had become so bad over the years that at last even the patient voters of Cleveland rebelled. They elected Harold H. Burton—later to become an associate justice of the Supreme Court—on a reform ticket in 1935.

Mayor Burton soon brought in Eliot Ness as city safety commissioner and ordered him to clean up Cleveland. Ness had gained some specialized knowledge of crime as an Alcohol Tax Unit agent of the Treasury Department in such cities as Chicago and Cleveland. If any man could do the job it would seem to be Ness.

Ness learned, however, that too much time had elapsed. The Cleveland Syndicate had put down roots. And, unlike "Scarface Al" Capone, its leaders were unknown. Ness was to vent his energy upon the Mayfield Road Mob while, somewhere in the background, the real bosses smiled and went silently about their business.

CHAPTER THREE

Business in sugar is not all it is cracked up to be.
Angelo Porello

THE CLUES were a trail of blood across the snow, a kernel of corn, and two bodies in a ditch.

It was 1 A.M., January 29, 1920. Fourteen days after the Volstead Act to enforce Prohibition became effective, Cleveland had its first bootleg murder. It was to remain a mystery as did most of the ones that followed.

Mr. and Mrs. Sherman Ransopher were returning from a Salvation Army meeting. They walked along unpaved Bader Avenue in the Brooklyn district. Snow on the road reflected enough light to make visible the foot of a man. It was sticking out of a ditch. A closer look disclosed that three bodies were in the ditch.

Only two remained when Ransopher returned to the scene with help. But police found a bloody trail leading down that lonely road and ending in a well-traveled highway. They also found a hat with a kernel of corn stuck to the crown. The "glue" was dried blood.

The investigation revealed that the first two victims were from Buffalo. They had come to Cleveland to enter the liquor business and had been warned to leave. One of the dead men, it developed, had a brother who had heeded a warning to go back to Buffalo. The warning came, he said, from men who carried revolvers and badges.

Despite the kernel of corn, the real struggle for control of the corn liquor business did not begin until about 1925. As elsewhere, the first pangs of thirst were satisfied by the liquor already in stock. The whiskey was diverted to bootleggers, and then the alcohol. In Cleveland, Abraham and Louis Auerbach were quite helpful. Southward in Cincinnati was George Remus, king of them all.

In those first years of Prohibition the man considered Cleveland's most powerful bootlegger was that ex-circulation manager of the *Plain Dealer,* Thomas Jefferson McGinty. McGinty's, at 2077 West 25 Street had an apparently inexhaustible supply of good liquor, and McGinty was in the wholesale as well as the retail end of the business.

McGinty had tried professional boxing as a career before bootlegging, a fact which gave him something in common with Morris Kleinman, later a top man in the syndicate. It was the young Irishman's skill with his fists which qualified him to be a newspaper "circulator." But, as McGinty liked to tell it, one day he was flat on his back in the ring, knocked there by "Battling" Schultz. His manager, Jimmy Dunn, was in a ringside seat.

"There sat Jim in solid comfort," McGinty said, "yelling 'Get up, get up.' And there I lay, a bruised and bleeding mess. 'Well,' I says to myself, 'I'll get up if I live, but it'll be as manager.'"

With help from his friends who sponsored a benefit which raised $5,000, McGinty became, instead, a fight promoter. Even after he turned bootlegger, he continued to promote sports events. The "Tom McGinty Derby Special Train" to Louisville was a regular event each May. Through his association with Haas and Strong, McGinty became a racetrack owner and can be credited with later bringing the syndicate into that field.

But in 1924, United States Attorney A. E. Bernstein was calling McGinty the "King of Ohio Bootleggers." Raids on his joint were ineffective. McGinty seemed immune to surprise. There were those who said that Executive Order No. 73 had something to do with it, as far as police were concerned. But the reaction to the Ohio Gang had begun in Washington—a brief period of housecleaning—and the "federal heat" was on.

Two undercover agents were assigned to the case. One was

Fred Rickey, brother of Branch Rickey, manager of the St. Louis Cardinals. Trading on McGinty's interest in sports, Rickey won his confidence and took the evidence to a federal grand jury. McGinty and ten associates, including his brother and his brother-in-law, were indicted and convicted. McGinty was sent to the federal penitentiary at Atlanta for eighteen months.

The brother-in-law, James Gaul, was sent to the workhouse instead of the penitentiary so his pension as a retired Cleveland fireman would not be endangered. Reporters noted that when Joe McGinty arrived at the prison he gazed at the imposing white marble and commented:

"It looks like the new library back home."

Tom McGinty continued to operate his place on 25 Street after his release from prison. Eliot Ness tried to raid it ten years later. But McGinty was aware the first phase of the bootleg era had ended. The warehouses had become depleted. Permits for withdrawal had become scarce. There was no longer a supply of "good liquor" to be had. McGinty turned to gambling, and to race tracks. Eventually he would ally himself with the syndicate and get back into the liquor business, but meanwhile, a new situation had developed. The second phase of Prohibition had begun.

Demand created a new supply, and new kinds of opportunities. At first there was little organization, little pressure. Development was along community lines, and communities were based on such things as religion and race. In each community a leader arose to dominate the economy and eventually to control it. The serfs—retail sellers, drivers and runners, distillers and brewers—needed his help in arranging protection from police, from other competitors. They needed the credit he could supply. The leaders were always men of some business ability and much natural ferocity. They had to be—to be leaders. It was sometimes necessary to fight to retain authority in a given area or, if opportunity offered, to expand at the expense of someone else.

The new industry was, of course, based upon home manufacture. The volume depended not upon a few giant breweries or distilleries, but on thousands of small ones. This had the advantages of decentralization—a raid or a number of raids couldn't cripple the business—and it also had the disadvantages. One of these, the absence of quality control, was to be a big reason for the growth of the smuggling industry and, ultimately, for Repeal. Too many people died drinking rotgut. There was no way to regulate the thousands of individuals operating their own stills, no way to set standards. Nor is there any record that anyone attempted to do so.

As the demand for the product grew, new pressures appeared. Superbarons began to develop their power based on their ability to supply the raw materials of the industry in the volume required. Inevitably, since this proved to be the key to the industry, battles for control developed on this higher level too. Since the principal ingredient needed to make corn liquor was corn sugar, the struggle became known as the "Sugar War."

John and "Big Joe" Lonardo were long-time merchants with offices at Woodland and East Ninth Streets in what was called the "commission house district."

The district was a slum area containing thousands of small, drab houses, many without electricity or plumbing, some little more than open sheds. It was a place where newly arrived immigrants huddled, most of them remembering warmer climates in Italy or Sicily. When houses were needed for the distilling of corn liquor, the cooperation of these frightened people was easily obtained. Usually, they were supplied with cheap, homemade stills, and with the raw materials needed. For their work, and for the addition of a still to an already crowded household, they received a small commission on the sale of their products. Thus the name, "commission house."

But it was many months before the name was applied. Because the neighborhood was so poor, because its people lived with the natural fear of immigrants plus the all too familiar fear of the Mafia, because of the very decentralization of the process, little was known about what went on. Individually, the stills were too small to bother with. Collectively, they produced a vast amount of corn liquor.

The Lonardos were born in Sicily, but they came to Cleveland early. "Big Joe," who weighed nearly 300 pounds, arrived shortly after 1900. Liking what he saw, he sent for John. Later a third brother, Frank, made the trip and was welcomed into the growing business. After Prohibition the principal commodity they handled was corn sugar. Prior to 1925, they worked for the nickel trade, but even this required the cooperation of several hundred of their countrymen. Joe, the pioneer, was the "don." In a community which had known a long series of "black hand" murders even before Prohibition, a don was a powerful individual.

No one ever estimated the number of stills "Big Joe" controlled, but Ralph Kelly, writing in the *Plain Dealer* in 1933, called it "enormous."

The Lonardos' rise to power was not without incident. Strange things happened to competitors, many of them deadly things. Louis Nobile, for example, moved away from the Lonardo territory to 2681 East 51 Street. Word was he left owing money. In his new location he went into the corn sugar business in a small way. This was not considered quite ethical for a debtor. A short time later, on June 17, 1926, his body was found in a vacant lot where it had been flung from a passing car. It was obvious someone wanted him found—an anonymous telephone call told police where to look.

About that same period Angelo "Chink" Bottaro sold a lot of corn sugar. This seemed interesting in view of the fact that a short time before seventy 100-pound bags of sugar had been stolen from a warehouse on Woodland Avenue. Angelo got a call. Would he like to look at some vacant houses with a view of installing a still in one of them? Flushed with the chance to become a big operator, Bottaro agreed. He drove away with a stranger. Later the car was found parked in front of a vacant house. Angelo was still in it but in his head were several bullets.

Then there was Luigi Colafato. At age thirty-five he was on his way to becoming a sugar baron. He bought a store at Woodland and East Twenty-second Street, bought a diamond ring, a diamond stickpin, and two cars. A short time later he was taken for a ride at midnight. His body was dropped in Shaker Heights, a Cleveland suburb.

There were many other murders along the way, but, undeterred, the Lonardo brothers waxed prosperous. Big Joe moved his family to Shaker Heights, following the example set by earlier immigrants. To display his success, "Big Joe" visited the old folks back home in Sicily. This was a mistake. While he was living it up in the town of Licati, competitors back in Cleveland grew bold and started grabbing. Perhaps they wanted a home in Shaker Heights or a trip to Sicily. It is not always a good idea to set a precedent.

When the home-manufacturing industry really got going in 1925, Cleveland was ninth of American cities in the number of murders. Before Prohibition ended, it was tied for third.

Despite the killings that accompanied the rise of the Lonardos, one set of competitors was not eliminated. In the Woodland district was a group of stills controlled by the seven Porello brothers. They were ambitious and unscrupulous too, but they were also cautious. They waited for an opportunity. A so-called bootleg joke provided it.

Victims of the "joke" were self-styled "tough guys from the East"—Jack Brownstein and Ernest Yorkell. They arrived in Cleveland in September, 1927, a Cleveland worried about a rumor that Prohibition was about to be modified. Such an event could ruin business so tempers were short. Something was needed to relax tension.

Brownstein was the sharp dresser, an alleged jewelry salesman from Philadelphia. Yorkell, who looked like a hood, had once traveled in a side show with the billing of "Young Hercules." For Cleveland he had prepared a new act. He looked tough while Brownstein talked tough: "Pay up or we'll bump you off." The extortion racket. It had worked in Buffalo and Pittsburgh, but the hoods of Cleveland found it funny.

The team started at the top and worked their way down. One of the first persons they approached was Thomas J. McGinty. When the victim didn't pay after a few threats, the boys ended up begging for a handout. McGinty passed the word and everyone agreed it was just the tonic needed for the times.

In desperation the boys decided to try once more. They told a friendly waitress they were going to get a lot of money "or we're not coming back." They didn't come back. Their bodies were found tied with clothesline in Amber Park. Each had been shot many times in the head and body as if someone had taken his time with the task and enjoyed every minute of it.

It was all very amusing, but the biggest joke was yet to come. Word spread in some circles that the men had been killed because they were a threat to a local beer baron. Even the police laughed at that.

The police did more than laugh. They rounded up some suspects, and in so doing, they gave the Porello boys their opportunity. For one of the suspects was Charles Colletti, a bodyguard for the Lonardos. Another "hired companion," as the newspapers put it, of the Lonardos was also jailed at the same time.

On the night of October 13, 1927, the Lonardos received a telephone invitation. They were asked to come over to play some cards and discuss mutual problems. The Lonardos had not been seen without bodyguards for years, but the opportunity to perhaps buy out the Porello clan seemed too good to pass up. Big Joe and John went to the barbershop of Ottavio Porello at 10902 Woodland Avenue, and through it to a cardroom in the rear.

No one was quite sure of the sequence of ensuing events. But shortly after 8:30 P.M. Big Joe fell to the floor. Two men, one on each side, had fired seven bullets into his body.

John Lonardo was hit too, in the left leg and in the stomach. But he was younger than his brother and not as fat. He chased one of the killers through the barbershop and onto Woodland Avenue. In front of the butchershop next door, the killer halted. As John charged up, the killer hit him with the butt of his pistol. The blow landed squarely on the forehead, and John fell on the stone steps of the butchershop and died.

Police learned several months later that Anthony Caruso, owner of the butchershop, had been standing in the shop and had seen the face of the killer. But the knowledge was not gained until after Caruso was shot down at the door of his garage. The investigation revealed that Caruso had decided to reveal the identity of the Lonardo killer after a $10,000 reward had been posted. Before he could do so, he was silenced.

There was one other witness to the original killing, but he wasn't much help although he talked freely. His name was Angelo Porello.

The Lonardos ceased to be a major factor in the bootlegging business, a fact which perhaps explains why Frank Lonardo, the remaining member of the family in Cleveland, managed to outlive his brothers by two years and one week. Then he too accepted an invitation to play cards and was shot in the rear room of a cigar store.

Times were changing in other ways. People were getting sick of the poison being manufactured in the slums of the Woodland district—so sick that many died. More important, it was no longer necessary to drink it. Again the demand had created a supply. The third phase of the Prohibition period was under way—the rum-running phase. Good liquor was pouring across Lake Erie from Canada in a tremendous flood. The household still was becoming outmoded.

But although the business was going down hill, there was still enough of it to require some killings. The Porellos had profited by the deaths of the Lonardos, but not as much as they could have expected. For there was another force at work.

Lawrence Lupo, a refugee from Brooklyn, New York, moved in on the scene. A fight promoter in the same class as Tommy McGinty, Lupo first made the newspapers in 1927 by killing a former deputy sheriff at an inn. The ex-deputy was reported to be in the slot machine business. Lupo went to the inn with Nathan "Nate" Weisenberg, a slot machine agent. For some unknown reason, he testified, the ex-deputy assaulted him and he had to shoot in self-defense.

This tale was sufficient to free Lupo from official wrath, but apparently some others didn't accept it. A month later someone shot Lupo, putting out an eye and smashing his nose. He had a new nose installed by a plastic surgeon.

With Lupo at the time his nose was shot off was a business associate. At that time he was calling himself Albert C. Polizzi, but most people called him "Chuck." They didn't want to confuse him with Alfred Polizzi who was known as "Big Al."

The presence of Chuck Polizzi, while meaningless at the time, has great significance in the light of later developments. Polizzi was to become a very special member of the then developing Cleveland Syndicate. His association with Lupo indicated that the boys on Mayfield Road were taking a hand in the home-manufacturing business.

Once Polizzi had his foot in the door, however, he found he could get along without Lupo. On May 4, 1928, the body of one-eyed Lupo was thrown out of a yellow roadster at Orange Avenue and East Twenty-fifth Street. Polizzi and an associate, Charles Colletti, the ex-bodyguard of the Lonardos, said they didn't know who took their friend for a ride.

Nate Weisenberg was more fortunate. He lived almost two decades and became known as the "Slots King of Ohio" before being taken for a ride. By then his empire was worth dividing.

There were other more immediate problems. The seven Porello brothers were still in business. They had begun their trek to America in 1907. Like their neighbors, the Lonardos, they had come from the village of Licati in Sicily, and had settled in the Woodland district near Twenty-fifth Street and Woodland Avenue. That intersection became known to newspaper readers as "the Bloody Corner." Following the death of the Lonardos, some of the Porello boys became so prosperous they too were able to move to the suburbs.

The threat of the Mayfield Road Mob, represented as it was by Chuck Polizzi and Frank Milano, caused the Porellos to seek confirmation from higher authority for their role as successor to the Lonardos. As a result, the first known meeting of the Grand Council of the Mafia took place at the Hotel Statler on December 5, 1928. It didn't get the publicity a similar meeting received at Apalachin, New York, in 1957, but it got more notice than anyone could have wanted. The trouble started when Cleveland patrolman Frank Osowski became suspicious at the sight of a group of men entering the hotel at 4:30 A.M.

"The men looked both ways and pulled their hats down as they entered the hotel," Osowski testified.

In the Cleveland of that day more than the suspicions of a patrolman would have been required to trigger a raid on a leading hotel. There is reason to believe, but no proof, that the Cleveland Syndicate saw an opportunity to embarrass some rivals. In any case, the hotel was raided. Twenty-three men and thirteen guns were found in one room.

Among those arrested was Giuseppe Profaci. (By the time he was picked up at the Apalachin Convention he was well known as Joe Profaci, boss of the Mafia in Brooklyn.) Others in the group included some of the top gangsters in the country. The host was Sam Tilocca, a close associate of Joe Porello. Tilocca owned the only "Cleveland gun" found at the hotel. Another man was Giuseppi Palmero. The newspapers noted he was held "for investigation in connection with the murder of eight persons in Italy."

Eventually most of the men were given suspended sentences on condition they leave Cleveland and stay away for one year. Temporarily, many were released on bond provided by the Porellos.

The incident was very unfortunate and if it didn't win any friends for the Porellos, who could be blamed?

The Porellos needed friends. Things got worse instead of better and by July 5, 1930, they were bad indeed. On that day Joe Porello and his friend Sam Tilocca decided the time had come to make a deal with the Mayfield Road Mob. Together they went to 12601 Mayfield Road where Frank Milano maintained a saloon and social headquarters. At about 2:30 P.M. both men were dead. Joe Porello died in the saloon with three bullets in his head. Tilocca was shot five times but managed to make it to the street where his new car was parked. He never reached the car.

A witness told police that present in the saloon at the time of the shooting were Frank Milano, Alfred "Big Al" Polizzi, John Angersola, and Charles Colletti. All were well-known members of the Mayfield Road Mob, and all, with the exception of Colletti, were to become better known as associates of the Cleveland Syndicate. "Wanted" circulars were distributed.

The men in question denied the story and the police, reasonable as ever, accepted the denials. But the murder forced an investigation of Milano. Expressing surprise to learn Milano had been operating a tavern at the location for years, the police went to his home next door. There they found a supply of whiskey and beer, some slot machines, and a number of automatic rifles and shotguns. Also found were account books, canceled checks to politicians and bootleg figures, as well as other records.

County Prosecutor Ray T. Miller—later mayor of Cleveland—was quoted as saying the records were "valuable," but for legal reasons not clear to laymen it was necessary to return them all to Milano.

After the shouting began to die, the surviving Porello brothers donned black suits and buried their brother. Three weeks after his death it was necessary to bury another one. James Porello was blasted with a shotgun as he stood in a grocery store ordering lamb chops for Sunday dinner. The meat counter fronted a plate-glass window. Someone fired from the street.

The surviving brothers buried their second brother, then complained of hard times. There was only one bright spot. Brother Rosario was in the penitentiary. He had been picked up carrying a revolver at the time of the Lonardos' murder, and was presumably safe. "They can't kill him" said Ottavio Porello.

Ottavio was wrong. Rosario was paroled in January, 1932. With his four remaining brothers, he went into a Catholic retreat. This proved dull and by February 25, the boys were back in action. But not for long. Three men entered a back room where two of the Porellos were playing blackjack with Dominic Gueli. They fired revolvers. Raymond and Rosario were killed instantly. Gueli lived two hours. A fourth man who had stopped for a bottle of pop was killed.

The fall of the Porellos was dramatized when in September, 1932, Angelo Porello was arrested back on lower Woodland Avenue where the family had begun its rise. He was charged with operating a still—one of the small ones that formerly thousands of "serfs" had operated on a commission basis for such barons as the Lonardos and the Porellos.

There was a bloody sequel to the "Sugar War." Mrs. Christine Colletti, age eighteen, was taken for a ride and dumped in Barrett Road with a bullet in her head. She had married Tony Colletti, nephew of the ex-bodyguard of the Lonardos and associate of "Big Al" Polizzi.

Tony had married Christine a few days after the murder of Joe Porello and Sam Tilocca in Frank Milano's saloon. He murdered her, police said, because he discovered she had been unfaithful to him.

Tony went to jail. On the morning his trial was to begin, he was found hanging by his trouser belt. Two prisoners, both charged with gang murders, were in the cell with him but said they had heard nothing. A deputy sheriff forty feet away hadn't heard anything either.

Normally that would have ended the affair. But Colletti had lawyers who announced their late client had given them another account of Christine's death. She was killed, they said, because she had seen the murder of Porello and Tilocca and had threatened to reveal what she knew when he accused her of infidelity.

According to the lawyers, Colletti told them that Christine was taken from his car by the Mayfield Gang. Police then arrested him, they said, and beat a confession from him.

This story might have been ignored had not Ernest Hopkins,

an investigator for the Wickersham Commission then investigating the Prohibition problem, used the Colletti case in an article in *Nation* to illustrate third-degree methods of police. The mayor appointed a commission to investigate, but it could find no proof to support the story. Mayfield Road Mob members declined to testify and the commission lacked power to force them to talk. It didn't want to try the third degree under the circumstances.

Murders continued after the Corn Sugar era ended, but on a reduced scale. While the Mayfield Road Mob won for itself a reputation of ruthlessness, its members came under the influence of more thoughtful individuals who believed the bribe, as a general rule, was more effective than the bullet. Not all the hot-blooded boys fresh from Sicily could accept such moderation, such indirectness, and they became the exception that proved the rule. Others like the Angersolas, the Polizzis, the Licavolis, did accept the uses of bribery and lived to become old as well as rich.

Behind the reputation of the Mayfield Road Mob, the silent men who formed the Cleveland Syndicate were content to hide. They gained the power, they took the profits. If others got the glory, so much the better. The Mayfield Road Mob became a legend—the Cleveland Syndicate became, and remained, a fact. In the years to come it became national, then international in scope.

But it began with Lake Erie.

CHAPTER FOUR

Morris Kleinman is the Al Capone of Cleveland.
Alvin E. Giesey, 1931

BENJAMIN NADEL was not one of the brighter intellectuals produced by the Jewish community which had moved from the Woodland district to the East 105 Street area. He didn't even look smart.

Dull eyes gazed at the world from beneath a low forehead, and found little to smile about. As a boy he had hung around the street corners with other loafers. As a youth he was arrested for plundering a boxcar. Later he worked in a handbook, and was suspected of peddling narcotics.

Just another punk—or so it seemed. But suddenly in 1925 Nadel began to change. He bought new and flashy clothes, a big car. He carried himself with a new confidence. It was obvious to all that Ben Nadel had established a connection—he was on his way up.

The mystery deepened when the *Ranger*, a sixty-five-foot cabin cruiser, was seized at the mouth of the Huron River west of Cleveland with 680 cases of liquor on board. Loafing near a shack on the shore was Nadel. Parked near the shack were three automobiles and a truck.

A year later, in 1926, a former United States submarine chaser was captured on Lake Erie by the Coast Guard. It was loaded with liquor consigned to Nadel, came the report. It was another of "Nadel's boats."

With each capture, Nadel's prestige grew. It was assumed, and correctly so, that for every boat seized many, many more got through. The United States Department of Commerce estimated that of all the liquor then being smuggled into the United States, two-thirds came across the border from Canada. And that, for practical purposes, meant the Detroit River and Lake Erie.

But, as sometimes happens when a man gets publicity, Nadel found himself in trouble. He was convicted of harboring one Pat McDermott at a time when McDermott was being sought for the murder of Don Mellett, editor of the Canton (Ohio) *Daily News*. Newspapers, by and large, can sleep soundly through certain kinds of civic corruption, but when an editor is murdered they awake with a vengeance. Nadel fought the conviction in all the courts, and lost. By March 20, 1928, he was a bitter man. Rumor spread along Mayfield Road that when Nadel gave himself up to the sheriff, he might talk. He might tell who really owned "Nadel's boats."

It was 1:30 A.M. on March 21, when the bodies of Nadel and an associate, Morris Goldman, were found in a car parked on the side of Lost Nation Road near the point where the Chagrin River enters Lake Erie east of Cleveland. Nadel had fourteen bullets in him; Goldman had twelve.

Police investigated and found a room where Nadel and Goldman had lived. In the room they found nitroglycerin, dynamite percussion caps, and some opium. They did not find the answer to the two questions everyone was asking: Who killed Nadel and Goldman? Who really owned "Nadel's boats"?

There were those who said the two questions required only one answer.

It was 1933 before part of the answer to the second question was provided. Morris Kleinman was indicted for income-tax evasion. He failed to file returns for the years 1929–30 while depositing at least $1,674,571.24 in eight separate bank accounts. Now he disclosed that he and three partners owned "Nadel's boats."

Questioned about the formation of the syndicate, Kleinman gave the following account of his business activities:

Q. What was the beginning of it?

A. I had some partners.

Q. Who were those partners?

A. I don't like to mention any names.

Q. Give the reason why you don't want to mention their names.

A. I just like to answer all the questions that concern myself.

Q. Why?

A. I might get myself into some trouble or something like that by giving these names.

Q. In what way?

A. I might get hurt some way by giving their names.

Q. You mean bodily harm?

A. That's right.

Q. Do you have any other reason than that?

A. I said I was afraid of bodily harm. I don't care to get them mixed in it. I don't know where they are at.

Q. When did you hear from them last?

A. I haven't heard from them for a long time. I don't remember how long.

Q. What was the understanding when you and these partners went into the business? The liquor business?

A. Just to buy and sell liquor and divide the profits.

Q. At the beginning how many persons were there?

A. Four or five—four.

Q. Four?

A. Yes, four.

Q. How much money did each partner put up?

A. I don't remember.

Q. Do you remember about the value of the capital of the partnership at the beginning of the business?

A. About $15,000.

Q. What part did you put in?

A. I put in about $3,750.

Q. You mean that that was the value of interest in that distilling plant which had been in operation prior to that time?

A. Yes, sir.

Q. What was the first purchase of equipment that you made?

A. A boat.

The questioning continued, but Kleinman remained steadfast in his refusal to name his partners. Perhaps he remembered Ben Nadel. Years passed before more information crept into the record. Twenty years later, Sam Tucker, in a petition filed in the United States Tax Court, stated:

"For some years prior to 1936"—the case at issue involved a property acquired then—"Messrs. Moe Dalitz, Sam Tucker, Louis Rothkopf, and Morris Kleinman were associated together in various enterprises . . . associated together as sort of an entity in various and sundry business transactions involving laundries, real estate, night clubs, and casino operations. They have always been equal partners in these various and sundry transactions."

The "sort of an entity" was the Cleveland Syndicate.

2.

The Cleveland Syndicate: Moe Dalitz, Morris Kleinman, Sam Tucker, and Louis Rothkopf. Other names were added over the years. Some like Chuck Polizzi and Tommy McGinty achieved near-equality. But, as Tucker put it in 1953, the original four remained as equal partners in every undertaking. Find one, and the three others were nearby. From Buckeye Enterprises in 1932 to the Lookout House in 1941 to the Las Vegas Desert Inn in 1950, to the Nacional in Havana in 1954, it was one for all and all for one. When Rothkopf died mysteriously in 1956, the remaining members carried on, still equal partners even in Garden Farms, Inc., a Las Vegas tomato patch, in 1965.

Dalitz, who came to be regarded as "first among equals" in the syndicate, was born in Boston on December 24, 1899. His father had become an American citizen four years earlier. The family moved to Ann Arbor, Michigan, in 1901, and opened the

Varsity Laundry, serving generations of University of Michigan students. Moe Dalitz was later to refer to it as "the family laundry," distinguishing it from others he acquired over the years in Detroit and Cleveland.

In 1915, Dalitz entered Central High School in Detroit. At the time, he was living with relatives at 726 Brush Street. But the man who later handled millions of dollars proved to be a poor student. He failed four subjects and dropped out of school without finishing the eleventh grade.

Perhaps one reason for his poor scholastic record was preoccupation with extracurricular activities. For he had become an associate of Joe and Benny Bernstein in the Purple Gang.

The reputation of the Purple Gang was built late in Prohibition, but the gang came into being as a group of neighborhood thieves about the time Dalitz entered Central High School.

Two shopkeepers on Hasting Street in the heart of Detroit's Jewish community were discussing the looting of a store by the gang.

"Those boys are tainted," said the man whose store had been wrecked. "They're off-color."

"Purple," said his sympathetic companion. "That's what they are, purple."

"The whole bunch of them," replied the first man, "they're all purple. They're the purple gang."

The name stuck only because the gang for years confined itself to preying upon its own people and the angry shopkeeper's remarks were repeated again and again as outrage followed outrage.

Moe Dalitz, aware that his parents had achieved a respectable laundry business in Ann Arbor, began calling himself Davis. He used many other names as well, but as late as 1936 in Kentucky he was indicted as Maurice Davis in connection with an illegal dog track.

The Purple Gang reached maturity when it was hired in the early 1920's to "protect" certain owners of cleaner's and dyer's companies from labor organizers. Realizing the possibilities, the gang set up their own racket and forced anyone desiring to operate a laundry to join and pay "dues" of up to $1,000 a week. It became necessary to murder a few holdouts like Sam Sigmund and Sam Polakoff.

Interestingly enough, it was in this same period that Moe Dalitz and his brother, Louis, went into the laundry business. The first company began operating as the Detroit Supply System in 1920. It was incorporated in 1924, as the so-called "Cleaner's and Dyer's War" raged hotter. The Michigan Overall Cleaners was then organized and merged with Detroit Supply to form Michigan Modern Overall Cleaners.

Moe Dalitz' interest in the Detroit cleaning and laundry business continued long after seventeen members of the Purple Gang were tried on extortion charges in 1928. The McClellan Committee learned in 1957 that as late as 1949, when the Detroit Institute of Laundering was confronted with a strike, Dalitz was contacted and he arranged an easy solution. The institute paid $17,500, and James Hoffa, an old Detroit boyhood chum of Dalitz, ordered a "sweetheart contract" accepted by his union which previously had rejected it.

Louis Dalitz was two years older than Moe. Twice in 1922 he was arrested on liquor charges in Detroit, and was found guilty and fined $100 on one of them. But with the laundry business booming, Louis turned his attention to it. Other laundries in Detroit were developed over the years— Dalitz Brothers Company, Inc., became Colonial Laundry which, in 1951, merged with Michigan Industrial Laundry, which, in 1959, merged again to become the Michigan–U.S. Industrial Glove and Laundry Company.

Moe Dalitz apparently did not share the opinion of Owney "the Killer" Madden who invested $350,000 in a New York laundry and was quoted in 1930 as saying:

> These legitimate rackets, there ain't no sense to them. You've got to wait for your money.

Dalitz, while investing heavily in the illegitimate rackets favored by Madden, continued to put some of his profits into the laundry business. He built a laundry empire in Cleveland similar to the one in Detroit.

The "legitimate rackets" were secondary in the early days, however. The Purple Gang was but one of several groups seeking domination in Detroit where bootlegging was but one of several rackets available. Gambling flourished as well as labor racketeering, and competition was fierce. Occasionally one gang or another would find it necessary to "import" additional "troops" from New York or St. Louis.

Two "massacres" gave the Purple Gang its reputation. The first was in 1926 when three St. Louis "imports" were mowed down by machine guns at the Milaflores Apartments. The second was in 1931 when the Purples turned their machine guns on the "Little Jewish Navy," and killed three "Admirals" in the Collingwood Manor Apartments.

It was the latter killing, following as it did the murder of crusading radio reporter Jerry Buckley in 1930, which aroused Detroit to demand a cleanup. The Buckley murder had come on July 23, 1930, and was credited to the Mafia. Buckley had led a campaign to recall Mayor Charles Bowles on the ground he had failed to stop wide-open gambling. The campaign had just resulted in victory and Buckley had just broadcast the results when three men entered the lobby of the LaSalle Hotel and shot him eleven times. Many of the Mafia members had been imported by the Purple Gang. Among those fleeing Detroit were the Licavoli boys, Thomas and Peter, who had come originally from St. Louis. They invaded Toledo and it was there Thomas—he was better known as Yonnie—"took a fall" when beer baron Jackie Kennedy was murdered. Back in Detroit, the Purple Gang scattered after the Collingwood Manor Massacre. Eventually, in one of the ironies of criminal history, Peter Licavoli and his forces returned to Detroit and became known as the Purple Gang. Apparently the name was just too colorful to die.

Moe Dalitz, meanwhile, had broken away from the original Purple Gang. Long before the Collingwood Massacre, he had moved to Akron, Ohio. But old associates from Detroit, such as Sam Stein and Abe Moss, would become important in the Cleveland Syndicate's rum-running operations. Even more important was Peter Licavoli. Dalitz saw no reason why people of Jewish and Italian descent could not cooperate for mutual profit. This attitude of reasonableness was expressed in dealings with the Mayfield Road Mob of Cleveland, and, later, when Dalitz joined the Army in 1942. At that time he listed his religion as "preferably Jewish." The other side of the coin was shown in 1948 when he teamed with Sam Stein to ship warplanes to Egypt for use against Israel.

A medium-sized man—five feet, nine and one-half inches tall and about 163 pounds—Dalitz liked hunting and women. He was married in 1925, divorced in 1939, married again in 1945, divorced in 1951, and married for the third time in 1953. But most of all he liked money.

In Akron he met Sam Tucker, and, shortly thereafter Kleinman and Rothkopf. And soon the money started rolling in.

3.

In 1951 James H. Brink, who called himself a "sportsman," was asked to tell the Kefauver Committee how the Cleveland Syndicate obtained control of his casino near Covington, Kentucky. He said he dealt first with "Mr. Tucker, Sam Tucker, whom I always had and still have in high regard, who seemed to be the gentleman of the boys."

The Tucker family, consisting of Louis and Jennie Tucker, a daughter, Ann, and three sons, Jacob, Samuel, and Garson, were late in reaching the United States from Russia. Sam was fifteen years old and his personality could be called "old country" in character. Perhaps that is why he seemed to be "the gentleman" of the syndicate.

Sambo, as he was known, managed to get two years of high school and six months of business school before going to work. The family prospered, and twelve years after reaching Cleveland it was able to buy property at 5700 Central Avenue.

Unlike Dalitz, Tucker married but once. He picked the former Louise Kaplan, a widow with one child, and the marriage lasted. Like Dalitz, Tucker took care of his relatives. Brother Jacob was given titles in various companies Sambo bought or created. The companies dealt in everything from real estate to automobile tires. Garson, who called himself "the kid brother," was brought to the Beverly Hills Club outside Newport, Kentucky, when the expanding syndicate forced the owner to give it away. Garson managed the restaurant while Sambo handled the swank casino. When the Beverly folded in 1961, Garson moved to Miami to manage a giant motel his brother had acquired.

This pattern of indirect involvement was typical of the way syndicate members allowed their relatives to benefit from their illegal activities, while, at the same time, keeping their hands clean. Such an approach differed from the Mafia where crime was a family affair and sons, in-laws, and cousins were expected to do the dirty work along with the head of the clan.

The one exception was Louis Rothkopf, who became widely known as "Uncle Louie." Show girls, for whom Rothkopf had a special fondness, used the name, but only after a younger edition of the Rothkopf applied it. Bernard Rothkopf, son of Benjamin, was Louis' nephew. He worked for "Uncle Louie" in Cleveland-area gambling joints until 1950 when he was given an administrative post at the Desert Inn in Las Vegas. College-trained as befitting a second-generation junior partner, Bernard later received $22,500 and a small piece of the Desert Inn as his share of his uncle's estate.

Louis Rothkopf was born in Cleveland in 1903. Like his partners he had a limited education, getting only three years of high school. He married Blanche Morgan in 1929, but the couple had no children. In later years, after wealth and respectability had been achieved, the Rothkopfs loved to rent pony stables and entertain visiting children.

Unencumbered with a family, Rothkopf lived well and traveled widely. He became highly regarded as "the best still man in the business," and in the early days specialized in the erection

CARNEGIE LIBRARY
LIVINGSTONE COLLEGE
SALISBURY, N. C. 28144

and operation of the largest illegal distilleries ever found in the United States. In the course of such activity he became close friends with Frank Costello. The relationship was valuable in establishing cooperation between the Cleveland Syndicate and the boys in New York.

But despite the kind heart which made Rothkopf cross the street to avoid meeting men who owed him money, "Uncle Louie" was the principal suspect in several murders. The most famous was the killing of William E. "Raring Bill" Potter, ex-councilman of Cleveland. Morris Kleinman was also sought in that murder.

Born in Cleveland in 1896, Kleinman was the oldest of the hard-core members of the syndicate. His father operated the Liberty Poultry Company and Morris and his brother, Fred, took over the business at early ages. But Morris was bored by chickens and sought other means to a better life. He became a boxer, winning the city lightweight championship. A factor in his favor, then and later, was his claim to kinship with Sam Haas. The relationship was distant, but real enough to be a value to a young man seeking to rise in the world.

Marriage gave Kleinman a wife named Gizella, a daughter named Mandell, a son named Allen, and a brother-in-law named Louis Kowit. The latter took over the poultry business and ran it for the family. Morris Kleinman quit thinking in terms of chicken feed.

When his fists failed, he tried a little bookmaking. The contacts proved useful later, but he dropped his "scratch sheet" temporarily as big opportunity beckoned. The corn-sugar business was on the decline. Something would have to replace it. Kleinman got the "feel" of the racket by opening a brewery. It also provided contacts.

4.

Exactly when and how the four partners got together remains their secret. Each had entered the business individually. Dalitz, with his experience in Detroit as a guide, was first to begin actually smuggling. He had established connections at various supply points in Ontario, and had an export dock at Leamington, downriver from Detroit. By 1926, the syndicate was in operation, as the loss of the *Ranger* and the *Hannah,* two of "Nadel's boats," indicated.

Kleinman, in his 1932 statement, said the Liberty Poultry Company was important to the bootlegging business. A secretary at the company, Miss Sylvia Regar, confirmed that Kleinman would bring checks to her at the office of Liberty Poultry and instruct her to deposit them in any of several bank accounts maintained for the purpose.

When money was withdrawn from one of the accounts, Kleinman or his partners told Miss Regar the amount desired and she drew the check. Miss Regar didn't know the real names of the partners, Kleinman added. "She knew who they were by seeing them only. She didn't have any association with them."

Other accounts in other banks were maintained by the individual partners, each using an assumed name. "William Martin" was a favorite alias of Moe Dalitz, but later he called himself "Bennett."

Some indication of the widespread nature of the operation was given when Kleinman named Joe Massei as one of the "people in Canada" who acted as banker in the purchase of Canadian booze. Individual transactions were called "loans" and many involved as much as $10,000 each.

Joe Massei was to become one of the biggest gangsters in the country. The arrangement with him was part of the working alliance Dalitz had formed with his old Detroit connections and with the Mafia. It was called the "Combination," consisting, as it did, of both Jewish and Sicilian elements. Long after the Prohibition era ended, the "Combination" continued to control gambling and related rackets in Toledo, Youngstown, Buffalo, Pittsburgh, Port Clinton, and to a lesser degree, in Detroit. One of the higher-ranking members of the "Combination" was Peter Licavoli, brother of Yonnie.

The Detroit end of the Cleveland Syndicate's rum-running operation was headed by Abe Moss, who, like Dalitz, had come up with the original Purple Gang. A retired federal agent who worked Detroit in those days told the author about a telephone wire tap which was installed at Moss' headquarters. It was revealing. Each morning someone would call Canada to discover how many cases of liquor had been shipped during the night. A second call was made to Joe Galbo, who handled the receiving end to see how many had been delivered. If the two totals didn't tally, "there was hell to pay." Individual bootleggers were scared of Galbo and afraid to cheat.

The phone tap revealed also that the liquor went out of Detroit in railroad boxcars. Crates were marked "Auto Parts." Shipments were made to points all over the Middle West and, on occasion, to Newark, Boston, and Philadelphia.

Not all conversations overheard concerned liquor. Sam Stein, a close friend of Moe Dalitz, had a mistress who sometimes used the office phone to order silk shirts for Sam at $25 a pair. Stein, it was obvious, didn't share the opinion voiced about that time by Dutch Schultz, boss of booze, among other things, in the Bronx. The "Dutchman" was famous for small economies —he didn't waste a bullet—and a friend one day took him to task for not dressing like other successful gangsters of the era. Dutch dismissed the subject in one short sentence:

"Only queers wear silk shirts."

The telephone tap ended when the federal agent was given a new man as an assistant. Within twenty-four hours after explaining the operation to the friendly young man, the agent heard Moss spreading the word to his customers that his telephone was tapped.

Shortly thereafter the agent was transferred. He had just discovered that a traffic manager and rate clerk of the Chesapeake & Ohio Railroad were involved in the movement of liquid "auto parts." Parenthetically, it should be mentioned that the C & O was part of the railroad empire acquired by the Van Sweringen brothers of Cleveland. Years later, the Cleveland Syndicate was to have an "understanding" with some C & O officials at White Sulphur Springs, West Virginia.

The traffic manager complained to the agent's new boss, a political appointee just off a Montana cattle ranch. The boss hated sheepherders in the best cowboy tradition. He ordered the agent to destroy his report, and transferred him to the Northwest on an undercover assignment. The traffic manager told the agent, for good measure, that "you'll grow up someday and recognize the realities."

Business involving the East was not a matter of one-way traffic. The hazards of the business being so unpredictable, it was often possible for one area to have a surplus of liquor while another area was experiencing a deficit. Arrangements were evolved, after some earlier violence had shaken out the less cooperative, to help keep the customer happy. Thus at times Canadian liquor went east from Detroit, Toledo, and Cleveland, and at other times Canadian booze brought up the St. Lawrence and around and down the Atlantic Coast, went west.

Kleinman stated that much of the liquor bought by the syndicate in Canada was purchased from a group of Canadians known as Peerless Carriers, Windsor, Ontario. The liquor purchased in New York, he said, was bought at the Claridge Hotel.

No additional questions were asked Kleinman about his Canadian and New York sources. As became apparent later, the investigation of Kleinman was rather unique. Had the matter been pursued, however, this picture might have emerged:

The bulk of the liquor business in the East was controlled—after the bloody shakedown—by what was first known as "the Big Seven" and later "the Big Six." Involved were gangs in New York, New Jersey, Philadelphia, and Boston.

The major forces to survive the era have since become known as the Eastern Syndicate. While oversimplification is necessary, they consisted, in part, of the New York Mob made up at various times of such individuals as Meyer Lansky, Benjamin "Bugsy" Siegel, Louis "Lepke" Buchhalter, Jake "Gurrah" Shapiro, Irving "Waxey Gordon" Wexler, Owney "the Killer"

Madden, "Big Bill" Dwyer, and Mafia components represented by Joe Adonis, Charles "Lucky" Luciano, and Frank Costello. There was also Arthur "Dutch Schultz" Flegenheimer, but he broke with the organization and died independent.

This collection of hoods has sometimes mistakenly been identified as either THE Syndicate or THE Mafia. If you assume the first, then the presence of the Mafia can easily be explained. But if you call it *The* Mafia, and put Luciano or Costello in as "Boss of all the Bosses," it is difficult to explain the presence of the large non-Sicilian, non-Italian group. The answer, of course, is that this was merely the New York Mob, of which the New York Mafia was but a part.

The other half of the Eastern Syndicate became the forces represented by Abner "Longie" Zwillman of New Jersey. Back in the rum-running days, however, Zwillman was but part of what was known as the Reinfeld Syndicate. Zwillman actually began as a strong-arm boy and worked his way to equality with Joseph H. Reinfeld.

The Reinfeld brothers came to the United States from that part of Poland seized by Austria during the Partition. Arriving prior to 1910, they worked as bartenders, tailors, and truckmen. Ultimately they became allied with Harry Bronfman and his three brothers in Canada who were in the hotel business. But the turnover in booze was even faster, so the Bronfmans went into the liquor business. They formed several corporations, among them the Atlas Finance Company, which served as the investment arm, the Atlas Shipping Company, and Northern Export Company. The parent organization was, of course, Distillers Corporation–Seagrams, Ltd., which owned distilleries.

Procedures varied, but most common was for Atlas Shipping to deliver consignments of liquor to Northern Export on the French-owned islands of St. Pierre and Miquelon in the St. Lawrence. Northern Export would re-export the liquor and it would be taken to Rum Row off the east coast of the United States. The Reinfeld-Zwillman end of the combine took over at that point. Sales offices were maintained at 60 Park Place, 1030 Broad Street, and 1451 Broadway, in New York. Other offices were at Newark, New Jersey. A customer would visit one of the sales offices, pay his money, get a receipt. At a scheduled time, he would go out into a boat beyond the three-mile limit to the waiting "rummy," present his receipt, and collect his merchandise. The responsibility, and the risk, from that point on was his. If the customer didn't have a boat available, the syndicate would rent one to him.

The beauty of the operation, from the point of view of the syndicate, was that, technically, it had remained within the law during the various phases of the smuggling process. The law wasn't violated until the customer took the liquor inside the territorial waters of the United States, and it was the customer who had violated it. In one effort to defeat the "High Seas Operation," the three-mile limit was extended to twelve miles on the theory that shuttle boats couldn't go that far from shore. It was a vain hope, but it did give the Coast Guard more room in which to maneuver.

While the Reinfeld Syndicate was officially estimated to have collected some $60 million during Prohibition, the individual members sought even more profits by engaging privately in the retail end of the business. Men like Zwillman set up their own distribution system and bought, as other customers, from the combine.

The best customers were, individually and collectively, the New York Mob. In fact, the entire concept had been largely the brainchild of Arnold Rothstein. He had been first to import liquor and had assigned to Waxey Gordon the job of distributing it. Rothstein dropped out when he realized the business was too large for one man to control. Gordon carried on and was soon joined by Dwyer and Costello. The "Big Seven" followed.

Headquarters were divided. Retail matters were handled from the Belvedere Hotel. The wholesale end—arrangements with Reinfeld and resale to such groups as the Cleveland Syndicate which couldn't meet the boats—was arranged at the Hotel Claridge. It was there Kleinman went to buy, and on occasion, to sell.

That the relationship between the New York and the Reinfeld syndicates was closer than mere buyer and seller now seems obvious. The Eastern Syndicate was even then in process of formation. When the Canadian branch of the Reinfeld Syndicate invested in certain race tracks south of the border, it was "Big Bill" Dwyer who appeared as fiscal agent and American representative. And when the fourth phase of the Prohibition era began, the New York and Cleveland boys found themselves as officers of the same corporation—Molaska. Together they produced illicit alcohol long after liquor became legal.

Yet the working relationship whereby the Reinfeld Syndicate supplied the East, and the Cleveland Syndicate catered to the Middle West was such a natural division it was put on a formal basis when the National Syndicate was organized.

But that was for the future. Back on Lake Erie the "Big Jewish Navy" ruled, while, in Cleveland, citizens gave thanks that good liquor had supplanted rotgut and wondered who really owned "Nadel's boats."

CHAPTER FIVE

THE CHAIRMAN. Have you ever been convicted of anything?
MR. TUCKER. Not that I know of.
Kefauver Committee, 1951

DANIEL J. EBERLE wasn't very important to anyone except himself, but he was unhappy. And even a little man can become dangerous if he is unhappy enough.

The trouble began back in 1927 when a man calling himself Larry Davidson employed Eberle to bring booze from Canada to the vicinity of Toledo. Eberle made many trips before being overhauled on November 22, 1927, and captured.

Sentenced to eighteen months in Atlanta Penitentiary, Eberle was soothed by an agent of Davidson who promised to pay $25 per month during his incarceration if only he wouldn't mention Davidson's name. When Eberle agreed, he was given $50 in advance, but after arriving in Atlanta he received only a few $10 checks.

This annoyed the prisoner and upon being released early in 1929, he hurried back to Lake Erie. In a Sandusky hotel he finally found Davidson and asked for the money he felt was past due. Always a quick man with a promise, Davidson said he would pay up but, meanwhile, would Eberle be interested in a new job? It would pay $50 a week and $75 per "pass" from Canada. Not only that, it was a promotion. Instead of a speedboat, he would be captain of the fish tug *Neptune*. Eberle promised to think it over and Davidson invited him out to his cottage at Harbor View. The cottage was well located on Lake Erie near the mouth of Toledo's Raisin River.

Eberle accepted the invitation, but before going to Harbor View a few days later, he contacted some of the officials he had met when arrested in 1927. A group of Prohibition Bureau agents drifted into Harbor View and rented cottages near the one occupied by Larry Davidson.

When Eberle reached Harbor View—after the agents had become established—he found his bitterness justified. Davidson gave him $10 on the debt, more promises, and a chance to stick his neck out again as captain of the *Neptune*. Eberle was taken to Sandusky to inspect the boat. Among those in the party were Moe Davis and a George Martin. Eberle still turned the job down and, as quickly as convenient, made his excuses and departed.

The *Neptune* was owned by United Fisheries at Sandusky. On May 14, 1929, it was sold to a George White of Erie, Pennsylvania, but the bill of sale was never found. Kleinman later admitted the Syndicate paid United Fisheries "about $4,000" for the boat.

Meanwhile, the Prohibition agents were becoming chummy with Davidson's crew. Some of the men, such as George Martin and Clarence Andrews, had been hired in Florida to man the boats of the "Big Jewish Navy." And business was steady as liquor designed for the Toledo area was brought in. On several occasions when the *Dart* and the *Judson* arrived loaded with booze, the agents played the role of good neighbors and helped load the liquor into waiting cars and trucks. Records do not indicate if they were paid for their trouble.

The operation created considerable excitement in official circles. It seemed possible that at long last a clue might be obtained to the leaders of the syndicate. Orders went out to continue the good neighbor policy as long as possible. On May 28, however, Martin J. O'Boyle, a former Prohibition agent and a member of the Thomas McGinty Irish section of the syndicate, visited Harbor View. He recognized one of the "neighbors" as a former colleague. Before the "Proes," as Prohibition agents were sometimes scornfully called, realized what was happening, O'Boyle gave the alarm and the gang fled. Only one man, George Martin, was captured. He gave a statement implicating some of the smaller fry, but the trail to the big shots had come to a dead end.

The interlude at Harbor View had not been unprofitable, however. The *Dart,* the *Judson,* and the *Neptune* had been placed on the Coast Guard's "Wanted" list, and were eventually seized.

Boatswain J. Dailey captured the *Neptune* at 12:15 A.M., June 7, 1929. He and his two-man crew on the CG-2262 found the *Neptune* running without lights and boarded her approximately 100 yards off the end of the West Ninth Street pier in downtown Cleveland.

Aboard the rummy was George White, who listed Leamington, Ontario, as his home. A second man, called "Captain West" by White, pointed a revolver at Surfman Charles P. Ricer as he entered the pilothouse. Holding the sailor immobilized, the rum-runner leaped overboard and, according to the report, "it is assumed he got ashore as he did not have far to swim."

The boat proved loaded with sixty-three sacks, or "hams," of assorted liquor. Each sack contained twelve quarts. There were fifty-eight sacks of beer and ale with twenty-four bottles to the sack.

In a statement, White said he was hired in Buffalo, and went to Sandusky aboard the *Neptune,* and then to Leamington. The liquor was loaded there and the run to Cleveland began.

"This Captain West was a hard-boiled guy," said White. "He steered right in past the breakwater last night and didn't seem afraid of meeting the law. The only thing he seemed afraid of was hijackers. When I heard a bump as the Coast Guard boat came alongside of us last night, I thought it was hijackers and I took a dive into the sacks where the liquor was. I was afraid to show my head because I thought I might get plunked. . . ."

In his report of the capture, Dailey noted that the manner in which West piloted the boat into the harbor "indicated he was not a stranger to these waters. . . . When he jumped off the boat and started swimming, he struck straight out for shore as if he knew what he was doing."

United States Attorney Wilfred J. Mahon was quoted as saying "the bold attempt to land the $35,000 cargo of the *Neptune* is evidence that a powerful booze syndicate is trying to run rum into Cleveland's very harbor."

The only individual to get more than a rap on the knuckles out of the entire investigation was Larry Davidson. He was sentenced to a $3,000 fine and five years in prison. Daniel Eberle had collected at last.

2.

Boatswain Dailey, assigned to patrol Cleveland Harbor, remained busy as, despite occasional losses, the syndicate continued to transport Canadian liquor in volume across Lake Erie. While ports from Detroit to Buffalo were not neglected, Cleveland remained a popular "liberty" town for bootleggers.

On June 9, 1929, only two nights after the seizure of the *Neptune,* Dailey and his crew spotted the clinker boat *Helen* at 3 A.M. The rummy was approximately 100 feet from the outer breakwater in Cleveland's harbor, off Fifty-eighth Street. She was running without lights. The Coast Guard cutter, approaching from open water, cut off her escape. The *Helen* fled along the breakwater for a short distance, then gave up as her pursuer gathered speed. Dailey, watching through nightglasses, saw the *Helen* stop and put her nose against the breakwater. Two men leaped to the wall and vanished into the darkness.

After getting reinforcements, Dailey sent two men in each direction along the breakwater, but they found nothing. The boat, its motor still running, was boarded. Found aboard were 120 cases of Canadian liquor, twelve quarts to the case. The boat was later identified by Kleinman as belonging to the syndicate.

Dailey was getting close to a syndicate landing area when on August 3, 1929, he was ordered to investigate a burning boat off the mouth of Rocky River west of Cleveland. Moe Dalitz owned a boat dock there and at that boat dock many successful "passes" ended.

The *Red Boy,* loaded with liquor, had almost reached the boathouse when it caught fire. Dailey, arriving in the ex-syndicate boat, the *Judson,* found the burning boat abandoned. The lake was searched but no one found. Meanwhile, three of the *Red Boy's* gasoline tanks exploded. Nevertheless, it was taken in tow. A Cleveland fireboat came out to meet the *Judson,* and the *Red Boy* survived to reach port where it burned to the water's edge.

Approximately 300 sacks of ale and 200 sacks of beer were salvaged from the hull, along with the motor. Without equipment seized from the syndicate, the Coast Guard might not have been able to function.

Dailey continued his crusade against the syndicate and on November 29, 1929, aided by a sudden blizzard, he scored twice in a single day. He was roaming Cleveland harbor at 1:30 A.M. when he took his first prize. The weather was bad, and getting worse when he spotted the *Idle Hour* running without lights abreast of West Thirty-eighth Street. Dailey's crew was forced to fire a volley of rifle shots to bring the forty-five-foot boat to a halt. A man using the name Harry Wilson was arrested and 350 sacks of assorted Canadian whiskey was seized.

Eight hours later, the Coast Guard station received a call that a large boat had gone ashore on the breakwall. A storm had blown up during the early hours and the *Honey* had crashed into the wall. Two men were found near the wrecked boat, clinging to the ice-covered rocks. But when questioned they said they had been fishing on the sea wall and had slipped. Since no one had seen them near the boat they were released. Boatswain Dailey found 100 sacks of Golden Wedding and Log Cabin whiskey in the cabin of the *Honey.*

Kleinman, in a 1932 interview, said the *Honey* was built to order at Detroit and cost the syndicate $7,500. The *Idle Hour,* which had a capacity of 300 cases, was bought in Canada for "about $6,000."

Asked how the purchase of boats was handled, Kleinman explained:

"One of my partners would be over in Canada and just look around for a boat. He would find out about a boat, and, if it was a good boat, he would buy it. He would mention who he bought it from but I wouldn't pay any attention."

The *Sambo-G,* Kleinman noted, with a capacity of 2,000 cases, was the largest one lost by the syndicate. It was custom built at Port Stanley, Ontario, and cost "about $8,000."

But the syndicate didn't believe in putting all its booze into one, or several boats. One unverified report had it that a submarine was used. A federal agent at Detroit discovered that a "torpedo" loaded with booze was a reality. The metal shell was attached by cables at both ends to winches located on either side of the Detroit River. Several cases of liquor would be loaded on the Canadian side and the "torpedo" would be pulled across the river bed to the United States. The winch on the other side would then pull it back for reloading.

This worked well enough but it was rather impractical on the scale the syndicate needed. So, to supplement the boats, the syndicate began using barges.

Law-enforcement agencies learned about the barges as a result of information obtained during the brief period of fraternization at Harbor View in May, 1929. Moe Davis, one of the names mentioned, was located and a telephone wire tap established. It was much later before Davis was identified as Dalitz.

Beginning in July, much of Davis' activity dealt with barges. On July 20 he talked to a Canadian beer agent at Port Colborne, Ontario, near the eastern end of the lake. Davis was forced to tell the agent that the "tug captain has pulled away" and "you'll have to wait until he gets back." Shortly thereafter Davis called Edward J. Downing in Buffalo and asked if the tugboat was in yet.

Three days later Davis was in Buffalo calling Sambo Tucker in Cleveland. Tucker was told the "deal went through" and to wire $8,000 to a man in Port Colborne—not the one who had missed the tug. The money was for the purchase of 100 cases of whiskey and 600 cases of ale. Davis gave orders for John O'Boyle, brother of Martin, to come to Buffalo and lend a hand.

Tucker followed instructions. The money and O'Boyle were dispatched as directed. Next day Davis again called Tucker to inform him the boat would be in Cleveland that night, but because of bad weather only 100 cases of liquor and 300 cases of ale had been loaded.

Meanwhile, the steam tug *Ballinas* left Port Colborne for Cleveland with four barges including the *Pershing* in tow. On the way to Cleveland, the expedition was overtaken by the *Idle Hour* with John O'Boyle aboard, and 400 cases of liquor and ale were transferred to the barge *Pershing*. At 9 P.M. that night —July 24, 1929—as Davis had promised, the *Pershing* docked at the foot of West Ninth Street, Cleveland, and the liquor was unloaded and hauled away by truck.

Investigation much later confirmed that the cargo was originally purchased by the syndicate and loaded aboard by Edward J. Downing. The captains of the four barges had assisted in transferring the cargo from the *Idle Hour* to the *Pershing*, under the supervision of O'Boyle, in the middle of Lake Erie.

Another case involving the canal barge *Loretta* was uncovered. Officials got word that 1,159 cases of liquor had been loaded aboard the *Loretta* at Port Colborne, and discharged at Buffalo on October 23, 1929. Special agents hurried to intercept the *Loretta* then in tow through the Erie Canal to New York City. Some empty sacks and three quarts of Canadian liquor were all that remained of the original cargo.

William Lear, captain of one of the other barges in the tow, said that on the night of October 22 while docked at Buffalo he had heard a tug's whistle and looked out of his porthole. It was just before midnight, he said, and the *Loretta* was being towed away from the docks. At daybreak he looked out again to discover the *Loretta* had been returned to her original position.

More information came eventually from Eugene Downey, a crewman later arrested. Downey admitted that Downing hired him to help smuggle liquor into the United States, and said he was aboard the *Loretta* when it unloaded its cargo at Buffalo. He told of another transaction involving the barge *India* and a rummy named the *Sonora*. A cargo of ale was put aboard the barge in mid-Lake Erie, and towed to Cleveland where John King (Angersola was his real name) accepted delivery for the syndicate.

Shortly after Downey talked, he was found shot to death in Buffalo, thus confirming the fears of a Hedger Transportation Company official. The company owned the *Loretta,* and the official had discovered its illicit cargo, but he did not report it, he said, because "somebody told me to keep my damned mouth shut or be bumped off."

The investigation continued, disclosing many instances where barges en route from New York via the Erie Canal were intercepted in Lake Erie and loaded with liquor for discharge at Cleveland. The same procedure was used on the return trip to New York.

On January 20, 1930, a federal grand jury at Buffalo indicted three of the four members of the syndicate, listing them as Moe Dalitz, Sam Tucker, and Morris Kleinman. Also named in the conspiracy indictment were John O'Boyle, Edward J. Downing, and assorted barge captains.

Some thirteen months later, on March 10, 1931, the indictment was dismissed on motion of United States Attorney Richard H. Templeton. He gave as the reason his belief that since much of the evidence had been gained by the telephone wire tap, it would be difficult to make voice identification of the defendants. This was especially true, he added, since the investigating officers never had an opportunity to talk to the defendants in person.

Twenty years later Dalitz told the Kefauver Committee that all he knew about the Buffalo indictment was what he read in the newspapers. "I don't think I was indicted," he added. "I think it was a mistake. I don't think it was me."

Tucker was equally vague. "I don't remember being tried or convicted," he commented.

Out in Detroit, Peter Licavoli had not been so lucky.

3.

Lawrence Fleishman, slender, dark, and newly married, was a border patrolman stationed in New York in August, 1928. In September he was serving as an undercover agent in Detroit, where the best disguise was the uniform of a border patrolman.

Following the example set years before by the Ohio Gang in Washington, many federal agents assigned to stem the flow of liquor across Lake Erie had become corrupt. It was Fleishman's secret assignment to ferret out such men. Bootleggers were to be secondary to this objective.

Posing as a rookie, Fleishman swept floors and stored contraband for a few days before being assigned to accompany veterans on night patrol. After a few nights he was accepted as a "regular" by his colleagues, who never dreamed he was writing detailed accounts of each night's misadventures.

On November 15, 1928, Fleishman reported at 1 A.M. and "was detailed to land patrol at Ecorse and Wyandotte with Inspectors Mack and Miller in a Buick coach." They detoured by way of a lumberyard which Miller said was actually a "cutting and shipping plant for carload lots."

A "cutting plant" was a place where good liquor was watered down. Quality was sacrificed to quantity, at no decrease in price per bottle but at a great increase in bottles.

There was no sign of activity so the patrolman agreed to look it over later. "We then drove to Wyandotte and saw the Wyandotte picket boat crew which consisted of Inspectors Velroy and Davenport. Jack Dillon was there trying for a go." (A "go" was permission from official agencies to bring the booze ashore. A bribe was usually a preliminary unless a permanent arrangement had been worked out in advance.)

Fleishman said his patrol went to Ecorse and "at about 7 A.M. at the foot of State Street saw Bill Brewer. He wanted a 'go' and got it. Brewer said he would attempt to bring his stuff over if it wasn't too rough." Later, after some more exploring and a check on Dillon, they met Brewer again. "He wanted to know if $50 would be all right to split three ways. Mack said, 'Can't you make it $60?' and Brewer replied, 'I guess I'll have to.' He handed Miller a roll of bills and talked for a few minutes and then we drove away. . . ."

The $60 was divided equally. Fleishman listed the serial numbers on the bills he received. The hunt continued. They met a fellow agent, Mickey Craig, who told them he had knocked off a distillery for the owner's rival in exchange for twelve cases of whiskey.

On the way back to the base the patrol again went by the lumberyard visited earlier. It bore the name Cumberland Timber Corporation, and it was open for business. "They were making boxes, evidently for shipping liquor. At the side door we heard a lot of activity and looked in and there were a number of men in there. Mack recognized one and said, 'Here comes a friend of mine.' A fellow came out and said, 'For God's sake, where did you fellows come from?' He seemed pretty well upset. He said for us to beat it and he would fix us later."

The border patrolmen went back to their base and discussed the matter. "We decided not to put the thing off too long. Mack told me the fellow who came out and spoke to me was Pete Licavoli." It was just another name to Fleishman. They made arrangements by telephone to meet Licavoli at 6 P.M., "and I went home and went to bed. . . ."

"About 5:40 P.M." his report continued, "Mack came to my apartment. . . . I got dressed and went along with him. On the way he told me it was a bunch of Jews who ran this place and Pete Licavoli had a 25 per cent interest in it."

They went to the Big Four Carting Company, through several doors, and into a well-hidden restaurant. It appeared to be a rather exclusive place with very high prices. They also served drinks. Miller was already there talking to Pete Licavoli, and while we were sitting there a fellow known as Lou Simmons came in and sat down with us. They seemed to be waiting for another fellow who came about 6:20 P.M. They called him Sam. He was a Jewish fellow. . . .

We all had dinner and drinks. I drank one small glass of beer. They finally came to an agreement, $400 split three ways. . . . It was further agreed that they were to be left alone and they were going to pay off on a weekly basis. . . . They seemed to think Miller was dissatisfied and wanted him to assure them that he would not molest them. Miller said that if he was going to knock them off he would give them at least two weeks notice. . . . Before we left, Sam asked if we wanted a bottle and Pete went to get them. He returned in a few minutes with three paper bags and gave one to each of us. Mine contained a quart of Robert Walker's Imperial Whiskey.

Next day Fleishman worked with another crew, but the procedure was the same. They collected from Joe Galbo, among others. On the way back to the base one of the men commented that it was pay day for the Border Patrol. The other member of the trio commented: "Yes, you get paid on this job too."

Two days later, Fleishman's patrol consumed more liquor than it confiscated, and his two colleagues slept during most of the tour of duty. One awoke long enough to pass on a rumor he had picked up—that about forty men were going to be fired and some of them indicted. The other patrolman shrugged it off. "He said it was practically an impossibility to indict anybody on a job like this owing to the difficulty of securing evidence."

When Fleishman reported the rumor, he was immediately pulled off the job. A few days later a large number of border patrolmen were arrested as they returned from their night patrols. Eventually, most of the 150 men then on river patrol were fired, and eleven patrolmen along with sixteen rum-runners were indicted. Among those convicted on bribery charges were Peter Licavoli, Joe Galbo, and Joe Massei. Licavoli got two years in prison and a $1,000 fine.

Fleishman, who had collected $1,700 in bribes during his short tour in Detroit, turned in his "loot" and headed back with his young wife to New York. Twenty-five years later, after his appointment as deputy commissioner of the Bureau of Customs in charge of enforcement, he recalled his meeting with Licavoli as one of the high spots of his career.

In retrospect, it *was* a notable achievement. Licavoli was to advance in his chosen field even faster than Fleishman in his. But in 1928, according to the undercover agent's own report, Licavoli owned only one-fourth of the operation. The identity of "the bunch of Jews" who owned the rest was not discovered for many years. The practice of cutting local people in as junior partners was one the syndicate perfected when it expanded its gambling operations outside Ohio. The Licavoli incident had proved its value.

Another federal agent who submitted a confidential report a few months later came closer to putting the Detroit operation into perspective. He learned, he said, "it was all part of one big ring stretching from Detroit to Niagara Falls." Among field men directing operations at Detroit in the temporary absence of Licavoli was "Black Leo" Cellura, later to be quite famous. John "King" Angersola, together with Angelo Polizzi, were handling distribution in the Cleveland area, and Joe DiCarlo was in charge at Buffalo and Niagara Falls.

This was "the Combination," that association of the syndicate and the Mafia. The Big Four of the syndicate was usually far in the background, making deals, putting up the money. The Mafia members handled the actual details of transportation and distribution. As big a man as Licavoli was sent to get three bottles for Fleishman and his crew, while Sam, the "Jewish fellow" who had offered it, waited at the table with his guests.

Similar arrangements existed in another phase of the syndicate's affairs. Beer was almost as important as liquor, and the supply from Canada was constantly supplemented by huge distilleries at home. Some alcohol was being produced as well.

4.

A beer plant at 1700 Merwin Avenue, Cleveland, was seized early in November, 1929. It was a huge thing with eighteen 1,000-gallon vats. The syndicate, as Kleinman later admitted, spent $4,000 to remodel and camouflage the building housing the distillery. Six men worked there, none of whom had the slightest idea who the owners were.

A year after the Merwin Avenue plant was seized, Cleveland police discovered another one at 6902–6912 Lexington Avenue. It was even larger, and had been equipped with a network of secret passageways and hidden doors. Kleinman said that just the brick and mortar necessary to disguise the operation cost $5,000.

A third plant was found at 1513 Prospect Avenue. It boasted nineteen steel vats with a capacity of 1,500 gallons each, and two wooden vats holding 8,000 gallons each. On the floor were 200 bags of sugar, and fermenting in the vats were the contents of 580 bags.

Alvin E. Giesey, one of the federal agents who investigated Kleinman's income, once noted:

> It seems that sometime in 1929, one of the largest stills raided in this city was found within 100 yards of this office. Newspapers at that time made a sensational story of the raid, and it was cited how large that still was and that if it had exploded there would have been little left of the adjoining buildings, which would have included this office, and these examining officers would not now be writing this report. Kleinman has admitted that the equipment was part of his operations.

But even local stills, as well as one at 105 Furnace Street, Akron, were not enough properly to supplement the flow of liquor across Lake Erie. The occasional purchase of additional supplies from New York has already been noted. The syndicate also bought in Galveston, Texas, as Department of Justice agents discovered when they seized a boxcar alleged to contain rags. Among the rags were found 752 cases of Canadian whiskey.

The liquor had originally been shipped via St. Pierre and Miquelon, around the east coast. But instead of stopping at Rum Row, it proceeded on the good ship *Marshal Frank* to a point some fifty miles off Galveston. There it was purchased over-the-rails at $17 per case. Additional costs including freight and handling brought the total to $35. This was still some $10 under the price being charged just across the Detroit River, where the competition for the available supply was tremendous. United States Customs officials discovered that more than 35,000 cases a month were being cleared from Amherstburg, just below Detroit, for shipment primarily to Harbor View and Toledo.

It was all very profitable, even with the occasional loss of a boat, a barge, a still, or a boxcar, but the syndicate was looking ahead at the same time. Sooner or later the good times would end. Diversification was important, the boys at the Hollenden Hotel headquarters decided. Thus it was that while the liquor business was to continue long after Prohibition ended, the gambling business was well launched before Repeal.

The Mayfield Road Mob cooperated as usual.

CHAPTER SIX

A rose by any other name would smell as sweet.
William Shakespeare

THE OFFICIAL REPORT was filed February 8, 1931:

William Potter, No. 1842 Rudwick Road (rear) has been missing since 4 P.M. February 3, 1931. Married; age, 45; height, 5′ 9″; weight, 175 to 180; build, stocky; complexion, fair; hair, chestnut; no beard; occupation, real estate salesman; wearing a dark blue suit with a red pin stripe; wearing in his vest pocket a white-gold hexagon watch; light gray with black band hat; black oxfords; also wearing a dark gray mixed overcoat with plade (cq) lining.

An unofficial report was also written:

Detective Nichols and I investigated the missing persons report of William Potter by interviewing his wife who stated that Mr. Potter left home about 9 A.M. February 3, 1931, to transact some business, and the last she heard from him was when he called her by phone at 4 P.M. informing her he had some business he had to attend to and would be a little late getting home.

Mrs. Potter also stated that on February 6, 1931, she received a phone call from an unknown woman who informed her that an auto which contained papers with the name William Potter and with the same address of 1842 Rudwick Road, was parked in front of 880 Parkwood Road, and that she, Mrs. Potter, went to this address and had this auto which was the property of her husband towed to her home.

Mrs. Potter informed us that she did not want an official

report of the absence of Mr. Potter made until further word from her. We were instructed to make an official report by Lt. Jones. . . .

A few hours after the first official report was filed, another was prepared. It was addressed to Cornelius Cody, chief inspector of detectives:

> With Sergeant Hogan and Detective Buttner, I investigated the murder of William E. Potter, age 45 years, of 1842 Rudwick Road, who was found murdered in Suite 4, 880 Parkwood Drive, about 5 this P.M. by Mrs. Fred Laub, janitress of this apartment.
>
> We went to the scene of the crime and found the body slumped on the couch in the living room. The upper part of the body on the couch and the legs on the floor. The body was fully clothed and the hat under the body. The head and body were badly swollen and decomposed and had probably been there since Tuesday evening, February 3, 1931, at which time Potter was last seen alive.
>
> The body was conveyed to the County Morgue where a post [mortem] was had which disclosed a bullet wound from the left to the right through the head just back of the ear. Bullet was found in the dried blood in the couch and is a 38 steel-nosed bullet. There was also a laceration on the left side of the head where a bullet had grazed the skin and passed through the hat and went into the side of the wall and was later recovered.
>
> In the pockets of the dead man was cash $1.78, watch, chain, and knife, and papers of no value.

Thus began Cleveland's most famous murder case. For Potter was more than the real estate salesman indicated by the police report. He was ex-City Councilman Potter, a man who had been close in the past to the Republican political machine headed by Maurice Maschke, a man who had exercised great influence and knew where the bodies were buried.

The cry "Who killed Bill Potter?" was as loud and sustained in Cleveland as Chicago's "Who killed Jake Lingle?" or Detroit's

"Who killed Jerry Buckley?" Cleveland newspapers carried small front-page "boxes" at intervals noting that it had been thirty days, or sixty days, or 1,000 days since Potter's death, and repeating the officially unanswered question.

Not that Potter even mistakenly, as in Lingle's case, wore the mantle of crusader that Buckley rightly deserved. The newspapers were not so interested in avenging a good man as in exposing the criminal-political connections that, while obvious to all, were yet so difficult to describe in specific detail. Potter had been indicted in 1929 in connection with some very messy land scandals also involving Sam Haas and E. P. Strong, the political heirs of Mark Hanna. After a sensational trial, he had been officially acquitted, but his political career had been temporarily wrecked by the publicity and in the following election he was defeated—more by the desertion of his friends who found him too "hot" than by his enemies. Their fears had soon been justified, for Potter was again indicted, this time for perjury in connection with statements he had made at his trial.

Under economic pressure as well, Potter had been forced to sell his home and move to an apartment. Police learned he had been seeking money from various sources, explaining he had to have it to pay legal expenses in his upcoming second trial. "Rarin' Bill," as Potter was known, still had friends, but they seemed reluctant to help. The word passed that Potter had to be sacrificed. He was too much of a political liability. The public needed a burnt offering. Thus the "heat."

Investigating police learned that the room Potter was found in had been rented by a mysterious L. M. Marcus on January 8. Marcus had paid a deposit, accepted a key, and said he would move in later after his wife arrived from Philadelphia. He had not been seen since—but, added the landlady, he was not Mr. Potter.

Other tenants said they had seen a man in the kitchen of the suite on February 3, and a blond woman was also there. Police, after some tests, concluded Potter died in the suite on that date. The person who last admitted seeing him alive was City Clerk

Fred Thomas, who said Potter left City Hall about 4:15 P.M. that day.

A police bulletin was issued:

> Det. Bur.—WANTED FOR MURDER—Make every effort to apprehend a white man, 30–32-5-9-145, slim build, dark compl., black eyes, long thin nose, looks like a Jew and said that he was Jewish, wearing blue fuzzy o'coat silk lined and looked expensive, was full length, black suit, long, narrow, pointed black oxfords, light soft hat, was very well dressed. This man, who rented the murder apartment, can be identified. No. 2, a very attractive-looking blonde woman about 22 years of age, no further description, who was seen in apartment about day before murder. Wanted for murder of William E. Potter.

Much of the police investigation that followed was inconclusive as to evidence in the case, but it was revealing as to conditions in Cleveland in general.

On February 21 a detective reported he interviewed various people who told him they had: one, been invited by Potter to a spaghetti supper at Euclid Tourist Camp; two, asked to enter the real estate business by Potter who then said he was too broke to buy a drink to seal the partnership; three, been asked to sell a home which recently had been damaged when a still blew up in a back room. The investigating officer said he was "satisfied Potter had no connection with the still."

Next day a lead to the blond girl, identified as Betty Gray, alias Akron Mary, was discovered. A detective reported:

> There is a woman by the name of Fan McAffee in Akron, Ohio, who owns a high-class Speakeasy which is patronized by a high class of people, and the place, as well as herself, is well known by members of the Akron Police Department. . . . [The woman was supposed to be a] friend of Akron Mary and smart. So is Akron Mary, who does not associate with every man that comes to the place; in fact, she is known as a high-class girl and she is well known by all the politicians.

The well-dressed man who rented the room was identified as "Pittsburgh Hymie" Martin, and police began a search for him.

Armed with a photograph showing a dapper Hymie in the company of three other men, police prowled the city.

By then the officers thought they understood the motive for the murder. Martin had tried to "shake down" some former associates. Years later, the Kefauver Committee was told:

> It was alleged that Potter had been killed because it was feared he was about to expose some crooked deals. The police had traced checks written by a city official to the Prospect Advertising Company, operated by Moe Davis (Dalitz) and Maurice Kleinman.

The Prospect Advertising Company was what newspapers called "a gambling rendezvous," a combination handbook, accepting bets on horses, and casino. The checks mentioned by the Kefauver Committee witness had been sent to Dalitz, Kleinman, and a Dave Langman. They covered gambling losses. Police also located records of telephone calls from the gambling joint to Martin in Pittsburgh. It was learned that Martin visited Prospect Advertising when the liquor business brought him to Cleveland.

As winter gave way to spring and summer followed, police continued their search for Martin. But they were also looking for various members of the syndicate. As early as February 23, witnesses were being asked if they knew Moe Davis. On July 27 a detective reported he "spent the balance of the time, throughout the Jewish district in the east end, on the lookout for Louis Rhode, alias Collins, wanted in connection with this murder." Rhode was one of the several names used by Louis Rothkopf.

The Kefauver Committee was told: "Moe Davis and Lou Rothkopf were with Pittsburgh Hymie until a few hours before the slaying. Davis was also with Hymie until an hour prior to the arrest of Hymie who was charged with the murder of Potter."

Trails led into strange places. About August 17 this memo was handwritten at police headquarters:

> Woman called Freed [he was district attorney] says that

Hoot Gibson and Morris Kleinman are at Sam Miller's on Harvard Avenue. This woman heard them talking, and they said they were with H. Martin at murder of Potter.

Next day a detective reported:

Spent considerable time at the big barn on Harvard Ave. that is operated by Sam Miller as a gambling joint on the lookout for Harry Katz, alias Hoot Gibson, and Morris Kleinman who are supposed to frequent this place. . . . These men did not appear here tonight, and we did not find their automobiles parked in this vicinity.

As far as can be learned, this is the first official notice taken of a syndicate gambling joint that became famous as the Harvard Club. It soon moved from the "big barn" to swanker quarters where, eventually, it attracted the attention of Eliot Ness. The Sam Miller mentioned was "Gameboy," brother-in-law of Mushy Wexler, co-operator of the wire service, and later a syndicate troubleshooter in Kentucky and Miami Beach.

Ultimately, after public interest in the case had died somewhat and new sensations developed, Martin was arrested in Pittsburgh. None of the syndicate figures sought so long was charged with anything. Martin was convicted and sentenced to life imprisonment. But, as Gaston B. Means would say, there was "no ultimate conviction." A new trial was granted, several key witnesses abruptly changed their testimony, and Prosecutor Ray Miller lost a case. Miller went on, despite the loss, to become mayor. Martin went back to Pittsburgh and prospered in the gambling business.

Even before the case was settled, Martin had received convincing evidence that his friendship with Cleveland Syndicate leaders remained strong. They cut him in for a piece of the Thomas Club, one of the first syndicate casinos in the Cleveland area. True, because of all the rumors, his name wasn't listed anywhere. But it can now be revealed that Martin's interest was represented by a nominee, Alfred "Scotty" Goltsman.

A former bodyguard of Pittsburgh Hymie, Goltsman continued

to represent Martin's interest when the Arrow and, later, the Pettibone Clubs were opened. Martin's name never reappeared, but Goltsman continued as a junior partner in the syndicate's Kentucky casinos until 1961. He died in 1963.

The link between the syndicate and Martin was exposed once again in the summer of 1965. He was discovered to be the operating director of the numbers racket in South Florida. Backing, and bankrolling him, as usual, were the overlords of the syndicate: Kleinman, Tucker, and Dalitz. An old friend of Cleveland days, George Gordon, supervised Martin for the syndicate.

There was but one difference. By 1965, Martin had acquired a new nickname. The underworld of Miami knew him as "Fat Hymie." Yet there are those who say murder is unprofitable.

2.

The syndicate's interest in gambling was spurred somewhat as evidence mounted that the third phase of Prohibition was coming to an end. Rum-running was getting a bit risky, and profits were becoming harder to conceal. Proof of this was provided when, in the middle of the Potter investigation, it was learned that Kleinman's income taxes—or rather, the lack of them—were being investigated by the Bureau of Internal Revenue. There was little doubt a case could be made. Kleinman had neglected to file returns for 1929 and 1930.

Heading the investigation was an agent named Alvin Giesey. He so impressed Kleinman and Kleinman's associates that shortly after the investigation ended Giesey resigned and went to work for the syndicate. Indeed, he was to prove helpful even before submitting his resignation.

Something of the history of the investigation was once supplied by Giesey:

> Following a wide-spread rumor about certain activities of certain individuals operating in this vicinity, the examining officers called upon newspaper reporters and others familiar

with such operations and learned that a particular rum-running organization was headed by Morris Kleinman.

Knowing that persons engaged in such a trade would have no records from which to determine income, and desiring to have some information other than common rumor before proceeding directly with the taxpayer, the examining officers' first efforts were toward the location of bank accounts.

On Monday morning, September 15, 1930, the Merchants Trust and Savings Bank, Cleveland, was closed by order of the State Banking Department. Shortly thereafter, a certain check on hand September 15, 1930, was honored, being treated as a preferred claim against the bank. The payment of this claim excited the characteristic curiosity of newspaper reporters and much adue (cq) was made about it. The examining officers learned that on September 9, 1930, a check payable to cash in the amount of $15,320, was drawn by Frank Clark. . . .

Investigation revealed that several checks on the account of Frank Clark had been deposited to the account of Max Davis. It was then learned the checks were payment for a boat dock at Clifton Park Lagoon on Rocky River, east of Cleveland. It was just off this boat dock that the syndicate's boat, *Red Boy*, was found burning and abandoned in August, 1929. The dock had been bought by William Martin.

Kleinman was later to identify William Martin as the alias of one of his three partners. Officially, Martin was never identified by his real name. [The report noted, however, that]

on July 4, 1930, a boat exploded in the boathouse on this property and a passing craft pulled a burning boat into midstream where it burned to the water's edge and went down after the one man on board had been taken ashore. This man was taken to Lakewood Hospital where he was given first aid treatment, and he departed from the hospital before the police or the hospital had obtained any information. Thereupon the boat was raised and the police department made strenuous efforts to find this man, for evidence was found of a liquor running business at this property.

Had Giesey gone back to the newspaper reporters, they might have aided him in his quest for William Martin. Under date of August 13, 1930, the Cleveland *Press* had a story about "Moe Davis, reputed Lake Erie rumrunner," giving himself up for questioning in a murder case. "Until yesterday," the story continued, "Davis had been missing since July 4 when he was burned in a gasoline explosion which set fire to his cabin cruiser, *Natchez*, in a Rocky River lagoon. Davis was taken to Lakewood Hospital that day but never returned for treatment which had been advised." Instead, according to the story, he had gone to New York.

After questioning, Davis was released. The murder police asked him about was that of Morris Komissarow. Oddly enough, his name featured in the income-tax probe of Kleinman.

Giesey noted that Miss Sylvia Regar, the busy secretary at Kleinman's Liberty Poultry Company, deposited checks for Komissarow at Merchants Trust, and, on occasion, deposited checks drawn by Komissarow to the "Frank Clark" account. It was with money from the "Frank Clark" account that Moe Dalitz, alias William Martin, had bought the Rocky River boat dock. Another item from the account was a bond forfeiture. It was discovered that Harry Wilson, captured aboard the rummy *Idle Hour*, had not appeared for trial and it had been necessary to fork over the $5,000 bond.

It was also discovered that Komissarow had been in Lorain the night Fred Hentrie, wounded captain of the *Sambo-G,* had escaped through the hospital window. A girl friend of Komissarow had visited Hentrie earlier in the day and arranged details of the escape.

Yet Komissarow had been found in August, 1930, floating in Lake Erie off that same Rocky River lagoon where Dalitz had been burned on July 4. Police found it difficult to determine exactly when the bullet had been placed in his head, but, from the condition of the body, they figured it had been there since sometime in early July. Whoever fired the bullet there hadn't intended for it to be found. A rope had been wrapped several times around the body and fastened to a fifty-pound anchor. The word "Navy" was stamped on the anchor. Whose "Navy" wasn't indicated. The rope had become unwrapped.

Police never figured out why Komissarow was killed. For that matter, they never learned why Moe Dalitz' boat burned either. But, after questioning Dalitz, they said he obviously had nothing to do with the murder.

No doubt it was another coincidence, but the man who first reported Komissarow missing was Solly Hart, a rum-runner of some reputation who shared a hotel room with the unfortunate Komissarow. Hart, it developed, was a suspect in the Potter murder as well. He was considered quite handy with a gun and, in fact, finally went to prison for carrying one.

Many other interesting facts were emerging from the investigation of Kleinman, so in February, 1932, when Giesey went to Kleinman with some questions, he found him cooperative—up to a point.

A "deal" was made. Kleinman—realizing the rum-running business was about finished—agreed to give some details if he was promised immunity from prosecution. With that promise in his pocket he made a long statement on February 2, 1932. It appeared, at first glance, to be a frank statement, but closer study revealed Kleinman had told investigators nothing that was not already on record somewhere—details of boats seized, stills captured, and bank accounts kept under a dozen different names. He was careful not to reveal the name of a single partner or give details of a vast new joint operation with the Eastern Syndicate, which was just beginning. But, despite the agreement, Giesey did not press for additional details.

Ultimately, however, the case got out of Giesey's hands and top Treasury officials began pointing toward a prosecution of Kleinman. Charges of broken promises led, finally, to a conference in Washington on December 19, 1932. Representing what was inaccurately called "the taxpayer," meaning Kleinman, was Martin McCormack, a former United States Attorney. Representing the government was a battery of officials including the legendary Elmer L. Irey, chief of the Treasury Department's intelligence agencies. According to an individual present at the conference, McCormack stated flatly that he had told Special Agent W. E. McElveen:

> that I wouldn't let my client tell him his own name or give any information unless I had his word of honor that neither he nor his department was interested in a criminal prosecution . . . that I brought Mr. Kleinman up there and that I used the following words: 'I told you, Morris, but I am telling you again in the presence of these gentlemen that this information that you are about to give can be used against you to criminally prosecute you, but I have the word of the estimable gentlemen, I have the word of an honorable United States officer that such would not be the case,' and said, 'Am I right?' and they all three nodded in assent.

Irey and the other officials maintained that the promise had referred only to prosecution by the Prohibition Unit, and not for income tax evasion. But McCormack insisted that not only had he understood there would be no criminal prosecution but "I was given to understand by Mr. Maschke that such a promise was made to him that there would be no prosecution of any kind."

Maurice Maschke was Republican boss of Cleveland, but Franklin D. Roosevelt had just been elected President two weeks before. It is doubtful if Maschke's name carried much weight in Washington on that particular day. In any case, Irey and his associates refused to honor any agreement granting immunity, and on February 3, 1933, Kleinman was indicted for failure to file income tax returns and for evasion of income taxes for the years 1929 and 1930.

Apparently needing some time to get his affairs in order, or perhaps seeking some Democratic friends in the new administration, Kleinman vanished until August 12, when he was arrested in Washington.

It was a clear, cold day on November 27, 1933, when justice

could be delayed no longer and one of the syndicate's top bosses stood in federal court while his attorney entered a plea of guilty.

Again the charge was made that Kleinman had been promised immunity, but the defense attorney—a new one—acknowledged "the government was in possession of enough evidence to start this case and prove it without the disclosures by Kleinman."

For admittedly evading taxes on gross income of $1,673,554, in 1929 and 1930, Kleinman was sentenced to four years in federal prison and fined $15,000. A reporter noted the sentence was received without "dramatics."

The occasion was dramatic enough to require no gesture. The event was historic as far as the Cleveland Syndicate was concerned. It was the first time a major syndicate partner had been convicted. In the thirty years and more of operations to come, it would remain the only time a major conviction of a major partner was not beaten.

Income-tax evasion investigations were the downfall of such men as Al Capone and Waxey Gordon. The men of the Cleveland Syndicate were more durable. They learned from their mistakes.

Kleinman was to serve thirty-three months before being paroled on September 1, 1936. But he escaped most of the other consequences of his sentence. Upon being released he appeared before the United States Commission and swore he was a pauper—thus canceling the $15,000 fine. The government also attempted to collect a compromise settlement consisting of additional income taxes of $30,579.49; penalties of $22,934.62; and $4,804.65 of accrued interest. Kleinman "proved" he was broke and in debt. His only income, he said, upon being released from prison, was $75 a week from the Liberty Poultry Company, which was now owned by his brother-in-law. It seems, Kleinman explained, he signed over his 50 per cent interest in the company in return for payments of $50 weekly to his wife "while he was away." Meanwhile, the bank had foreclosed on the Kleinman home at 11411 Whitmore Avenue.

It was all very sad, this picture of the great now fallen, and all the Internal Revenue agents involved were touched. They recommended, unanimously, that an offer by Kleinman to settle the debt for $1,000 be accepted. It was accepted. Shortly thereafter, Kleinman's financial fortunes began to improve rapidly.

3.

The syndicate also had some arrangements to make while Kleinman "was away." As a working member of the organization, his usefulness had been impaired the moment he came under active investigation. His sentence only fixed the limits of his temporary retirement.

Adding to the headache were the problems of expansion. Not only were plans afoot for the fourth phase of Prohibition, but the new emphasis on gambling involved issues requiring special handling. More than ever, cooperation with members of the Mayfield Road Mob was essential.

The addition of Charles A. "Chuck" Polizzi as a member of the board and temporary substitute for Kleinman was the solution.

Why the Jewish leaders of the Cleveland Syndicate found Polizzi so uniquely qualified was a question that puzzled many people. And it was not the only thing about Chuck that seemed mysterious. There was his relationship to "Big Al" Polizzi, for instance.

Alfred "Big Al" Polizzi had the proper background. He was born in Sicily and spent his childhood there. Arriving in Cleveland, he quit school at age fourteen to sell newspapers for Mickey McBride. In the twenties he was a suspect in assorted murders, bombings, extortions, and other crimes. He was a friend of the Milanos, as well as other powerful Mafia leaders.

In the files of the Cleveland Police Department is a memo from a former sergeant of detectives. It concerns Chuck Polizzi:

> First contact I had with the above man, Charles Polizzi or Albert C. Polizzi, was in the year 1923 when he and his cousin,

Alfred Polizzi, alias Big Al, were in a restaurant next to the Grand Theater, which was located at Bolivar Road and East Ninth Street. They had bootlegging there. After they left this place, they loitered about the downtown district and took up with such men as Frank Milano, Charles Colletti—now deceased—John, George, and Fred Angersola, alias King. They were also known as bodyguards for Joe and John Lonardo and were seen frequently with these two men and around their headquarters at East Ninth and Orange.

In the year 1926, Polizzi, along with the others mentioned, loitered in a speakeasy at 7310 Lexington Avenue run by Frank Milano and Louis Cohen. We raided the place and put Milano out of business. They then took up headquarters in a restaurant on Hugh Avenue. On October 8, 1927, Ernest Yorkell and Jack Brownstein, two Philadelphia gangsters, were found shot and bound in Cleveland Heights. These two men were shaking down local bootleggers and investigation showed they were last seen in the restaurant with the Polizzis, Milano, King, and other gangsters. We arrested the entire gang, but all were released.

When we drove them from the restaurant, they went to Mayfield Road and made their headquarters at Tony Milano's Mayfield Road Inn, 12020 Mayfield Road, and Frank Milano's beer parlor, East 125th and Mayfield. On June 28, 1928, I arrested Polizzi, along with Charles Colletti, as suspects in the murder of Lawrence Lupo. Due to insufficient evidence, both were released. They then continued to hang around with the others mentioned along Mayfield Road, up until the time he [Chuck] married, and not much was seen of him. Later he became connected with the slot machine racket, and was also in the coal business. I have not seen him in the last seven years, but heard he was one of the large operators of slot machines but keeps himself in the background.

This is a very interesting memo on several counts. Note first the confusion as to the name—Charles Polizzi or Albert C. Polizzi?

Polizzi was known as Albert C. Polizzi from his first appearance of record in 1920 until after his marriage to Miss Angela

Page, 11919 Mayfield Road, on June 29, 1930. Sometime later he began calling himself Charles A. Polizzi.

The activity of two men, one calling himself Alfred and the other Albert Polizzi, caused considerable confusion in underworld as well as law-enforcement circles. The nicknames "Big Al" and "Chuck" were efforts to solve the problem, but as late as 1951 the Kefauver Committee had trouble separating their criminal records.

In addition to uncertainty as to the correct names, the Polizzi boys had a problem in deciding their blood relationship. Most people assumed they were brothers, and they did nothing to destroy the illusion. But when "Big Al" Polizzi was asked by the Kefauver Committee, this exchange took place:

> The CHAIRMAN: Is he your brother, Chuck Polizzi?
> Mr. POLIZZI: No; he is not a brother.
> The CHAIRMAN: How did he happen to have the same name? Is he related to you?
> Mr. POLIZZI: There are a lot of Polizzis.
> Mr. NELLIS: Is he related to you?
> Mr. POLIZZI: Well, I have always considered him a cousin.

Later, at another session, the committee again asked the question and was told:

> "Well, I have always considered him a cousin. I don't know whether he is or not. I mean his name is Polizzi, and actually I never met his folks, so I wouldn't know."

This testimony from a man who did know that his wife was a second cousin of the wife of Tony Milano.

Other people tried to get information. In 1952, Chuck Polizzi was in United States Tax Court protesting a tax assessment. His wife, Angela, testified on his behalf. On cross-examination, she was asked:

> "Now is Al Polizzi any relation to Mr. Polizzi?"
> Mrs. Polizzi replied, "Well, there is a relationship there."

Investigators from several federal agencies worried occasionally about Chuck Polizzi's background. Conflicts developed whenever a casual check was made. On one official record his birthplace was given as Chicago, on another it was listed as Cleveland. Even the names of the alleged parents varied.

These investigators did not know it but buried somewhere in a federal record center was the answer. It had been supplied to a federal investigator in 1944, and the man who gave him the information was Chuck Polizzi. At the time it was but a detail in a vast and complicated black-market liquor probe. The agent included the information in a report, and forgot it. Twenty-one years later other agents confirmed it.

The answer explained a lot of things.

Chuck Polizzi was not really a Polizzi. His parents were Jewish refugees from Russia. They reached Cleveland around the turn of the century, as did thousands of others. They lived in the Woodland district, which was soon invaded by families from Italy and Sicily.

The parents of "Polizzi" died young. Their son, left an orphan, was "adopted" by a family named Polizzi who lived nearby. Alfred "Big Al" Polizzi and the orphan grew up together. A few families knew the secret, but to the world of Cleveland the Jewish boy was a Polizzi.

As if seeking added protection, "Chuck" adopted a name similar to that of his friend. It helped. So did the illusion that "Big Al" and "Chuck" were brothers. They had the same name, they were seen together constantly in the joints of Woodland and later Mayfield Road.

As a Jewish boy growing up in what had become a predominantly Italian-Sicilian community, "Chuck" would have had problems. As a Polizzi, as the brother, or, at the least, cousin, of "Big Al" who was born in Sicily, he would have had prestige. It was that simple.

And the decision of the Cleveland Syndicate to employ "Chuck" Polizzi as a replacement for Kleinman was also that simple. Whatever Polizzi might call himself, or be considered, he was of Jewish stock just as were Sam Tucker, Moe Dalitz, and Louis Rothkopf. The parents of all had shared similar backgrounds. Moreover, "Chuck" as an assumed relative of "Big Al" Polizzi, and as a long-time associate of the Milanos and the Angersolas, was uniquely qualified to handle relations with the Mayfield Road Mob. With gambling becoming important, and with a huge new venture into alcohol production pending, co-operation was more important than ever.

Thus it was that Albert C. Polizzi, a man so broke in 1931 his tailor sued for a $119 bill, vanished to be replaced by Charles A. Polizzi, a man so affluent he listed his assets as $78,830 in a credit application in 1940. No longer did "Chuck" seek to be confused with "Big Al." He had become an individual in his own right.

And thus it was the police detective noted "not much was seen of him" after his name changed. As an associate of the syndicate, it was time to fade into the background and let the less fortunate graduates of Woodland and Mayfield Road take the glory and the blame.

Finally, it should be noted that "Chuck" Polizzi shared in more syndicate gambling operations than any other person bearing a non-Jewish name. When Kleinman came back, his old place of equality was waiting, but Polizzi retained high rank. Even "Big Al" could be proud of him. After all, "Chuck" had developed into what might be called "a cultural link."

4.

Morris Kleinman's attorneys were in Washington seeking vainly to win immunity for him when, on December 16, 1932, his associates formed the Buckeye Enterprises Company.

The firm was the first of several related ones, and it represented the formal arrangement as negotiated by "Chuck" Polizzi whereby the Cleveland Syndicate and the Mayfield Road Mob were to cooperate in selected ventures.

Testimony as to the efficiency of the arrangements was given when Frank Joiner was found on August 21, 1934. He had been buried head first in a lime pit, but a passing school dropout remembered his physiology course and recognized the bone he saw sticking out of the ground as that of a human heel.

Joiner had objected when "the Muscle," as his girl friend called it, wanted to take over the slot-machine business. His partner, Nathan Weisenberg, was more reasonable and lived another eleven years.

Based upon information supplied by Moe Dalitz in an official investigation, the partners in Buckeye were Dalitz, Tucker, Rothkopf, "Chuck" Polizzi, and from the Mayfield Road Mob, "Big Al" Polizzi, John "King" Angersola, Martin O'Boyle, and Harry Potter.

In the complicated financial dealings of the syndicate, nothing is quite as it appears. Thus O'Boyle represented the Irish faction as led by Thomas Jefferson McGinty, and Potter was the nominee of Sam "Gameboy" Miller.

Principal operation of Buckeye Enterprises was the Thomas Club, a plush casino just outside the city limits in a suburb known as Maple Heights. "Gameboy" managed it, assisted by his brothers, Dave "Honeyboy" Miller and Alex "Alky" Miller. Potter worked at the club. Years later, he was to serve as a nominee for syndicate members in the even plusher Beverly Hills casino near Newport, Kentucky.

Other companies listed by Dalitz included the Continental Supper Club, a combination restaurant and casino at 8591 Carnegie Avenue. Its business address was the office of Alvin E. Giesey—now in private practice as a tax expert. Wide-open gambling was featured, but the place closed a week after Reform in the person of Mayor Burton was elected in November, 1935.

The syndicate apparently liked the name, however, for they used it again some years later at Chesapeake, Ohio, across from Huntington, West Virginia.

Other inside-the-city syndicate casinos forced to close by Reform included the Shaw-Clair Catering Company at the corner of Shaw and St. Clair, and Superior Catering Company at 722 Superior Avenue. Again, Giesey's office was listed as the business address of both casinos.

It was Giesey who suggested that the income of Buckeye Enterprises be split for 1934 tax purposes after passage of a law permitting publication of tax returns that year. The theory was that a large sum attributed to one club might cause "heat." As a result, the Eastern Service Company came into being for one year only.

The Buckeye Catering Company was formed on or about January 1, 1935, to operate a slot-machine business previously conducted by Weisenberg and Joiner. Information about the early days of the business came from Christine Mace, a girl friend who met Joiner in Buffalo where he was establishing a slot-machine operation for Nate Weisenberg. She returned to Cleveland with him in 1927, and went to work as a secretary at the Harvard Avenue warehouse where the slots were stored. Joiner shared an apartment with her above the warehouse.

Pressure from "the Muscle" began in 1931, Miss Mace said, and by 1932, the boys from Mayfield Road were moving in. It was a step-by-step process, with the Mob first demanding 60 per cent of the profits on all slots outside the city limits, and then demanding a similar cut on machines inside the city. Weisenberg was ready to go along, but Joiner opposed it. He had already lost the Harvard Club to "Gameboy" Miller and James "Shimmy" Patton. The club had grown after being moved to Newburgh Heights, and Joiner resented his loss more every day. The slot-machine business was growing too, and Joiner resolved not to surrender the rest of it.

Joiner disappeared on the night of January 3, 1934, while Miss Mace was away in Buffalo. When she returned she discovered his records had also disappeared from their ransacked apartment. She reported him missing, she said, "but police didn't seem interested."

It was August 21 before Joiner's body was found in a pit beside what was called an "abandoned cottage" near Solon, Ohio.

Solon was a little community in southeast Cuyahoga County. Rothkopf owned property there. It turned out that the "cottage" boasted a six-car garage and a basement. Neighbors said the house had been owned by a bootlegger who had operated a brewery in the huge basement. A twenty-four-inch sewer pipe running from the basement to a deep ravine at the rear had been designed for a quick getaway.

Joiner, police said, had been living on borrowed time since July 5, 1930, when he watched gunmen shoot down "Big Joe" Porello and Sam Tilocca in Frank Milano's café on Mayfield Road. Now that he was blocking the path to slot-machine prosperity, he was filled with bullets, stripped, and dumped into the lime pit. Two partly filled sacks of lime and five pistol shells were found in that big basement.

Dalitz disclosed that he and his partners jointly owned 50 per cent of Buckeye Catering Company. Weisenberg and some of his old associates were allowed to keep the remaining half of the business—temporarily. Morris Haas was designated general manager and his brother, Sammy Haas, served as counsel. The business address was, of course, the office of Alvin Giesey.

In much the same fashion, the syndicate took control of the numbers racket. Men like Frank Hoge, Benny Mason, Willie Richardson, and "Hot Stuff" Johnson were "persuaded" to cut in the Mayfield Road Mob for a big portion of the profits. The men secretly associated with the Mayfield Road Mob were never mentioned.

The Cleveland Syndicate was altogether willing to take the cash and let the credit go. But its takeover of the gambling business was complete. The "Casino era" had begun, and, as if to give it moral justification, Gameboy Miller reported the Thomas Club was providing food and shelter for thirty indigent families in Maple Heights, and coal for twenty others.

It was a technique that was to become as standardized as loaded dice.

CHAPTER SEVEN

I invented the Save-All Pie Plate.
Jacob Stein

WITH THE PROBLEM of Morris Kleinman's substitute solved and the gambling business launched as insurance, the Cleveland Syndicate was ready to cash in on the fourth and last phase of Prohibition.

Liquor and alcohol had been diverted, home brew had come and largely gone, rum-running had enjoyed popularity—now the emphasis was to be on the operation of huge but illicit distilleries.

Such an investment gave promise of profits even after Prohibition ended—and no particularly astute businessman was needed to know the end was near. The warehouse supplies which had been consumed in the first phase would have to be replaced when Repeal came, and there would be a considerable lapse of time before good "legitimate" liquor could be put on the market. Then, too, the illegal product would be cheaper since federal and state taxes would not be added to the price.

The Cleveland boys were deep into the alcohol-production business by 1930—as Kleinman's records indicated—but their primary effort began in 1933. By then it was felt the opportunity was too large for one syndicate to handle. Old associates in the Eastern Syndicate were contacted and a joint operation was decided upon.

Records in the office of the secretary of state, Columbus, Ohio, show that Molaska Corporation officially came into being on November 25, 1933, just ten days before liquor again became legal. Incorporators were listed as two secretaries and a clerk in the offices of Sammy Haas in the Leader Building, Cleveland.

Officers of the corporation were listed but their names were also somewhat misleading:

President John Drew of New York, was, in reality, the Jacob Stein who had been a co-conspirator with Gaston B. Means back in the balmy days of the Ohio Gang. He had served briefly as a Department of Justice investigator and his testimony had helped send Means to prison. Later, in 1928 at Covington, Kentucky, he had been convicted in a giant liquor conspiracy known as the Wiedemann Brewing Case.

Vice-president Theodore Black of New York was a long-time associate of Stein, and had been involved with him in many alcohol plants along with well-known New York gangsters, such as John and Charles Polichek, alias Kramer.

Secretary Ray Tobien of Cleveland was a "front" for Charles A. Polizzi with whom he was associated in the Ray Coal Company.

Treasurer Sidney Kyman of Cleveland was a "front" for Sam Tucker. He was in the produce business and had known Tucker since they were boys on Hawthorne Avenue.

Assistant Treasurer Moses Citron of New York was a "front" for his son-in-law, Meyer Lansky, an overlord of the Eastern Syndicate and, at the time, co-boss with "Bugsy" Siegel of the "Bugs and Meyer Mob."

Director David Kyman of Cleveland was a "front" for Moe Dalitz. He was employed in the produce department of the Fischer Brothers Company.

Counsel of record was, first, Aaron Sapiro of Los Angeles, New York, and Chicago. He had to drop out after being indicted in Chicago with Al Capone, and his place was taken by Sammy Haas of Cleveland.

That was the official record. Others interested in Molaska included, in Ohio, such stalwarts as "Big Al" Polizzi, Peter Licavoli, and Charles Baron. In the East were included Louis "Lepke" Buchalter, Joe Adonis, Abner "Longie" Zwillman, Charles "Lucky" Luciano, and Frank Costello.

In the tangled history of Molaska Corporation can be found

the men and the associations upon which the structure of organized crime in mid-century America is based. It came into being as the National Syndicate was evolving, and its success had much to do with proving the value, and practicality, of cooperation by regional and cultural factions in a national association.

A closer look at affairs along the east coast is needed if the achievement of Molaska in supplying much of the nation east of the Rockies with illicit booze is to be understood.

2.

Rum-running in New York, as noted in Chapter Five, was largely the brainchild of Arnold Rothstein. He introduced the idea to certain lieutenants, such as Costello and "Dandy Phil" Kastel, Irving "Waxey Gordon" Wexler, and Jacob "Yasha" Katzenberg. Early in the game in a big way was "Big Bill" Dwyer, and soon the field was crowded.

The value of cooperation was not immediately apparent, but by 1928 a certain "drawing together" of rival mobs was apparent. A meeting was held on the twelfth floor of the Claridge Hotel, Forty-fourth and Broadway, and a merger was agreed upon. Joe (Doto) Adonis and Harry "Sweeney" Rosenberg agreed to quit a gentleman named Tony Caccino, and join forces with Katzenberg and his partners. Katzenberg later claimed they muscled in, but that was after he had become unhappy and returned to the narcotics business, to which Rothstein had introduced him.

A reason why Adonis, *et al.* were ready to quit Caccino was supplied by a retired federal agent who asked to remain nameless. Caccino had been an associate of Dwyer, and Dwyer was under investigation. To avoid testifying, Caccino had gone to an island in upper New York State. When discovered there, he reported he was too ill to leave. The agent was assigned to take a doctor to see Caccino and, if he was faking the illness, to bring him back.

The visitors were met by a delegation of gangsters and taken to a fishing lodge where Caccino was supposed to be convalescing. When they entered the big downstairs room, they found it crowded with more gangsters, some of whom were cleaning pistols and doing it in a conspicuous manner. They insisted the doctor go upstairs alone, and the frightened doctor obeyed. Soon he returned and in a loud voice announced that the patient was deathly ill and couldn't possibly testify. The hoods cheered this grim news, but the agent—a slender, dark-haired determined man—said that in that case he wanted to pay his last respects to Mr. Caccino. The boys, and the doctor, protested, but the agent went up the stairs.

> Caccino was in bed, [he related] and his beautiful Italian mistress was on a bed beside him. Caccino coughed and muttered that he wasn't long for this world. I called him a liar and told him to get up. The woman picked up a gun from beneath her bed and said she would kill me. Caccino laughed, took the gun away, and gave me his word he would come in next day. I went back downstairs and told the boys. The doctor still protested—until we were out of the house—that the patient was too ill. But Caccino was a man of his word as I knew he was—he came in next day and talked.

With Adonis and his associates in the association, it was decided to seek new sources of supply. Sam Blum of Chicago had set up pipelines to Charleston, South Carolina, and to Florida. Most of his booze came there from the Bahamas. He agreed to bring in 10,000 cases on each trip from Nassau. An outfit known as Stone's Express was to haul the liquor to a "drop" on Beckett Street in Brooklyn. But conditions being what they were, Blum had to arrange protection for his cargoes. He hired the Bugs and Meyer Mob, sometimes known in the trade by people who considered Lansky as kill-crazy as Siegel, as "the Two Bugs." However crazy the bosses might be, this forerunner of Murder, Inc., was efficient. It was also expensive, and after a few $30,000 expense accounts were turned in, the Mob decided to make the "Bugs" members of the combination.

The next development came when Charles "King" Solomon, boss of Boston booze, joined forces. He was to handle liquor landed by the Reinfeld Syndicate in and around New England, and ship it to New York via the New Haven Railroad. Stone's Express was also used to bring in the surplus. An average of six boxcars a week came in, each with 870 cases to the car.

Records show that, despite a halt during the hurricane season of 1928, 102 boxcars were shipped by "King" Solomon. Of the total, the "combination," as it was being called, got sixty. A group then headed by Dutch Goldberg took thirty-five cars because it was willing to pay a higher price. And the balance of seven cars was shipped on to the Middle West, to "a group headed by Louis the Chinaman who was in the laundry business in Detroit."

"Louis the Chinaman" was Louis Dalitz, brother of Moe Dalitz and his partner in various Detroit laundries. The retiring nature of the Cleveland Syndicate was never better illustrated than in the use Dalitz made of his brother as a front. Records show that at least some of the New York gangsters knew that "Louis the Chinaman" was in partnership with Moe Davis, but it was not until later they realized the real relationship. When they did, "Louis the Chinaman" was mentioned no more.

As to the nickname—almost anyone in the laundry business in those days ran the risk of being called "Chink" or "Chinaman."

In the latter part of 1929, Al and Bill Lillian of New Jersey joined the "combination" and were assigned to handle boat-loads that arrived off their territory. Jim Murphy's group of smugglers joined up, as did Jack Levinson and Eddie Michael's retailers.

It was 1931 before the easterners gave serious attention to alcohol production, thus beginning the final phase of Prohibition. The decision came at a meeting at the Hotel Belvedere in which it was decided to consolidate liquor sales offices at the Hotel Claridge. Smuggling was to continue, however, with the "combination" taking 60 per cent of the net profits and associate groups "cutting up" the remainder. But the new emphasis was to be on alcohol. Stills were set up near Kent Avenue in Brooklyn and at Forest Hills on Long Island.

Stone's Express, Inc., which had been used before, agreed to cooperate in the new venture but demanded that "Company" be substituted for "Inc." on trucks and buildings. A garage on Simms Street in Brooklyn became a "drop" for five-gallon cans and drums. An office was opened in the Chanin Building, 122 East Forty-second Street, under the name Tropical Molasses Company.

Molasses in dehydrated form was to be used as a substitute for sugar. It was cheaper and more efficient. Tropical Molasses imported it in 125,000 gallon lots from such firms as Molasses Products Corporation and Cuban Molasses Corporation. Tankers of the New York Barge Company, 11 West Forty-second Street, were used to transport the molasses.

But even as the Cleveland Syndicate continued rum-running while getting alcohol production under way, so did the eastern mobs. And the groups already cooperating to some extent were forced closer together when an overflooded market forced prices down. It was then the "Big Seven," forerunner of the Eastern Syndicate, came into existence. The organization of all top gangs on the eastern seaboard was formed primarily at the suggestion of Johnny Torrio—creator of the Capone legend—and lasted for about a year. Under the arrangement, each group could bring in only so much liquor at a time, and quotas were established according to previous volume. If one group disposed of all it had on hand, it could not buy more until the other groups had sold out too. The arrangement was clearly a violation of the Sherman Anti-Trust Act, but no prosecutions were reported.

One should not assume, however, that peace and harmony was the order of the day. Killings were common. Even a big shot might be double-crossed. Benjamin Baron, who worked as a transportation agent for the gangsters and the railroads, told federal agents what befell Sam Blum, the gentleman from Chicago who had been shipping booze in from the South.

Trucks from Stone's Express which met his boxcars would stop en route to an official destination of the cargo and drop off a few cases at an unofficial location. Thereupon, when the load did arrive, the gangsters were "shocked" to discover a shortage. Blum was shocked too—he couldn't understand what had happened. Sometimes as many as 100 cases from a total shipment of 870 cases would be missing. The New York boys righteously refused to pay the difference.

When, at last, Blum discovered the trick, he protested to Adonis. Joe agreed it was only right that Blum get his money and offered to collect it personally. He walked into the Claridge Hotel office one day and asked how much Blum was due. The figure was about $100,000, and Adonis demanded that amount. Katzenberg, serving as office manager that day, produced it, and Joe walked out.

The money was allegedly given to Blum, but since Blum disappeared the same day, Katzenberg always had his doubts. Meanwhile, Baron was notified by telephone to take care of arrangements for incoming shipments that normally Blum would have handled. Wondering what had happened to Blum, Baron went next day to the Claridge and asked Harry Rosenberg.

> Rosenberg didn't answer. I also asked Solomon and he didn't answer. I asked each as they came in. This included Joe Adonis, Meyer, the Bug, and Katzenberg. After this I was called into the Claridge in the presence of Joe Adonis, Bugs, Meyer, Solomon, and two strangers, and told if there were any questioning by police I was to know nothing.
>
> Later, [continued Baron] men from the South whom Blum had represented came to New York to straighten out their affairs and to find out what happened to Blum and their money. The mob told them that Blum had absconded. A new agreement was then made with these men. Bugs and Meyer took the money south with them and came back with bills of lading covering several weeks.

Baron played a minor role in an international venture of the Eastern-Cleveland Combination. In January, 1934, he was called to the Claridge Hotel by "Little Moe" Sedgwick, a recent addition to the high command. Sedgwick had been Waxey Gordon's alcohol man—Waxey's primary interest had been beer—but with both Dutch Schultz and Tom Dewey after Gordon, "Little Moe" had sought new connections. At the meeting, in addition to Sedgwick, were Siegel, Lansky, and Adonis. Baron was shown bills of lading and told to arrange shipment of thirteen railroad cars of liquor to Cleveland.

The liquor was part of a deal involving 700,000 gallons of alcohol purchased in Belgium and brought to New York by a ship chartered for the purpose. The Cleveland Syndicate's consignment was on its way as Baron had arranged, when part of it was discovered, turned back to New York, and confiscated on Pier 97.

It was to eliminate the risks involved in importation, as well as to cut the costs, that Molaska was created. When at last its stills—the largest ever found in the United States—were in full production, the only thing that had to be imported was molasses.

3.

Molaska Corporation was investigated at various times and at the same times by several federal and state agencies. If an example of the need for coordination of investigative agencies is ever wanted, none better than Molaska could be found. At a time when one agency was striving to link Moe Dalitz and Sam Tucker to the conspiracy, another agency was filing away the very evidence needed. Within the same agency there was confusion. Had agents in New York known what their colleagues in Cleveland knew, or vice versa, much more would have been achieved.

The necessary intelligence data was collected—but never coordinated. Even today, to get the complete picture, it is necessary to pull together reports from a dozen sources. The files of no federal agency, for example, contain any mention of the

"Stanton Avenue Arson Plot." Yet it was an essential background fact.

On November 30, 1932, smoke was observed coming out of a six-story building covering a square block of Stanton Avenue in the southeast section of Cleveland. Quick work by firemen prevented the ignition of 700 gallons of gasoline stored in twenty-four drums. The drums were resting on a makeshift wooden platform mounted on chairs in the basement. Surrounding the whole was a mountain of excelsior.

The property was owned, it developed, by the Beth Realty Company. The president of Beth Realty proved to be Edward P. Strong, that old pal of Nicky Arnstein. Henry Beckerman was vice-president and his law partner, Herman Felsman, was secretary. In default on the property were mortgage bonds of $315,000. Yet the property was insured for $800,000. A grand jury indicted Max Felsman, brother of Herman, and he was convicted of a charge of attempted arson.

Strong was reached in Florida by telephone when the plot was discovered. He told reporters he was astonished. Actually, he added, he was not involved, because he had given his stock in Beth Realty to Ungerleider & Company as security for his obligations there. Attempts to get Ungerleider's records before the grand jury failed—after all, the firm had President Harding's reputation to protect.

When at last the uproar died, as inevitably it did, the Stanton Avenue property became the site of Molaska Corporation's first dehydrated molasses-manufacturing plant. And, as already mentioned, Strong's old associate, Sammy Haas, eventually became attorney for Molaska. Haas' experience with arson plots had come some years earlier.

But perhaps the story of Molaska begins with Jacob Stein. There was some difficulty in making him admit he was Jacob Stein—he kept insisting his name was John Drew. Technically, he was right. When his background could no longer be concealed, he admitted he had obtained a court order in 1933 which transformed "Jacob Stein" legally into "John Drew."

After all the problems involved in getting that one fact established, investigators were naturally a bit skeptical of other statements by Stein. But some of them actually checked out.

Stein said that in 1932 he was contacted by one Manuel Leavitt about the possibility of manufacturing powdered molasses. Together they organized the Molasses Products Company in Albany, New York. This venture was unsuccessful, Stein said.

Other investigations, however, mentioned the Albany company as a supplier of many of the alcohol stills along the east coast. Its products were hauled by the bargeload to points as far away as Boston by such people as Benjamin Zuckerman.

For whatever the reason—possibly because new plants were needed—Stein left Albany and contacted his old friend and associate, Theodore Black. Stein, Black, and a bootlegger named Joe Darvin, had operated earlier from 55 West Forty-second Street, New York. They were associated with the Polichek brothers of Brooklyn, and with Abe, Isaac, and Nate Scharlin of Chicago. As operator of the Acme Feed & Supply Company, 612 North Michigan Street, Chicago, Abe Scharlin became one of Molaska's best customers. Still later he was associated with Johnny Torrio after that master craftsman of crime turned Chicago over to Capone and returned to the New York area to build a legal liquor empire under the name Prendergast-Davies Company.

In any case, according to Stein, his friend Black said he knew some people out in Cleveland and he went to Cleveland to talk to them. As a result, he continued, Black secured the financial support of Ray Tobien, Sidney and David Kyman, and a plant was constructed (installed is a better word) at Cleveland for the manufacture of dehydrated molasses.

This account was given with a straight face and apparently accepted with one, but investigators later checked it out. They talked to David Kyman and obtained a statement which said in part:

> For many years I have been engaged in the produce busi-

ness in Cleveland. . . . About two and a half years ago a party by the name of Moe Davis [Dalitz] called on me and stated that as he did not wish to use his name, would I permit him to use my name in connection with a corporation that he, Davis, was interested in. I had known Moe Davis for several years, and I told him that as a favor to him I would permit the use of my name in the Molaska Corporation.

I never paid anything to the Molaska Corporation for stock or other purposes, nor have I entered into the management or financial affairs of the Molaska Corporation except indirectly for Moe Davis. Any record of my name or contribution either for stock or other purposes has been solely for Moe Davis who put up said monies and funds in my name. I have never taken any active interest in the management of its affairs except on two or three occasions when I was present at meetings held in the Hollenden Hotel in Cleveland. . . . I really don't know what my connection is with Molaska, if any.

Sidney Kyman, for fourteen years in the produce business, also talked freely.

About two and a half years ago, one Sam Tucker came to me and asked my permission to use my name in connection with the Molaska Corporation. . . . I have never taken any interest, active or otherwise, in the affairs of Molaska Corporation, nor have I attended any of their meetings or put one red cent into that corporation. . . . I do not know John Drew, president of the Molaska Corporation, neither do I know Theodore Black, the vice-president.

Ray Tobien, president of the Ray Coal Company, said in part:

I have been in the coal business the past five years. . . . Associated with me in the Ray Coal Company is one Charles Polizzi, also known as Chuck Polizzi, who is the owner of one-fourth interest in the Ray Coal Company. . . . [It should not be difficult to guess who owned the remaining three-fourths.] Sometime ago I loaned Charles Polizzi about $5,000 which Polizzi invested in the Molaska Corporation, presumably in my name. The stock certificate subsequently was issued in my name and I endorsed this stock certificate over to someone whom I believe to be a party by the name of Sapiro in New York.

I have never taken any active interest whatsoever in the management or operation of the Molaska Corporation except to sign a quantity of blank checks as treasurer of said Molaska Corporation in advance for John Drew, the president. . . .

If Tobien seemed somewhat deeper involved than the other "fronts," it might well be because the Ray Coal Company existed primarily to supply coke and coal to the syndicate's stills throughout Ohio. Records revealed that Ohio operations of Molaska purchased coke from the company.

But, to return to the history of Molaska as recounted by Jacob Stein–John Drew, he told his interviewers that, shortly after the Cleveland investors were secured, it became necessary "to enlarge" the corporation. "One Moses Citron, a large produce dealer of New York came into the picture and supplied $121,000 of additional capital. One thousand shares of stock were issued under one certificate, and this certificate was placed in trust with Aaron Sapiro, Citron's attorney."

An investigator contacted Moses Citron and confirmed the "produce dealer" had invested in Molaska. According to the report of the interview, "Citron said he made this investment through a son-in-law, Meyer Lansky, who resides at the Majestic Apartments at Central Park West." (Costello lived there for some years too.) It was "through his son-in-law," the report continued, "he met Teddy Black. All business he did with Molaska was transacted through Meyer Lansky [who] represented to him that considerable money could be made in the molasses business."

According to Citron, Lansky owned the Elaine Food Company, 1501 Kings Highway, Brooklyn, "but that Lansky of late had been devoting most of his time to the Molaska Corporation."

Citron added, according to the report, that unfortunately his son-in-law was away on vacation at the time. He promised when Lansky returned he "would have him get in touch with us."

Meyer Lansky, famous as a partner in the "Bugs and Meyer Mob," was born Maier Suchowljansky on July 4, 1902, in that part of Russia which once had been Poland. He came to the United States in 1911 and was naturalized in 1928 in New York. Slight of build, only five-feet-six, he suffered from a complaint Dixie Davis ascribed to Dutch Schultz—he thought he was a Napoleon. His first wife was Anna Citron. Of their three children, one later graduated from West Point and, reportedly, never spoke to his father again.

At the time Lansky was said by his father-in-law to be on vacation, he was in Cuba wooing another man who, as did Napoleon, liked to be called a "sergeant." Much later, after Sergeant Batista returned from an exile in Florida, Lansky and some of his Cleveland associates in Molaska went back to Cuba.

Meanwhile, investigators asked Stein–Drew for more information about "Citron's attorney," Aaron Sapiro. Changing his story somewhat, Stein said Sapiro was brought into the organization by Citron because he could dispose of large amounts of dried molasses through his farm connections. He represented forty-five farm organizations, Stein continued, and was widely recognized as an expert on farm problems. Unfortunately, he got himself indicted with Al Capone in the Chicago version of the "Cleaner's and Dyer's War."

Aaron Sapiro—investigators kept calling him "Shapiro"—was, in many respects, as amazing as Gaston B. Means. He came to New York from California, and was indeed recognized as an expert on farm problems. The New York *Times* on September 23, 1930, carried a story identifying Sapiro as "the author of a cooperative marketing act which is in force in forty-one states." The story concerned a speech Sapiro made in Boston at a Chamber of Commerce dinner. In the speech, Sapiro assailed Herbert Hoover's "Farm Board" for what he called "gross inefficiency."

But on January 23, 1934, the *Times* was reporting from Chicago that Sapiro was on trial, one of twelve defendants alleged to have conspired to damage plants of cleaners and dyers. Among the defendants were Al Capone, already in prison, Murray "the

Camel" Humphries, Chicago Alderman Oscar Nelson, and Dr. Benjamin F. Squires, "former czar of the cleaning and dyeing industry." Sapiro was involved as counselor for the Chicago Laundry Owners Association.

The defendants were acquitted after a key witness and former Illinois attorney general killed himself, but Sapiro was soon on trial again in New York on jury-fixing charges. The *Times*, in reporting the case, identified Sapiro as the man "who attracted nationwide attention several years ago by suing Henry Ford for alleged anti-Semitic statements published in the Dearborn *Independent*."

Again Sapiro "beat the rap" after the first effort ended in a mistrial. He went back to California where respectability could be re-established under the shadow of his brother, a state supreme court justice.

Sapiro's address, and the New York address of the Molaska Corporation, was 500 Fifth Avenue. The building, a taller-than-average skyscraper next to the New York Public Library, was to be mentioned again some years later in another Eastern Syndicate liquor operation. But when Sapiro became involved in Chicago, he dropped out of Molaska and vacated the office.

The troubles of Sapiro apparently recalled to Stein some of his own. He told the interviewer that life could have been different after he invented something called the "Save-All Pie Plate." Unhappily, Nate Scharlin was pressing him for a personal debt so he transferred his patent rights to Nate in payment, and Nate turned around and sold them to a Chicago concern which proceeded to make a mint.

The interviewer tried to get Stein back to Molaska, but there wasn't much more to add, said Stein. After the Cleveland plant was operating, they opened another in Elizabeth, New Jersey. But problems arose, and all he wanted to do was to get out and leave Molaska behind just as he had left his career as Jacob Stein behind.

After all, he had children coming along. . . . That's why he changed his name. . . . He was John Drew now.

CHAPTER EIGHT

It was decided I had been having a pipe dream.
Robert Bridges

BY 1933 WHEN ROBERT BRIDGES REACHED CLEVELAND, he had developed a rather short temper. There was a reason. Back in Seattle a decade before, Bridges had been a cop. When President Harding came to town on his last trip to Alaska, officials borrowed Bridges' car. It wasn't really his—it had been loaned to him while his own jalopy was being repaired.

After Harding died, and while people were still able to grieve for him, it was discovered he had ridden in a stolen car. Bridges was blamed. It was years before he was officially vindicated.

Meanwhile, in disgust, he had wandered east and become a Prohibition agent in Detroit. Conditions there, as Lawrence Fleischman proved, were not conducive to high morale. Bridges became something of a "loner," trusting no one, caring only for his own reputation. He was transferred to Grand Rapids and, eventually to Cleveland, as an undercover man. The success of his mission exposed his undercover role, and the Cleveland assignment was made permanent.

Bridges' temper didn't improve any as he was taken by his colleagues around town on "get-acquainted" tours. One agent would point out a sharp-looking hood and say, "That's Maxie Diamond, a big-shot Jew racketeer." A few days later another agent would point out the identical person and say, "That's Frank Milano, a big-shot Italian racketeer."

"Finally," said Bridges, "I got sick of the whole business. When I found one of these fellows with a black overcoat and a white hat, I lined him up against the wall and went through his pockets to find out who he really was. And I found out that these agents, many of whom it developed were 'on the take,' didn't even know who they were taking from."

(All of which perhaps explains why investigators could announce later that the real name of Moe Davis was Fred Bennett.)

About the middle of 1933, there was a shake-up and most of the Cleveland agents were transferred. Bridges was one of three left in Cleveland. One of the departing agents tipped Bridges just before leaving that a giant distillery was in operation at Fifty-third and Sweeney. Bridges began an investigation "in my spare time."

An official report of the case dated October 10, 1934, states "the investigation regarding this still started in July, 1933."

Bridges began making "casual reports" on the distillery. No molasses or sugar could be seen entering the large brick building at 5301 Sweeney Avenue, and nothing ever seemed to come out. Yet a guard was posted at the door.

In August, 1933, Bridges and a colleague, H. D. Boldt, saw the guard leave the premises to get lunch. They took advantage of his absence to look in through a broken window—the doors being heavily padlocked. The building was absolutely empty, but Bridges noted the floor appeared to be covered with cinders.

On October 20, Bridges learned from records in the city engineer's office that an abandoned sewer of brick construction having an interior diameter of five feet ran close by 5301 Sweeney. The sewer also passed close by property at Fifty-fifth and Truscon streets on which were located the storage tanks of Molaska Products Company. Molaska Products, it developed later, was the predecessor to the Molaska Corporation.

When Bridges tried to get into the sewer, he found the manhole cover had been recently cemented down. Undaunted, the stubborn agent knocked off the cement and forced open the manhole, but upon entering was almost overcome with fumes.

Retreating, Bridges went to the fire department and, after some delay, arranged to borrow a gas mask and some lights.

But before he could return to the manhole, he received abrupt instructions to report to the Detroit office. On October 22, Bridges went to Detroit.

The official report of the incident notes Bridges was ordered not to go through the sewer, the implication being it was considered too dangerous. Bridges supplemented the report by saying he was "told it was a wild goose chase," and informed he was being put in charge of the Cleveland office.

"I had heard," Bridges said, "some previous talk through racket circles that to control me they were going to put me in charge of the district and maybe that would satisfy me."

Apparently the syndicate, assuming as usual that every man had a price, figured Bridges was bucking for promotion by his "spare time" activity, and, if promoted, would be happy. They were wrong.

> "I told the major in no uncertain terms what he could do with the appointment," Bridges said. "I told him I wasn't going to be responsible for anybody's actions but my own. Upon my return to Cleveland I was met at the depot by a prominent racket boy and these two agents. They complimented me on having been appointed head of the district. When I told them I had declined it, they told me I had cooked my goose."

A day or so later, Bridges continued, he was in the office of a man who controlled sugar in the Akron area. "I didn't even know his name at the time, but I had traced molasses and sugar through his operations and went to interview him. He told me to get the hell out. Said I had missed my chance to make thousands of bucks. They had gone to a great deal of trouble to get me appointed, I had turned it down, and he would talk only to the man in charge."

Shortly thereafter, Eliot Ness, the "Untouchable" from Chicago, was transferred to Cleveland as acting investigator in charge.

"Eliot Ness," said Bridges, "never made an arrest in his life."

Meanwhile, Bridges continued his investigation of 5301

Sweeney Avenue. On one occasion, he said, an agent was sent out from Washington to check his reports. It was a "bitter cold day," he recalled. "On the back of the brick building were yellow-stained icicles, a characteristic of an illicit distillery. The steam and fumes seep through the walls and stain the ice that hangs from buildings in a cold climate." Yet the man from Washington was not impressed.

Pursuing his lone-wolf activity, Bridges satisfied himself that molasses was being pumped through the abandoned sewer from the storage tanks some 700 feet to the basement of the Sweeney Avenue building. The finished alcohol was being pumped, he discovered, in another direction to an alleged gasoline station. Occasionally large tank trucks would seem to replenish the station's gasoline tanks. Instead, alcohol was pumped into the tank trucks, and hauled away.

It was August, 1934, before Bridges at last got the green light from his superiors. A conference was held, and, according to an official report, it was decided that "since there was so much smoke there must be some fire." Bridges was at last officially assigned to investigate.

Prompting the decision was a report "that a huge still is being erected somewhere in this territory and columns from this still [Sweeney Avenue] are being used."

On September 7, 1934—fourteen months after the official beginning of the case—Bridges raided the premises at Sweeney Avenue. In the party was his boss, acting investigator-in-charge Eliot Ness. The first discovery concerned the cinder-covered floor. It had one foot of rolled cinders on top, two feet of rolled clay beneath, and a thick concrete base.

Beneath that floor, well under the ground, had been a giant distillery. But it was there no longer. It had been dismantled and moved out.

From pieces of equipment left behind it was possible to deduce that the capacity of the still had been "in excess of 2,000 gallons daily." Six column stills had been used in the operation, the largest being four feet in diameter.

A galvanized iron flume or pipe containing several electric blower fans ran from the still room to a tall stack erected on the adjacent premises at 5221 Sweeney Avenue. Smoke from the boilers and fumes from the distilling room were thus disguised as belonging to the Sweeney Metal Company.

Water for the operation had been stolen from the city of Cleveland. A six-inch water line had been run across the street to a railroad roundhouse, and connected to the city's water mains. Bridges found the fittings used in tapping the mains had also come from the city. Electricity had been supplied in the name of the Oxford Machine Company. Power company records indicated the distillery began operations in November, 1932.

Other records indicated that Molaska Products Company "originally went into business as a means of providing molasses for this illicit distillery."

When the raiding party struck, it found five workmen in the employment of the Acme Boiler and Welding Company. They had been working for two weeks, they said, dismantling three large steam boilers. Since there was nothing illegal about the presence of three boilers, the raiders could not stop the men from working. But Bridges, suspicious as ever, "surreptitiously scratched my initials on the boilers." He had a hunch, he said, he might see them again some day.

He was right.

2.

Solomon Berman was fifty years old when he found himself saddled with civic responsibilities, but they were not unwelcome. After all, he had run for office on a platform which stressed the need to encourage new industry. And having won election as a Zanesville, Ohio, councilman, he was not without ideas when, on January 1, 1934, he was sworn in.

As he explained in a statement later, as early as December he had talked to Sam Goldstein about the problem. Sam had a son, Bernard, who worked at the Lubeck Brewery in Toledo, and knew one of the big shots there, an Abe Moore. And there was talk, Sam reported, that Lubeck might expand. So, here was a prospect. In fact, Moore had mentioned Zanesville as a possible site.

Early in the spring, Berman and a cousin, Lester Gold, went to Toledo to see Moore but learned Moore operated out of Cleveland. With the city footing the expense accounts, Berman went next to Cleveland to contact the elusive Moore. He took along Frank Bauers, a Zanesville policeman. Whether he wanted Bauers as a driver or a bodyguard was never made quite clear. There was some indication Berman was not as naïve as he appeared.

Moore was located, and proved very friendly. There was a good possibility Lubeck might relocate in Zanesville, he said. Things were not going too well in Toledo. He promised to pay the town a visit in the immediate future. Meanwhile, so Berman would have some tangible result of his trip, he gave the councilman a bottle of Lubeck's beer to take home.

Two weeks later Berman received a telegram which he proudly displayed to his fellow councilmen, the Senior and Junior Chambers of Commerce, and Charles J. Barron, a furniture dealer who also happened to be the city safety director. Abe was coming down on an inspection trip.

When Moore arrived he was met by an official reception committee which included representatives from most of the town's civic groups. All available industrial sites were shown. Moore displayed particular interest in the old J. B. Owens Pottery and Tile Plant, a sprawling three-story brick structure on North Dearborn Street. But following an official banquet at the Zane Hotel, Moore said they would hear from him later and departed.

"I've never seen or heard from him since," reported Berman.

At this point, some word on the company Berman and his associates on the city council and in the chambers of commerce were trying to attract to the city, might be in order. "Big Al" Polizzi, a member among other things of Buckeye Enterprises, told the Kefauver Committee rather bluntly that, "I started that company." Others involved from the beginning in 1933 were William Goldenberg, alias William Gerson, and Abe Moore. Goldenberg invested $42,787 in the company between January 27, 1933, and January 6, 1934.

Both Goldenberg and Moore, like Polizzi from Cleveland, had been associates in Toledo of Thomas "Yonnie" Licavoli, brother of Peter and, until convicted of four murders, boss of the Italian version of the Purple Gang. Early in 1934, Lubeck Brewery was cited for various violations, and in June, Goldenberg and Moore officially severed their direct connections. No one knew about Al Polizzi's role at the time.

No one knew, or at least would not admit to knowing, just how the effort to attract new industry paid off. But on August 3, 1934, a man registered at the Zane Hotel under the name of Harry Bender, of Cleveland. He opened negotiations with the owner of the tile plant, a Chalmer O. Mulligan, and after failing to lease the property agreed to buy it. Using the name Harry Smith, Bender took possession of the plant on August 17.

Proving once again the use of insulation, it was later learned that the real name of Bender, alias Smith, was Harry D. Bader. He came from Cleveland where he had $15 divided between a bank account and a safe deposit box—at least that's what was there when investigators looked.

Bader, this time as Harry Smith, registered again at the Zane Hotel on August 21, and stayed there until January 18, 1935. In the room next to him, with a connecting door, was William Goldenberg. Shortly after they arrived, work began on remodeling the tile plant and installing in it the "Baltic Feed Company."

Solomon Berman, the enterprising city councilman, said he first became aware his efforts had been rewarded when, sometime in September, he was in the rathskeller of the Zane Hotel. Several men invited him to join them at their table. Three were "Jewish," he said, and one "Italian." He later recognized one of them as Harry Bader. Another he knew as William Gerson proved to be Goldenberg.

Both Bader and "Gerson" had "large rolls," Berman said, and tipped the waiters generously after each round of drinks. They secured Berman's telephone number and, a few days later, summoned him to a room in the hotel. The "Italian" was there and he announced plans to do contracting work. Were there any local people the councilman would like to recommend? If so, send them out to the Baltic Feed Company with notes addressed to Mr. Holtz, and they would be taken care of immediately.

Berman noted that "I contacted William Watson, one of my political associates, and told him that if he knew of two or three good workers from our political organization who wanted work, to send them out to the Baltic Feed Company. I know Watson sent several men out there who were placed to work."

The councilman was also called upon to tell Bader and "Gerson" about the city's sewer system. Bader took him for a drive and Berman pointed out the points where Zanesville's sewerage emptied into the Muskingum River. At the time, Berman had been told there was a unique opportunity to secure a beer outlet by buying the Star Hotel "for a song." He looked it over, he said, but after January, 1935, the opportunity vanished. So did the Baltic Feed Company.

Another man who was given an opportunity to display civic hospitality was Charles J. Barron. Exactly one day before Bader took formal possession of the old tile plant, Barron resigned as city safety director. He said his resignation was "due to some differences I had with the mayor on certain policies."

With the problem of law enforcement off his shoulders, Barron could concentrate upon his furniture business at 335 Linden Avenue. And, pretty soon he had a new customer. Harry Bader, using the name "Bender," appeared "and purchased several chairs and a coal heating stove and said he was starting a feed plant down in the old J. B. Owens building and he requested me to deliver these items there."

Barron said he asked "if you are going to need any help out there," and when Bender said he would soon need "twenty or thirty laborers," Barron said he told him he could furnish some people and "would consider it a favor if you would put them on."

Bender was agreeable, so the former city safety commissioner became an unofficial employment agency for the Baltic Feed Company. Among the people he placed for work was his brother, Emory Barron. When Bender wanted a reliable night watchman, Barron sent Charlie Smitley out that very night. Other chores included personal intervention with the telephone company to get telephones installed. The biggest bit of business came, however, when Bender leased a house across the street from the tile plant, and Barron furnished it completely with new furniture, carpets, and draperies. When asked about this, Barron first said he had rented it himself to be used as a "love nest." He changed his story when told that a tunnel had been constructed beneath the street from the tile plant to the basement of the dwelling house.

The value of having a leading businessman and former safety director in one's pocket was illustrated one day when Barron dropped in on his successor, Ernest Graham, at City Hall. Graham remarked, he said, that Milton Stotts suspected "there was a bunch of gangsters" out at the Baltic Feed Company.

"I told Graham," Barron said, "I would be glad to go out there with Stotts and look the place over, which we did the following day. We met Mr. Bender there and he took us over the plant. There were no signs of any gangsters or any indications of bootlegging at the place."

Milton J. Stotts was chief of detectives in Zanesville. One day in the middle of September, he related, he was parked on Main Street about 5:45 P.M. "I noticed three foreigners who were strangers to me knock on the door of the Star Store, which was closed for the day. The janitor let them in. They were in the place about fifteen minutes and came out carrying a bundle. One of them laughed and said to the others, 'Well, we got the overalls, didn't we?' "

Stotts investigated and was told by Morris Hirsch, one of the owners of the store, that the men bought three suits of overalls and said they knew Mr. Levy, another of the owners. The detective followed the men to a hotel, got their names, and checked with the Canton Police Department. One of the three had a record "for running liquor." Upon checking again with the hotel clerk, he learned the men left every 6 A.M. "dressed up," and came back late in the afternoon "still dressed up."

Next morning another detective was assigned to tail them, and he "followed them all the way to the J. B. Owens Pottery plant. They drove up to the big doors and someone on the inside opened the door and the car drove in."

More curious than ever, Stotts went out to the plant in time to witness a truck loaded with gravel drive inside. When it came out empty, he stopped it. The driver was Chalmer O. Mulligan, Jr. The youth explained he was from Crooksville, Ohio—no insulation wanted there. His father had owned the property and still operated a small pottery plant in one corner. He was hauling the gravel, he said, for Mr. Bender, who was having a new cement floor installed.

Stotts continued his quiet investigation, attempting vainly to get information about Zanesville's new industry. The Chamber of Commerce knew it had a new industry, he said, but didn't know any details. A check of some license plates on cars seen at the plant uncovered the names of some more ex-bootleggers and bookmakers.

The inspection trip with Barron soon followed. Stotts said he looked for new cement work, but couldn't find any. His suspicions remained. More license numbers were obtained and Stotts contacted the house detective at the Hollenden Hotel in Cleveland. The detective, who must have been new on the job and naïve, actually checked out the names and reported they belonged "to an alky ring." The personnel at the Hollenden, headquarters of the Cleveland Syndicate, was seldom so cooperative.

Word came in that the odor of cooking mash could sometimes be detected near the tile plant and few doubts remained. Safety Director Graham told Stotts to expect to be contacted soon by Bender—and "to play along and get all the information you can."

On December 5, Bender called, and arranged a meeting. At 7:30 P.M. they talked in front of the courthouse.

> Bender said, "I understand you've been checking up on me and some of my boys," and I told him, "Yes, we don't want any gangsters in Zanesville. We've never had a bank robbery in our town and we're not going to have any." He then said that anyone who was with him was not in the bank robbery racket and he would guarantee I would never have any trouble with anyone associated with him.
>
> He then said [Stotts continued] that "I want to make you a little present," and he pulled out some bills and handed them to me.

The detective said he protested there was nothing he could do to help Bender, and was told Bender didn't want him to do anything "'other than if one of my boys gets picked up, you can stop them from being fingerprinted.'" He then gave Stotts two pints of whiskey which, with five $20 bills, was his reward for the evening. Stotts recorded the serial numbers on the bills at headquarters and waited for the next move. It came on January 3, 1935.

Bender called Stotts at home and arranged a meeting. "He asked if I had been hearing anything about their plant. I told him there were rumors there was a still out there. I asked him if it was his truck that was knocked off around Dennison about Christmas with 400 gallons of whiskey. He said, 'No, I thought you knew we make nothing but alcohol.'"

The conversation continued, Stotts said, and he asked if Bender were not worried about being raided.

"He said he was not worried about being knocked off as he had the state and federal fixed and that his outfit had connections right in Washington. If any knocks went in they would just be notified to move. He claimed they had been in business ten years and had never lost a plant, but had to move three different times."

Bob Bridges would have been interested in that.

Near the conclusion of the discussion, Stotts said, Bender asked how to approach the chief of police "as he would like to send him a present if he was sure he [the chief] would get it. He also stated that this was the first town he was ever in that he had such a hard time trying to contact officials. In most other towns the officials would run them to death for a payoff. He handed me a $100 bill and said, 'Here is a little Christmas present as I did not get to see you Christmas.' And he also gave me a package containing six pints of whiskey and said when I ran out to let him know and he would see that I got some more."

Stotts turned in the money and whiskey. Contact was made with a federal agent and the situation reported. The agent arrived in Zanesville on January 16, 1935, and asked "why we did not notify the boys in Columbus, and I told him that the director and the chief wanted to be sure this information got into the right hands. He told me he knew one of the Columbus men and figured he was a square shooter. The following day Forrest Trees, state liquor inspector, and Joe Redden, federal investigator of the Alcohol Tax Unit, came to Zanesville . . . they asked me how many men we could furnish. I told them they could have every man on the force. . . ."

Stotts ended his statement by recalling that Bender had invited him to a party at Cleveland where "I would 'meet some real fellows.' He mentioned that Mr. Moe Davis would be there, but, you see how I stand, we never made the trip."

In charge of the investigating team which came to Zanesville was Basil H. Minnich, an Alcohol Tax Unit inspector. Accompanied by Redden and Trees, he made a preliminary check of the tile company between 11 P.M. and 3 A.M. on January 18–19. Sounds and odors were sufficient to convince him a distillery was being operated. A federal search warrant was secured and a raid launched at 1:30 P.M. the same day.

> Upon entering [Minnich reported] I searched the eastern part of the building which was a three-story structure with a basement, and found it to be vacant except for an air compressor which was electrically operated and in operation. Two

> large bins extending from the first to the third floor and some shafts with pulley wheels presented the appearance of recent construction.
>
> I then went further west in the building and entered a large room described as an old kiln. . . . Three men were patching the floor with concrete near the northwest wall. From this room could be heard a roaring sound resembling the blowing of a furnace. I looked for an entrance into that part of the building from which the sound came, but could find none. Then I went on to the roof and assisted in breaking through a skylight near a large steel smoke stack. At this point the sound previously described seemed directly below. When we succeeded in breaking through, the noise below ceased. Inspector Redden then descended a fire hose to the room below. I went back to the old kiln room. After a short while, Redden found a door in the brick on the west side of the old kiln room. The door was concealed from the kiln room by a tall cupboard which had been placed there for the purpose. I proceeded through this opening and found . . .

What Minnich, Redden, Trees, and the others found was the largest illicit distillery ever captured—before or since.

The distillery contained mash vats which required 48,600 pounds of sugar, and 15,200 pounds of "Molaska"—dehydrated blackstrap molasses—to fill. From these ingredients 36,506 gallons of mash per day were made. By using continuous-process procedures, 5,000 gallons of 190-proof alcohol of the highest grade were produced every twenty-four hours. Twelve men worked two twelve-hour shifts to keep production going. The alcohol sold for $2 per gallon wholesale, and for as much as $2.50 per quart retail. Cost of production, including the price of protection, labor, fuel, and raw materials, was estimated at fifty cents per gallon.

Minnich's report was one of first impressions, however. It continued:

> I proceeded through this opening and found a large quantity of soft cane sugar, molaska, chemicals, large steel tanks, large mixing vats, two steam boilers, large storage tanks con-

> taining a quantity of alcohol, a machine designed for filling five-gallon tin containers, electric motors, a ventilating system, fifty-gallon steel drums, a large quantity of five-gallon tin containers, etc.
>
> From this room I followed a tunnel running east under the old kiln room, into another room in which was installed a complete alcohol distillery. From this room I observed the mouth of another tunnel running east which, upon subsequent investigation, I found terminated in the cellar of a dwelling house located east of the tile plant.

The occupant of the house, Minnie Clara Barnes, escaped from the house at the time of the raid. So did a number of the distillery employees including Bader, alias Bender. The woman, investigation proved, had been living at the house "for the sole purpose of insuring the use of the escape tunnel in case of necessity."

There was also another secret exit from the room housing the distillery. A ladder led up to a trap door in the ceiling which opened into a tiny secret room on the first floor. The exit from the secret room was a hidden door which opened into a false toilet. Outside the toilet was still another room which featured a board fastened to the wall with four large nails. When a fifth nail was placed across the heads of the two center nails on the board, a signal was flashed to the distillery below by means of an electric buzzer.

Other electric alarm signals were installed in an elaborate network throughout the plant.

After the excitement ended, the investigators returned for a long and sober look. Three columns had been employed. One was a beer column—Lubeck had expanded to Zanesville after all. The beer column was made up of eight sections, each three feet high and fourteen feet in circumference. On each side of the beer column was a rectifying column of the same size for alcohol production.

Four steel cookers, equipped with steam coils, had a capacity of 7,400 gallons each. There were eight fermentors with a total capacity of 161,994 gallons; four yeasting tanks of about 800 gallons each. Beer production, in addition to the alcohol was estimated at 36,506 gallons daily. Both beer and alcohol were shipped out by the boxcar load. As Berman and his friends had pointed out when they first took Abe Moore on a sightseeing tour, the plant was near a railroad siding.

Cost of the plant was estimated as "at least $250,000."

Twenty-three defendants were indicted as a result of the raid, of whom twelve were ultimately convicted. Harry D. Bader, alias Bender, alias Smith, was sentenced to two years. He had fled through the tunnel, but had been captured in Kansas City after officials discovered he was related to Louis Rothkopf. It developed that Bader was living at a house in Kansas City while the owner of the house was living on Rothkopf's farm near Solon, Ohio, at a place called Chagrin Falls.

Goldenberg, alias Gerson, was sentenced to a year and a day. John O'Boyle, one of Thomas Jefferson McGinty's aides, escaped with a sentence of six months.

Meanwhile, Bob Bridges had come down from Cleveland to see the huge distillery. He examined the steam boilers found there and was not surprised to discover the marks he had placed upon them back on Sweeney Avenue in Cleveland. Rather ruefully, the investigators reported:

"This still was owned and operated by the Moe Davis Syndicate here in Cleveland. This plant almost in its entirety was formerly located at 5301 Sweeney Avenue, Cleveland. . . ."

The report also noted that ingredients used at the Zanesville plant included "dehydrated molasses sold under the trade name of 'Molaska,' a large quantity of which was seized. The manufacturer's name appearing on the containers of Molaska was The Molaska Corporation."

3.

Shortly before Bob Bridges was at last given the green light to investigate the Sweeney Avenue still, the Molaska Corporation closed its manufacturing plant on Stanton Avenue. Jacob Stein–John Drew, Teddy Black, and "Sambo" Tucker went to Elizabeth, New Jersey, and leased a factory from the Bethlehem Steel Company at 151 South Front Street.

The lease ran from October 1, 1934, to October 1, 1935, and the rent was $12,000. Tucker remained on the payroll of Molaska's New Jersey plant in a supervisory capacity. Production began December 1.

Meanwhile, back in Cleveland, arrangements were made to handle local distribution. Edward Udelson who, with his brother, Saul, operated a flour and feed company on Woodland Avenue, said he was approached in November about acting as the Cleveland distributor.

Udelson knew about molaska, he said, because he had earlier observed the boys at the Liberty Poultry Company using it to fatten chickens for market. Trust Kleinman's old family firm to have the latest wrinkle.

Shortly after Black offered the dealership to Udelson, a man giving the name of Hall showed up and paid in advance for 200 bags of Molaska. This convinced Udelson of the potential market, or so he said, and he ordered a carload from the New Jersey plant. Hall continued to buy large shipments from Udelson up to the time the Zanesville still was seized, then suddenly he stopped. After that only the chickens wanted Molaska.

Investigators were feeling sorry for Udelson and his lost business until they discovered that Harry Bader's wife was Mildred Udelson before her marriage. And she was related to Blanche Rothkopf, wife of Uncle Louie.

But back in Elizabeth, where Waxey Gordon once ran his beer through the sewers in pressure hoses, business was booming. In October the new plant received 91,775 gallons of molasses, and shipped out 473,133 pounds of Molaska. During its almost six months of operation, the plant received a total of 342,021 gallons of molasses, and shipped out 2,908,120 pounds of finished product. Much of the raw material came from the Cuban Molasses Company and was shipped to Elizabeth by boat. Records show that some of the Molaska was actually sold to candy and ice-cream makers, but the bulk of it went to alleged feed companies in the West and Middle West.

A check of telephone calls from the New Jersey plant to Cleveland revealed a strange assortment of people. Calls were noted to Melvin Strauss, 7500 Stanton Avenue, a trustee of Beth Realty Company which owned Molaska's Cleveland plant site; to Polster Electric Company, a manufacturer of electric equipment often found at illicit stills; to 2039 East 107 Street, a smoke shop which concealed a large handbook; to Louis Kowit, Kleinman's brother-in-law at Liberty Poultry; to Fred Bennett, 3609 Antisdale Road (the report noted that Bennett had recently been identified as the true name of Moe Davis); and calls to a variety of other people ranging from Fred Meyers of Freddie's Club to Martin Sweeney, identified as a congressman and law partner of former United States Attorney Martin McCormick. The latter had sought to gain immunity for Kleinman.

The official interest in Molaska's New Jersey plant was inevitable after Jerome Borden and T. Klein went to the office of the Manhattan Lighterage Company about September 1, 1934, and asked Captain William A. Long for aid in finding an industrial site. They had developed a secret process for converting molasses into powdered form, they said, and they needed a site with large storage tanks and waterfront facilities.

As eager as Solomon Berman to encourage new industry, Captain Long checked with someone in Proctor & Gamble and reported the Texas Oil Company had a terminal in the Baywell section of Elizabeth. Long recalled that Manhattan Lighterage itself had leased two field tanks for storage of oil and tallow. He promised to get in touch with Texas Oil.

By September 13 Jerome Products Company had been organized and had leased three buildings, two of which contained steel storage tanks, from Texas Oil. The buildings were located at 450 South Front Street, Elizabeth, not far by a strange coincidence from Molaska Corporation's manufacturing plant.

Tank storage included twenty-two tanks with a capacity of 30,000 gallons each, nineteen tanks with a capacity of 10,000 gallons, and seven tanks holding 1,000 gallons each.

It seemed an ideal location, an alcohol still situated in the middle of a forest of squat oil tanks and oil refineries. The finished alcohol could be stored in a tank then pumped by a pipeline to tankers tied up at the docks and transported up the bay to New York City.

But luck was running out—or was it that operations back in the hinterlands were better protected and more easily ignored? In any case, on January 26, 1935, the Alcohol Tax Unit at Newark got word a large distillery was being operated along the waterfront of Staten Island Sound—either on Staten Island or in Elizabeth. Considerable observation was required before the odor of fermenting mash was detected as coming from the Texas Oil Company property. On February 8 a tanker barge was seen tied up at the dock of Texas Oil, and a hose was spotted running from the barge to a pipeline on the dock.

Twenty-two men made the raid next day, and the story was worth a front page spot in the New York *Times*. The still was valued at $200,000, and was second in size only to the one at Zanesville. The *Times* quoted John D. Pennington, district supervisor who led the raid, as saying it was "large enough to flood New York and New Jersey with illicit alcohol."

Four men, all technicians, were arrested. Judge James T. Kirk fixed bail at $500. Later it was discovered the men had all given fictitious names, and they were brought before a United States Commissioner and the bail raised to $100,000 each. Representing the defendants at the hearing was Judge Kirk.

The story created such a sensation in sensation-weary Elizabeth that Mayor Joseph A. Brophy ordered police to start a drive on bootleggers. It was the first such drive "ordered here in some time," the *Times* noted.

One of the four defendants was Rubin Lubitsky, alias Birns, alias Harris. Only twenty-nine, he had an impressive arrest record and was considered a key, if minor, wheel in syndicate machinery. An undercover agent, C. W. DeWitt, was assigned to contact him and learn more about the operation.

DeWitt armed himself with a bottle of confiscated bootleg liquor, and roamed about Newark on April 23 until he met Lubitsky "and took a ride with him in his car up Central Avenue to the apartment of his girl friend. Lubitsky drives a big, black Buick. After telling Lubitsky I was contemplating putting up a still and needed a good column man, I asked him who was the last combination he had worked for. He said it was Charlie Kramer. . . ."

Kramer was an alias of Charles Polichek, an old associate of Jacob Stein and Teddy Black. He had won a temporary reputation as the successor to Waxey Gordon.

DeWitt persisted and next day Lubitsky confided that, in addition to Kramer, "Ben Siegel, known as 'the Bug,' had a piece of the Elizabeth plant, as did Charles 'Lucky' Luciano."

The association continued, and on April 26, after a stroll along Canal Street in New York, Lubitsky warned: "You should not wait too long about opening a plant as I have an offer to go to Cleveland."

On May 10, DeWitt reported he had learned that "C. K. [Charles Kramer] does selling, sets up plants. Jacob 'Gurrah' Shapiro, Louis Lepke, and the Bug, put up the money. Siegel looks like Edward G. Robinson, the actor. This mob wiped out the Waxey Gordon Mob, killed Max Hassell, Max Greenberg, Charles Solomon. . . ."

DeWitt was properly impressed, but, meanwhile, other investigators had tracked down John Drew and Moses Citron. They were impressed to learn that the day after the Elizabeth still was raided, the Elizabeth plant of the Molaska Corporation closed down, and on March 3, 1935, shipped its office furniture and fixtures back to Cleveland.

Announcing that Molaska Corporation had lost $70,000 on its manufacturing plant in Elizabeth, Stein–Drew said the company had no alternative but to seek reorganization through bankruptcy.

CHAPTER NINE

> I have had the privilege of fingerprinting manicured fingers.
>
> *Hugh Purdue, speaking of Lou Rothkopf,* et al.

THE PETITION was filed March 2, 1935, in the United States District Court for the Northern District of Ohio, Eastern Division. It quoted a formal resolution:

> Whereas the Molaska Corporation, an Ohio Corporation, engaged in the business of sugar, molasses and sirip [sic], is unable to meet its obligations and debts as it matures and is desirous of reorganizing in order that its assets may be preserved, its business continued and its creditors protected. . . .
>
> [Assets as of February 23, 1935, were listed as] a plant in Elizabeth, N.J., formerly engaged in the manufacture of powdered molasses in which $200,000 was invested; a plant at Cleveland, Ohio, principally engaged in the manufacture of powdered molasses; furniture and fixtures located at both Elizabeth, N.J., and Cleveland, Ohio; and patents and patent rights of no value except to the officers of the company.

Among the liabilities listed were a lease for the premises at Elizabeth, expiring December 18, 1937; a contract with Ira Merlis—a chemist who developed some of Molaska's formulas—for employment at $75 a week for five years; accounts payable in the amount of $23,215, and notes payable in the amount of $12,000.

Also submitted was a letter from John Drew as president of Molaska. In the letter he offered to take over Molaska Corporation and continue its business from the Cleveland plant.

Among other claims submitted within a few days of the filing of the petition were one for $200 by Alvin Giesey, Public Square Building, and one from Walter J. Salmon, president and treasurer of 500 Fifth Avenue, Inc., New York.

No data were given as to why Giesey was due money, but Salmon charged that Molaska "entered into a written lease under seal" for offices 4220 and 4223 in the building at 500 Fifth Avenue. The lease was for three years, from March 1, 1934, to April 30, 1937, and the annual rental was $2,800.

Judging from later developments, some of Frank Costello's associates took over the lease.

The United States since 1898 has had machinery to aid businessmen to carry on, and so in its hour of need Molaska was given help from the United States to survive the blows inflicted upon it by the United States. A special master was appointed to assist John Drew in reorganizing, and while the Molaska Corporation officially died a corporate death on November 15, 1935, the Molaska Company, Inc., came into being on October 9, 1935.

Records obtained from a source close to the Cleveland Syndicate also reveal that some of the individuals involved also received a degree of financial protection.

Buckeye Enterprises' partners—Dalitz, Rothkopf, Tucker, Chuck Polizzi, Al Polizzi, Martin O'Boyle, and John Angersola—each claimed a loss of $16,661.80 on income-tax returns for 1935. The loss was incurred, each said, as a result of an investment in the Molaska Corporation.

Other figures show the Cleveland group invested a total of $109,632 in Molaska, and the New York group put up $122,500. Not mentioned, however, were additional sums invested in distilleries.

So it was, while one set of federal agents were trying to prove Moe Dalitz and his colleagues actually were part of Molaska, another set of federal agents were debating with Dalitz as to the amount of losses he could claim from Molaska.

A compromise was reached. The members of Buckeye Enterprises were permitted to claim the Molaska loss, but each agreed to pay taxes on a prorata share of $50,000 added income for

1933, 1934, and 1935. The sum was agreed upon after Moe Dalitz admitted that "any newsboy thirty inches high knew we had to pay something for ice" [permission to operate]. Dalitz suggested $35,000 would be about right, but readily agreed to $50,000 when the matter was pressed.

Meanwhile, of course, Molaska Company, Inc., was in business. Reports were required during the early months while the business was still nominally under the supervision of the court. Some of the daily receipts showed a rather strange pattern. On June 11, 1935, sales were listed:

Atlantic Supply House, Inc., $10.05.
Reindeer Brothers, $17.15.
Ira Krupnick, $1,000.

On July 9, 1935, sales were listed:

Damsel Ice Cream Company, $4.55.
Eleanor May Candies, $4.50.
Golden Crust Company, $0.55.
Hasbrouch Drug Company, $4.50.
J. C. Immell, $2.75.
Ira Krupnick, $150.

As late as September 6, 1935, the pattern remained:

Lynwood Ice Cream Company, $4.46.
Paramount Creamery, $4.50.
Ira Krupnick, $1,000.

The Jenny Lind Company was the only one to give Krupnick any competition. It purchased Molaska at regular intervals at costs of $253, $361, $176, $240, and $481. But Ira was far and away the biggest and most frequent customer. He was also on the receiving end of cash paid out by the company, getting a check for $125 on April 13.

John Drew's name appeared the first few months as receiving $50 checks, but soon it vanished from the records. So, apparently, did Drew vanish, to be replaced by the mysterious Ira Krupnick. On January 31, 1936, the final report of the special master was approved and a final decree entered closing the case. The Molaska Company, Inc., was on its own.

Years later a John Drew appeared in Las Vegas as a partner of the Cleveland Syndicate. He held 5 per cent of the Stardust Hotel. When asked if he had ever used the name, Jacob Stein, he replied, "My life is an open book" and refused additional comment.

The "open book" appeared hard to decipher, but one item was found—a birth certificate at Madison, Wisconsin, showing the John Drew in question was born John F. Drew on November 21, 1901, in the village of LaFarge, Wisconsin.

But—the birth certificate was issued on July 30, 1952. It was based on what was called "a declaration of self."

The Las Vegas John Drew was alleged to have had interests in Chicago before going west. He was said to be closely associated with the Capone syndicate. Molaska's Jacob Stein, alias John Drew, had an associate who was indicted with Al Capone in Chicago, one Aaron Sapiro.

All of which may prove only that organized crime is really organized.

2.

Meanwhile, there was business to be handled, money to be made. On January 4, 1936, Sam Tucker invested $1.65 in a long-distance telephone call to a man in Scranton, Pennsylvania. The conversation:

Sam—"Hello, Pete?"
Pete—"Yes."
Sam—"Pete, this is Sam from Cleveland. Remember me?"
Pete—"Yes, oh yes. Sam, how are you doing?"
Sam—"All right; are you doing any business?"
Pete—"We are doing a little."
Sam—"Can you pick goods up?"
Pete—"Where? Out there?"

Sam—"Yes. I can give you all you want."

Pete—"I had a big wagon, but I lost it. I haven't got it back. I'm not equipped for long hauls, Sam. We make short runs around here."

Sam—"We've got the equipment, but it won't be worth it to send our equipment down there."

Pete—"What are you getting?"

Sam—"Two dollars, and that's the price in New York too."

Pete—"That's the figure here too. I picked up a load in New York yesterday at that figure."

Sam—"I can give you good merchandise at that figure if you can use it."

Pete—"I can use a hundred barrels a week."

Sam—"Will you pay two dollars and ten cents if I roll it in for you? I have to ask that extra dime on account of the risk to the equipment."

Pete—"You see, Sam, we handle only the dealers. We don't sell to saloons, so you see the dealers look for the cheap price too."

Sam—"How many does your wagon carry?"

Pete—"About forty barrels, and I could use double that right now. If you split the dime you can send me eighty."

Sam—"How about money?"

Pete—"I'll give you all you want. Pay you cash for the first load and four or five days on any other you send."

Sam—"Where will I send him? To this number I'm calling?"

Pete—"No, you take these two numbers—Scranton 6667 and 6871. It might get here at night, and if he gets either number he will be directed right."

Sam—"It might go out tonight or tomorrow."

Pete—"Shoot it tonight, because if you don't I'll have it on my hands over Sunday."

Sam—"I'll try to get it out tonight."

Pete—"Okay, I'll look for it tomorrow."

Sam—"Okay, Pete. I'll try my best."

Thus did two businessmen discourse, some thirteen months

after Repeal put an official end to the bootleggers and their era. The Molaska Company, Inc., operated huge new stills in Chicago and Buffalo, and perhaps other places as well. Federal agents learned of them long after they had closed. But Cleveland remained a distribution center, with the main storage plant located at the Railway Terminal Warehouse, 3540 Croton Avenue.

A "canning plant" was maintained at Park Garage, 2043 East 105 Street. Each day varying numbers of drums of alcohol would be taken to the garage from the warehouse and the contents transferred to five-gallon cans. Local customers were supplied from the garage as well.

The Diamond-T Garage at the corner of Eighteenth Street and Rockwell Avenue was used to house a fleet of syndicate trucks, and as a place to transfer empty cans from one truck to another.

Business offices were maintained at different locations which were changed regularly. Federal agents, operating a court-approved wire tap, were forced to shift the tap five times from October 8, 1935, to March 23, 1936. Conversations were guarded —the word "alcohol" was seldom mentioned, but such substitutes as "stuff," "merchandise," "vica," "white," "it," and "any" were popular.

Local customers were not permitted to know where the "canning plant" was located. Orders were placed by calling one of the "offices." The customer would then drive to the "office." A member of the syndicate would take his vehicle, drive it to Park Garage—and not always by a direct route—get it loaded, and return it to the customer at the "office."

The wholesale price in New York and Chicago ranged from $1.75 to $2.00 per gallon. It was sold in Cleveland for about fifty cents more per gallon.

Sam Tucker and Louis Rothkopf were the syndicate members most closely associated with the Cleveland phase of the operation. Assisting them were a host of Mayfield Road and 105 Street characters, among whom the most famous was Maxie Diamond.

Maxie was no relation to the better-known "Legs" Diamond of New York, but he had more intelligence and business acumen than the ill-fated "Legs." Cleveland's Diamond was a big-time gangster in every sense, and ranked just under the top men.

Diamond was born in 1902 in Russia. Of slender build, he was five feet, eight inches tall, and weighed 140 pounds. His arrest record began in 1917. A 1937 report said he had been "actively connected with illicit alcohol and liquor activities in Cleveland for fifteen years," and during Prohibition was one of "the leading men connected with a large syndicate smuggling large quantities of illicit liquor from Canada."

The report noted that Diamond, "together with his other associates in this combination, has been connected with numerous other rackets in and about Cleveland, being classified as the number one racketeer of northern Ohio. He was actively connected with numerous labor rackets, produce rackets, laundry rackets, cleaner and dyer wars and, together with his other associates, operated several big-time gambling establishments in and around the city of Cleveland. . . ."

One phase of the operation was explored by Alcohol Tax Unit acting investigator-in-charge Eliot Ness. In a report dated March 25, 1935, Ness mentioned Diamond, and some old Mayfield Road reliables, such as George "King" Angersola, and Tony and Frank Milano. His probe centered around a distillery operated by Fred Morelli on East Ninetieth Street, and a distribution center called "Hanna's Grill" at 2121 East Fourteenth.

Morelli saved all legal liquor bottles and labels from the grill, Ness complained, and took them home where they were refilled with illicit products. Color was added, and every effort made to duplicate the exact degree of proof called for by the labels. But demand outstripped his supply.

Following raids on the plant and on Hanna's Grill, Ness found records showing that 2,035 gallons had been purchased by Morelli "from Antonio Milano, brother of Frank Milano, a reputed vice lord and underworld king in Cleveland, who is reported to control by gunplay, torture and intimidation all rackets and vice in Cleveland."

Other suppliers included Diamond, who furnished 2,600 gallons on one occasion and 2,325 on another. Ness expressed surprise to find these businessmen paying by check, and keeping records. Al Capone had not been so well established.

The big problem was not solved—at least not in time to help the investigation. Where were the syndicate's big stills? In December, 1935, agents thought they had an answer. "Uncle Louie" Rothkopf arrived in Kansas City and with him a rumor that he was there to establish a new distillery.

Rothkopf was said to be about forty, to pay all his bills in cash, and to be very generous with tips. When speaking on the phone in the presence of hotel employees, he used Yiddish. There were frequent calls to David Finkelstein and Ralph Messina, two Kansas City bootleggers of some reputation. Many people of Italian descent found their way to the hotel suite occupied by Mr. and Mrs. Rothkopf, and after two weeks an arrangement was worked out. On December 16, Mrs. Rothkopf was overheard telling her husband to call Cleveland, station-to-station, right away. They wanted to talk to him "about the agreement." Shortly thereafter, the Rothkopfs left Kansas City. Within a few days the first of several shipments of alcohol arrived from Cleveland. Uncle Louie had been opening a territory, not building a still.

The boys in Kansas City were hard pressed financially if a call to Sam Schraeder's home in Cincinnati is an indication. Schraeder was an old rumrunner in the Cincinnati-Newport area who switched to gambling and became a junior partner in the syndicate's gambling operations. In years ahead he was to be second only to Sam Tucker at the plush Beverly Hills Club outside Newport. But at the time Messina's call came in on January 21, Schraeder had things to worry him. "My kid broke her leg," he told Ralph, "and the wife is up to the hospital."

Being a man of feeling, Ralph asked him to have "Joe" call him back anytime after 11 P.M. Joe obeyed, and Ralph asked for a favor.

"I want you to let us have $600," Ralph explained. "We've got to have it by Monday. Let me have it until the first."

Joe—[who was also "Doc" to Messina—was cautious]: "What do you need it for?"

Ralph—"Agendo [?] got $500 from the bank and said he would pay them back so the time is up. I told them to give me until Monday."

Doc—"Who is it? I can't hear you."

Ralph—"The Green Dago. The note was up last week and he wants his money."

Doc—"You got money coming on the second."

Ralph—"I know, but he won't wait that long."

Doc—"I don't like to do that. I hate to ask him for money. It will be awhile before we cut that money up."

Ralph—"I will send it right back to you. We've still got 225 gallons of stuff, and Jimmy will pay off soon. We have about $220 expense a week and we have those expenses whether the stuff moves or not."

Doc—"How much do you want?"

Ralph—"Five hundred."

Doc, or Joe, promised to talk to "him," whoever that was, and send along the money. Some social chit-chat followed. Ralph put his wife, Babe, on and she told Doc she missed him, then put Ralph back on the line.

Doc—"I'll talk to him tomorrow or Monday and send it to your house."

Ralph—"I'll send it back to you, Doc."

Doc—"Okay."

Ralph—"Good. See you when Uncle Louie comes there."

Doc—"All right. Goodbye."

Uncle Louis Rothkopf's travels continued, and on June 9, 1937, he was received at the United States Penitentiary at Lewisburg to serve a term of four years. Along with Diamond and several others in the gang—but not including Tucker or Dalitz—he had been sentenced on May 22, 1937, to four years and a $5,000 fine.

The Alcohol Tax Unit of the Internal Revenue Service had at last convicted a top man in the Cleveland Syndicate. It came some seven months after Kleinman won parole on his income-tax conviction. But there was no "ultimate conviction." Rothkopf served only eleven months. On April 11, 1938, the Sixth Circuit Court of Appeals ruled the conviction was based on evidence illegally obtained, that federal agents could not use evidence obtained by wire taps in federal court. A new trial was ordered but never held. Since there was little evidence other than that obtained by wire tap, there was no case.

A "secret and confidential" letter was circulated on April 12, 1938. It ordered an end to all wire taps then in operation, and added:

"It will be necessary for us to rely more and more on informants and undercover work to obtain information that we hitherto obtained by the cheaper and more direct means of the supervision of gangsters' wires."

The syndicate had scored a double victory of vast significance.

But Rothkopf's conviction marked the end of an era. Exactly one week before he was sentenced, the Molaska Company, Inc., was put in bankruptcy by a petition filed in federal district court. Ira Krupnick, who was to vanish with Molaska, was examined on June 19. The handwritten report of the examination is a court record. It shows Krupnick as president. It also shows M. B. Davis as vice-president.

The assets of the company were offered at sale at public auction. Total price received was $3,817.10. Krupnick acquired the company's 1934 Ford for $56. Offered for private sale were what the trustee called "three air fans and one lot of miscellaneous steam pumps located at Mitchen, New Jersey."

At last the location of one of the additional distilleries had been learned.

Among those having unsecured claims were Sammy T. Haas, $2,500, and the Ray Coal Company, $135.13.

The Cleveland Syndicate had quit the liquor business as a major endeavor. While it stood ready to invest as opportunities, such as black-market whiskey, came along, from 1937 on it concentrated its energies on gambling. Almost as if to symbolize the transition was a little story about Joe Kater, one of the defendants indicted with Uncle Louie.

Kater was arrested in the case while coming out of the Cleveland Trust Company where he had just withdrawn $6,100. Asked about it, Joe explained it really belonged to the Thomas Club. He had drawn it out for use at the club that night.

The publicity caused Sheriff Martin L. O'Donnell to declare he would raid the club if asked to do so by the mayor of Maple Heights. Under the circumstances, it seemed a safe thing to promise.

3.

It would be unfair to assume from the sheriff's attitude that the Thomas Club had never been raided. The record shows that it, along with the Harvard Club, received considerable attention shortly after Mayor Burton was elected on a reform ticket in December, 1935.

Burton received some unexpected help in his campaign. Sometimes, when the situation is ripe for reform, the "smart" boys make stupid mistakes or have a run of bad luck. Thus it was that, in addition to the customary corruption with which the newspapers were filled, the citizens of Cleveland read on July 22, 1935, a *Press* story which began:

"A roaring speedboat cutting across the smooth surface of Lake Erie, sounds of wild carousal, a woman's screams carrying a half-mile to shore, the boat's lights suddenly blinking out, and silence. . . ."

It was a good lead, good enough to make the jaded reader continue. He learned how a young lady employed at City Hall fell overboard during the "wild carousal" and was drowned. Others aboard at the time were City Safety Director Martin L. Lavelle, Marty O'Boyle, and various City Hall guys and dolls.

Lavelle was a former police captain. O'Boyle was an old rumrunner, a partner in Buckeye Enterprises and thus a junior member of the Cleveland Syndicate. He had achieved a degree of respectability as president of the Liberty Ice Cream Company. It was syndicate-owned, an outgrowth of the Molaska Corporation's more legitimate activities. O'Boyle's principal job, at the time, was representing syndicate handbook interests at City Hall.

Asked about his companion, Safety Director Lavelle said stiffly: "I have been acquainted with the O'Boyle family for thirty-five years." Citizens who could recall Police Captain Lavelle driving to work in a Rolls Royce didn't doubt it. But his position was supported by Mayor Harry L. Davis, and the reformers licked their chops.

Gameboy Miller, who had a well-developed political antenna, soon realized the boat incident would hurt. In an effort to repair the damage, he announced an added political assessment of $10 weekly on bookies using his Empire News Service. If Burton was elected, Gameboy warned, "all the books in the city might as well close."

But the bookies resented the extra charge. They were already paying the syndicate $100 a week for "protection," in addition to the $35 to $75 Miller and his brother-in-law, Mushy Wexler, charged for the wire service. Feeling the syndicate should be strong enough to handle any mayor, some of the bookies protested the new assessment and talked. That didn't hurt the reformers either.

Burton won, and, in looking for a successor to Lavelle, remembered Eliot Ness' work in locating that huge still on Sweeney Avenue. Good men were hard to find, or at least, to recognize, so Ness was appointed. Equally important, Frank T. Cullitan took over as county prosecutor, the post once held by Ray Miller. The sheriff was the veteran John Sulzmann, who devised the "home rule" policy his successor was to follow.

As previously noted, some in-city gambling casinos closed within a few days of Burton's election. But just outside the city limits, beyond the reach of Burton and Ness, were the plush Thomas and Harvard clubs. Gameboy, who started at the Harvard, had moved to the Thomas Club. James "Shimmy" Patton, a partner in the wire service, and Arthur H. Hebebrand were in charge of the Harvard. Scarcely anyone remembered the late Frank Joiner, who founded it.

The clubs seemed safe, but the gamblers had not counted on the enterprise of Prosecutor Cullitan. On January 10, 1936, he deputized twenty-five "private eyes" from the McGrath Detective Agency, and at dusk swooped down in separate raids on the clubs.

Little trouble was encountered at the Thomas Club. Neither Gameboy nor his two brothers were there when raiders arrived, but about 500 patrons were busy in the casino where blackjack, poker, chuck-a-luck, dice, and slot machines were available. One thousand silver dollars, apparently used as chips, were confiscated along with "two large sacks" of currency.

In the club's office, a small arsenal including tear-gas guns was found, along with a bundle of counterfeit $10 bills, and a list of eight addresses and telephone numbers. A notation on the list said the club furnished automobile service from the locations every fifteen minutes from noon to 6 A.M.

Raiders hitting the Harvard Club in Newburgh Heights had a different experience. The original party of ten men was commanded by assistant prosecutors Charles J. McNamee and Frank Celebreeze. Upon arriving at the door, they were told, "You can't get in here without getting your heads bashed in."

Guns appeared, "drunks" wandered out of the club and made threats. The raiders retreated, conferred, and decided they wanted "no bloodshed." A state of seige resulted—the deputies couldn't get inside, the gamblers couldn't get out.

Shortly thereafter, Shimmy Patton drove up in a new car with a bodyguard. Ignoring the deputies, he rushed into the club. A few minutes later he rushed out, went up to McNamee:

"If one of you tried to stick his God-damned neck in that door," he shouted, "we'll mow him down with machine guns. We've got them and we'll use them."

McNamee replied that he didn't want bloodshed and tried to arrange a truce to permit the patrons to leave the club in safety.

"The hell with that," shouted the portly Patton. "You aren't coming in here. If you do you'll get killed."

But, in the interest of the good citizens who comprised the club's customers, the raiders moved their seige line back a half block. Cullitan, who had led the raid on the Thomas Club, arrived, and a conference was held in a nearby gas station. It was decided to seek help. Calls were made to the city jail. After a conference there, the chief jailer called back to report, according to Cullitan, that "Sheriff Sulzmann was sticking to his home-rule policy." There would be no aid from that direction.

Meanwhile, out of the Harvard Club marched a steady line of men with overcoat pockets filled. No one bothered them. Trucks and cars loaded with equipment pulled out too, amid cheers from the crowds which now lined the streets.

Cullitan, becoming desperate, called Safety Director Ness. In turn, Ness called the jail and talked to William Murphy, the chief jailer. He said he told Murphy that, "As a citizen, I am calling on you to send deputies out there to protect the prosecutor."

Murphy replied, Ness said, "We can't send men out there without a call from the mayor of Newburgh."

It was then Ness collected thirty-three Cleveland policemen, just coming off duty. "I told the men," Ness said next day, "the city's responsibility for them ended when they crossed the boundary line. It was voluntary service to protect the prosecutor."

With sirens screaming, police led by Ness pulled up at the gas station where Cullitan and his frustrated raiders were waiting. They rapped on the door of the club, it opened, deputies and detectives in plain clothes entered. Ness and his uniformed men waited outside.

The club had been stripped. Only a large U-shaped blackjack table remained. Patton had disappeared. Art Hebebrand was still there, and he told the raiders to "act like gentlemen while you're in here or you'll wish the hell you had." With that advice, he retreated to an office and locked the door. When he wouldn't come out, Ness ordered tear gas fired into the office, but at that moment the door opened. Several men came out, but not Hebebrand. He had climbed up on a table and was gone out the window.

The office, including four safes, had also been stripped. As it was searched, a large van loaded with equipment drove out of the backyard and away. No one attempted to stop or follow it.

Next morning Ness issued orders to Cleveland police to arrest on sight, whenever they were found in the city, Gameboy and his two brothers, Honeyboy and Alky. Also named in the arrest-on-sight order were Hebebrand and Patton.

Ness' order created headlines, but achieved little else. The Thomas and Harvard clubs continued to serve the citizens of Cleveland. And the syndicate that owned them had already expanded its gambling operations far beyond the suburbs. It was now ready to move on to new opportunities.

One such opportunity developed near Cincinnati. It developed when Dutch Schultz was murdered in the Palace Chop House at Newark.

CHAPTER TEN

Napoleon was a short man too.
Dixie Davis

It is an unhappy commentary on disorganized law enforcement that three decades after organized crime formed a national syndicate there is still disagreement as to how it happened.

No well-informed person doubts the syndicate was created, but the answers to many questions remain buried in musty files. No one was ever assigned to research those files and pull together scattered intelligence reports from federal and local agents. Now many of the old files are being destroyed to make room for new, and the opportunity to get answers is dying with the elder statesmen of crime.

Thus amateurs and professionals remain free to debate details of who, when, why, and how. Was Johnny Torrio the master mind, or was it Louis "Lepke" Buchalter? Some say it was Charles "Lucky" Luciano. Others give the honors to Frank Costello.

For our purposes, it is immaterial. Important is that out of the "Big Seven" of rum-running days, out of the cooperation in joint liquor ventures, such as Molaska Corporation, out of the experience of such sophisticated individuals as Torrio, who built empires in New York and Chicago—out of all these and more, a national association did emerge sometime in 1934.

The date can be fixed with accuracy—not only because stool pigeons whispered about a meeting in New York or Atlantic City or Miami—but because certain things began to happen then and other things stopped happening.

The country was divided into territories. Wars ended between regional groups, between religious groups, between national groups. Meyer Lansky was assigned Florida and the Caribbean. His partner, Bugsy Siegel, got the Far West, including Nevada. The Eastern Syndicate came into being along the Atlantic coast, and assignments were made according to racket as well as geography. Thus Costello got slots, Lepke got the garment industry, Luciano got narcotics and prostitution, "Trigger Mike" Coppola got numbers, etc.

Broadly speaking, the Cleveland Syndicate obtained the Middle West—outside of Illinois, of course, where the successor of Al Capone held sway. In lieu of that, the Cleveland boys were given Arizona by way of compensation. It might not have seemed a bargain at the time—"only sand and lizards," as one hood put it—but it had potential. For one thing, it bordered on Mexico.

The confirmation of power, for that is what it amounted to, can be demonstrated by words as well as deeds. J. Richard "Dixie" Davis, the "mouthpiece" of Dutch Schultz, wrote a series of articles for *Collier's* magazine in 1939, after getting out of prison. The series was entitled, "Things I Couldn't Tell Till Now." Among the things he told was how, when the National Syndicate was being formed, "Moey Davis became the power in Cleveland, and anyone who questioned it would have to deal with Lucky and Meyer and the Bug."

While the identity of Lucky Luciano, Meyer Lansky, and Bugsy Siegel was well established, it is interesting to note that a man as well informed as Dixie Davis did not know that "Moey Davis" was really Moe Dalitz. The incident can be blamed on metropolitan myopia, perhaps, or on the skill with which Dalitz had insulated himself, yet it is important in view of the mystery attached to a dying remark of Dixie's old boss, Dutch Schultz. But more of that in a moment.

With the green light glowing, the Cleveland Syndicate began to expand. The Arrowhead Club near Cincinnati was an early objective.

The club was located in Clermont County in a community

known as Branch Hill. It had operated for several years under the direction of Joseph Bauer. Local law-enforcement officials, such as Frank A. Roberts, "tolerated" the club because it catered to the wealthy who lived in the Indian Hills section of Cincinnati, and employed the poor who lived in Branch Hill.

As Clermont County prosecutor, Roberts said he "never felt obliged to enforce laws to the letter." But one day he got the urge. Bauer was told he couldn't reopen the club when the winter season of 1934–35 arrived. Bauer, a local man, accepted the situation. "He was a real gentleman," Roberts explained.

The gentleman died suddenly and mysteriously—years later no one wanted to discuss it—while Roberts was "on vacation out west." He returned to discover that Sam Nason, formerly Bauer's assistant, had reopened the club on a more lavish scale than ever. Roberts said he didn't know who was behind Nason. He didn't find out until fifteen years later when Moe Dalitz admitted to the Kefauver Committee it was the Cleveland Syndicate.

It became a patented syndicate operation. Roberts told of an instance in which a minister new to the community came to him to complain about the club's gambling. Before Roberts could act, he said, the minister withdrew his complaint. He had just discovered the club gave the church $75 monthly toward his salary. Anyone familiar with the Thomas Club would have recognized the hand of Gameboy Miller.

The Kefauver Committee noted that the Cleveland Syndicate never sought complete control in any area in which it operated. Instead, it made great use of local lieutenants, giving them pieces of the operation and even letting them operate smaller joints independently.

At Arrowhead, Sam Nason became the local lieutenant. A native of St. Louis, he went to Cincinnati as a child and managed to finish the seventh grade. He married across the river in Newport, Kentucky, and worked as a bootlegger and bookie in that wide-open area until becoming associated with Bauer. The syndicate, which enjoyed good relations with a number of Cincinnati-Newport characters such as Sam Schraeder, found it could work with Nason.

After the takeover, Gameboy, that casino troubleshooter, was sent down from Cleveland to put the operation on an efficient basis. Coming along as an observer was Joe Zucker, alias Baker, a New York representative of the Eastern Syndicate and for many years a lieutenant of Frank Costello. Baker apparently acted as a liaison man between the two groups for he also accompanied Dalitz and "Big Al" Polizzi on an inspection trip to Arizona.

The Arrowhead Club, while not a major casino, was nevertheless the syndicate's first investment in an area it was soon to dominate. The next logical conquest appeared to be the Coney Island Race Track just outside Cincinnati on the northern side of the Ohio River. Coney Island was controlled by Dutch Schultz. How Dutch got Coney Island is a story in itself. It went back, as so many things did, to Arnold Rothstein.

2.

Max Greenberg of Detroit and Waxey Gordon approached Rothstein early in the Prohibition era with a proposition which was discussed on a Central Park bench in New York. It resulted in Rothstein's venture in rum-running and, later, in an alliance of Greenberg and Gordon that lasted until some of Dutch Schultz' boys stuck a gun in Greenberg's ear in Elizabeth, New Jersey, in 1933. While Gordon crawled out the window in the next room, Greenberg's head was blown off. For good measure, the Dutchman's boys also knocked off Max Hassell, who left $213,000 in a safe deposit box.

Dutch got his start, as did Lucky Luciano, working for "Legs" Diamond, who, in turn, protected Rothstein's interests and did a little hijacking on the side. Inasmuch as "Big Bill" Dwyer had built up the first major bootleg empire, "Legs," naturally, made Dwyer's trucks a frequent target. Ultimately Rothstein got a bit tired of Diamond, who killed for pleasure as much as for profit, and passed the word Dwyer could take him. The first attempt in October, 1924, failed. Diamond outlived Rothstein by three years, but his gang broke up almost immediately and went over to Dwyer.

Already there and with high rank was Owney "the Killer" Madden, who, many years later, was to become known as the "Sage of Hot Springs, Arkansas." Owney and Dutch became friends and partners. They were alike in many respects, essentially individualists. Both built up vast empires, and both fell victim to progress when the trend toward organization and unity made independence dangerous. Owney was sent back to prison for a while and released on condition he stay out of New York. He went to Hot Springs and, in time, became an elder statesman. Dutch was not so fortunate.

But, in those early years, Dwyer towered above his lieutenants. And when, as was described in Chapter Five, rumrunning became big business, Dwyer was there. He had a piece of the Reinfeld Syndicate, his principal task being that of distribution.

The Reinfeld Syndicate made so much money it didn't know what to do with it. And the Canadian branch, the Bronfman brothers, looked for investments in other fields. The Atlas Finance Company, one of several subsidiaries formed to help handle the liquor business, became the instrument by which investments were made in the United States.

In July, 1941, the Florida Racing Commission held a series of secret hearings in Miami to inquire into the ownership of Tropical Park Race Track at Coral Gables. The findings were so sensational they were never made public for fear the truth would destroy the pari-mutuel betting system upon which the state depended heavily for tax revenue. And the Commission may have been right.

The testimony disclosed that Sam Kantor had been operating a dog track on the future site of Tropical Park when in 1931 pari-mutuel betting was legalized in Florida. Frank J. Bruin, then general manager of Madison Square Garden in New York, promised Kantor he would finance the construction of a horse-race track. Tropical Park was built at a cost of $879,000. It was only after it was constructed that Bruin revealed the money came from the Atlas Finance Company of Montreal. Shortly thereafter, "Big Bill" Dwyer appeared with a power of attorney from Atlas Finance to act as its American representative and fiscal agent.

Atlas, with money to spare, went into other race track ventures. It owned a track at Jacksonville, Florida, and it bought control of the Coney Island Race Track at Cincinnati. But ultimately, as the liquor profits dwindled and rumrunning ceased, Atlas sold—or gave—its stock to its United States associates.

Thus, as the testimony at the 1941 hearing revealed, Tropical Park came under the control of Dwyer's associate, Owney "the Killer" Madden, and John Patton, the notorious "Boy-Mayor of Burnham, Ill.," and Capone lieutenant. As a final item in the strange tale the Florida Racing Commission tried to bury, it should be noted that Patton's stock was placed in the name of "M. Powell." She proved to be a relative. She also proved to be the wife of a noted American newspaper editor who was "best man" at the 1909 marriage of Arnold Rothstein. "M. Powell" was maid-of-honor.

Of such details are fashioned the relationships which hold together the fabric of our society.

Dutch Schultz acquired Coney Island Race Track from Dwyer when Owney "the Killer" got Tropical Park. He also obtained the services of a strange genius, Otto "Abbadabba" Biederman. Abbadabba was known on Broadway as an official race-track handicapper at tracks in which Dwyer was interested. Dutch gave him additional duties. According to Dixie Davis, Schultz' attorney, it was Abbadabba's job to help Dutch rig the payoff number of the numbers racket.

A little man physically, Dutch had big ideas. With wealth from his beer racket rolling in, he had branched out in every direction. Among other things he bought the Piping Rock Club at Saratoga, New York, from Nick the Greek in 1933. His biggest venture outside beer and alcohol was the numbers game.

For millions in those dark Depression days, the only hope

of getting out of the economic rut was to "hit it lucky with the numbers." The racket is particularly vicious in that it preys on poor people. While the investment may be no more than a dime or quarter, it is still important to the individual paying it out, and like pinball profits, which are measured in nickels, it becomes a source of tremendous profits when enough people play.

The odds are heavy against winning even when the racket is not rigged, but the big operator invariably will cheat to increase his profits. Thus the winning number might be the closing stock market quotation for the day, or, as in the case of Schultz, the final three digits of the pari-mutuel betting total at a particular track. To the uninformed, such a procedure seemed fixproof, and in the belief they were being given a fair chance, thousands in East Harlem and elsewhere invested daily in "numbers" or "policy," as it was called.

Abbadabba's special assignment, according to Dixie Davis, was to compute the number that had received the least action from the suckers—the one requiring the smallest payoff—and to arrange for the final mutuel bet total to reflect that desired number. When the boss owned the race track, this wasn't as difficult as it sounds. When he didn't own it, a small bet at the last second would produce the desired results.

It was all very profitable; however, Dutch was having new difficulties with his associates. He ordered some of Gordon's boys killed and got that situation well in hand, but a greater danger arose—the National Syndicate. Dutch was not asked to join.

The reason, in addition to his personal unpopularity, was the general belief that "Uncle Whiskers" was about to take care of Dutch in the same way he took care of Al Capone and Morris Kleinman—a stretch in prison for income-tax evasion. Dutch, apparently expecting the same thing, fled into hiding.

It was while Dutch was in hiding that the National Syndicate was organized. Since he was not a member, his empire was fair game for anyone daring to take it. With the "Dutchman" in hiding and apparently doomed to stay there or go to jail, not too much courage was needed. So Lepke took over Dutch's $2,000,000 restaurant "protection" racket, and "Trigger Mike" Coppola took the numbers racket under the wing of the Mafia. Many of Schultz' men switched sides even as Dutch had done when years before the word passed that "Legs" Diamond was no longer a good bet.

Schultz, a surprising fellow, came out of hiding after eighteen months. He got his income-tax trial moved twice—first to Syracuse, where a mistrial resulted, and then to the little border town of Malone, New York. A classic job of public relations convinced the good citizens that Dutch was a much persecuted fellow who wouldn't harm a fly. After all—he just sold a little beer. The jury chosen from the good citizens acquitted Dutch.

It was a shock to the "smart" boys, but they weren't about to return the assorted rackets they had stolen. After all, Dutch's fortune was estimated at $7 million. He had enough to live on. Dutch seemed to agree. He settled down in Newark and tried to pick up what pieces were left.

One of the pieces was the Coney Island Race Track at Cincinnati. And yet, according to the recent division of the country, it belonged to the Cleveland Syndicate if the syndicate had the courage to take it. A little more courage was required, now that Dutch was back in circulation. The view from Arrowhead was tempting though. The race track was just down the road a ways.

On October 23, 1935, Dutch Schultz was shot in the Palace Chop House & Tavern, 13 East Park Street, Newark. Also mortally wounded were Abbadabba Biederman, Abe Frank, and Schultz' chauffeur, Bernard Rosenkrantz.

The Chop House had become Dutch's headquarters. It was convenient to the Robert Treat Hotel, where he lived. Twice daily the restaurant was cleared of customers and turned over to Dutch for use as a private dining room. There was a small room making an "L" at the end of the main barroom, and it was there with two bodyguards at the door that Schultz transacted his business.

On October 23, the group was working at a round table in the center of the room. Overhead was an orange-colored electric light. Light came also from the wall where eight-foot mirrors reflected dull yellow electric lights hanging between them.

Jack Friedman was tending bar in the outer room when two men came in with hats pulled down, overcoat collars pulled up. They told Friedman to hit the floor and stay there. He dived behind the bar. The men went in the side room and the shooting started. Dutch was in a washroom adjoining his "office" when he was hit.

Years later, when details of Murder, Inc., the enforcement arm of the syndicate, became known, it was learned—or at least reported—that Dutch was killed to prevent him from murdering New York District Attorney Thomas Dewey. Schultz allegedly was worried lest Dewey succeed where the "feds" had failed. The National Syndicate was afraid, however, that Dewey's death would cause so much "heat" as to ruin the rackets. Thus Murder, Inc., was to "execute" Dutch to save Dewey.

The story explained a lot of things. It did not answer some questions. Among the minor mysteries that remained unsolved were Dutch's deathbed statements.

For Schultz lived almost twenty-four hours after being shot. Admitted to the hospital, he described himself as of the Jewish faith. When he knew he was dying he called for a Catholic priest and said he wanted to die a Catholic. A police stenographer sat by his bed, hoping to get a statement that might reveal why Dutch was shot. He got, instead, remarks such as:

"Please crack down on the Chinaman's friends and Hitler's commander. I am sore and I am going up and I am going to give you honey if I can. Mother is the best bet and don't let Satan draw you too fast."

The stenographer asked: "Who shot you?" Schultz gasped, "The boss."

A few minutes later he was dead.

Police learned that Dutch's boys sometimes called him "Hitler." Thus, they reasoned, "Hitler's commander" would be Schultz' boss—the one who, he said, killed him. That was considered to be—you name it—Lepke, Luciano, Costello, etc.

But who was the "Chinaman" and who were his "friends?" Dutch had asked that the Chinaman's friends as well as Hitler's commander be cracked down upon. No one had a theory there.

The answer, of course, is simple. The "Chinaman" was "Louis, the Chinaman," and that was Louis Dalitz. The Chinaman's "friends" were Cleveland Syndicate members who, even then, were trying to take away one of Dutch's few remaining possessions—Coney Island Race Track.

The New York boys had never bothered to learn—as Dixie Davis illustrated in 1939—that Moe Davis was really Moe Dalitz. Back when they were shipping booze to Detroit, it went to "Louis the Chinaman and Moe Davis." Dutch was involved in some of those shipments. In dying he didn't blame the Chinaman, didn't ask for a "crackdown" on the Chinaman. It was the "Chinaman's friends" he was worried about.

And why was he worried at that particular time? He, along with Abbadabba Biederman, had just returned from Cincinnati where a racing meet at Coney Island Race Track had ended.

Information about Schultz' visit to Cincinnati comes from Edwin Garrison, a hoodlum who, later in life, was to win the distinction of making the F.B.I.'s "Most Wanted" list twice in five years.

A Newport, Kentucky, native, Garrison received two years of business school education. Like Abbadabba, he was something of a mathematical genius, and he worked with Abbadabba as a race-horse handicapper and numbers-racket fixer.

During his long career, Garrison had many narrow escapes —not the least of them the time he burned the old Beverly Hills Club for the Cleveland Syndicate and killed a child in the process. For many years, though, he told associates the narrowest escape he ever had was the time in Cincinnati he missed the train to New York. He was scheduled to go to Newark, he continued, with Abbadabba and Schultz. When he was delayed, they went on without him and within hours of arriving they were shot at the Palace Chop House.

Investigators puzzled for years at the papers they found on that round table the night Dutch was hit. One strip of adding-machine tape carried a long list of figures totaling $827,253.54. Among the figures were entries of $313,711.99 and $236,295.95. Dutch must have been adding up his monthly income, was the answer police agreed upon. Actually, Dutch and Abbadabba were simply going over the pari-mutuel figures from the Coney Island meet which had just ended. To suggest, as some writers did, that Dutch had managed to get back part of his numbers racket is to insult "Trigger Mike" Coppola, who never gave back anything.

As the Dutchman lay dying, his mind wandered here and there. But very much in his subconscious was the knowledge that Coney Island was a very valuable property and the "Chinaman's friends" were trying to take it away. Those facts ranked as important to Schultz as the fact that some syndicate boss wanted to kill him.

And thus it was when racing next resumed at Cincinnati, the track had a new name, River Downs, and new owners, the Cleveland Syndicate.

United States Tax Court records tell the story in detail. Coney Island went into receivership. Moe Dalitz "learned" it could be acquired cheaply. According to a statement by Sam Tucker, Dalitz "knew he could not be a party to the actual operation of the race track, but he was interested in acquiring it with his other associates, for the purpose of the real estate venture and with the idea in mind of leasing it to a race-track operation. Mr. Davis was acquainted with one Samuel T. Haas, of Cleveland, Ohio, whom he knew was acquainted with Mr. E. P. Strong, who was engaged in the business of operating race tracks. . . ."

Thus it went. The charter members of the syndicate—the Mayfield Road Mob was not cut in on this deal—Dalitz, Kleinman, Rothkopf, and Tucker put up one-third. Haas and Strong, those old associates of pre-Prohibition days, put up the rest. The transaction was left in Strong's name. "Mr. Strong," said Tucker, "was to form a corporation known as the River Downs

Racing Association with the understanding that the company would enter into a lease with River Downs, Inc., for the purpose of conducting horse-racing operations."

It is interesting to note that one of the "fronts" whose name was used in the new corporation was Harry Rose. He was also listed as an official of Molaska Company, Inc. when it went bankrupt.

According to Tucker, who was trying to save himself some money in tax court, the corporation had troubles. Not the same kind Dutch Schultz had, but after the first meet in 1936 a flood came along in 1937 and washed away all the barns and part of the grandstands. There was no question about the flood—downriver it covered much of Louisville and was rated the worst in history. In order to finance repairs, Tucker said, it was necessary to borrow money from the Jacobs brothers of Buffalo. It was not the first or the last time the syndicate dealt with Louis Jacobs and his kin.

In 1948 Strong died. It was then, for the first time, that news of his partners in River Downs became public. Some financial readjustments followed and River Downs, Inc. "sold" its stock to Daleview, Inc. This was largely a paper transaction, with the syndicate members owning Daleview. The settlement resulted in a net long-term capital gain of $373,838.13. Of this, Haas received $124,612, Strong's estate, $124,612, and Kleinman, Tucker, Dalitz, and Rothkopf, $31,153.18, each.

An accountant was able to study the complex transaction and, on the basis of the facts as they were admitted, conclude that each member of the syndicate invested $83.33 in River Downs in 1936, and got back $31,153 in 1948. But that wasn't all. On March 15, 1950, Daleview, Inc., sold its assets to River Downs of Ohio, Inc., for $470,000.

Like many other syndicate business ventures, the trail goes on and on. Henry Green, a native of Elizabeth, New Jersey, was the principal investor in River Downs of Ohio. His background included work for Tommy McGinty at Thistle Downs Race Track, Cleveland. In 1940 he opened Randall Park near

Cleveland as the sole owner, and the track folded within four days. Apparently learning a lesson, he joined others to operate tracks in Cleveland, and in 1950 bought the Cincinnati track. In 1955, there was another sale. Green went to Las Vegas, worked with the syndicate boys at the Desert Inn, and was indicted for income-tax evasion. . . .

And so it goes. In 1965 the track was sold again.

3.

With the conquest of Coney Island, the syndicate was in a good position in the Cincinnati metropolitan area. It liked the setup. Cincinnati once had been as corrupt a city as existed anywhere, but the scandal resulting from Arnold Rothstein's fixing of the 1919 World Series at Cincinnati led to a reform movement. Gangsters were driven across the Ohio to northern Kentucky and for a decade they had flourished. Newport, a city of 30,000 even then, had a national reputation as a wide-open town.

The federal agent who was sent after Tony Caccino in New York, and who consorted as an undercover agent with Capone's men in Chicago, said Newport exceeded them all for concentrated vice. He told of going to Newport in 1929 as an undercover agent. With a newly made "friend," he went to a bootlegger to make a "buy." The bootlegger sat in a chair. The chair was leaning against the wall. Flies buzzed around the man's open mouth.

"He's asleep," said the native. "We'll come back later."

Before they could come back they learned the man had been murdered three days before. His killer had propped him up in a comfortable position and left him. It was considered rather amusing in Newport.

All of which was not important to the Cleveland boys except insofar as it indicated a certain tolerance on the part of citizens and law-enforcement agents. Cincinnati was clean. Its population, and those visitors who came there for conventions, needed entertainment. To get it they had to go outside the city. The opportunity seemed to justify expansion. The decision to cross the river was logical. It was helped along when the Arrowhead Club began having problems.

The problems were all the fault of those slot machine people, Prosecutor Roberts recalled. If they had been less greedy, there would have been no necessity to act. The slot situation became so bad it couldn't be tolerated, "and it wasn't consistent to let another form of gambling operate."

Thus it was on November 19, 1937, Roberts raided the club. Nason was arrested and ultimately fined $1,000. Much gambling equipment was seized but it wasn't destroyed. The county had just opened a new courthouse at Batavia. The gambling equipment was converted into furniture and installed in the courthouse. The grand jury room got a crap table with the felt removed and the legs cut short.

Indicative of the cross currents always to be found in an enterprise so massive as organized crime was the fact that while the raid by Roberts got exactly three paragraphs in the Cincinnati newspapers, five miles away, it received a half-page spread in the Philadelphia *Enquirer,* nearly a thousand miles away.

The Philadelphia paper included the feature spread complete with pictures in its Ohio edition.

Such journalistic enterprise can be understood if it is realized that the *Enquirer* at the time was owned by Moses Annenberg —a man who considered it wise a short time later to escape with three years in jail and an assessment of $8 million rather than face a jury on an income-tax evasion case.

Annenberg was the creator of Nationwide News Service, among many other things, and in 1937 some of the Cleveland boys, including Mushy Wexler, Gameboy Miller, and Mickey McBride, were making threatening noises. Thus a raid on a Cleveland Syndicate gambling joint might conceivably be embarrassing if given enough publicity. Annenberg's newspaper gave it publicity. Apparently no one else did. Early in 1940 Annenberg went to jail. The Cleveland boys took over his wire service and renamed it "Continental Press."

Several efforts were made to persuade Roberts' successor, Ray Bradford, to let Arrowhead reopen. A series of "reputable businessmen" came to him, he said, with the message: "Name your price." Bradford's secretary made notes of the offers. The men said Bradford would even be permitted to raid the club occasionally. "The only thing we had to do was warn them before we raided them," he added. But, "I was supposed to enforce the law," and all offers were rejected.

Nason moved on to Elmwood Place where the syndicate opened the Valley Catering Company, a casino-café. Still later, in 1944, he ran the Fox and Crow Club at Montgomery, Ohio, for the expanding syndicate. It was a plush casino.

Nason also obtained a piece of the Northern Kentucky Company. It operated a syndicate handbook for many years at the Yorkshire Club in Newport. This group as late as 1961 reported for tax purposes gross bets of more than $200,000 monthly.

The boys who cooperated with the syndicate were well repaid. Those who didn't had problems. The syndicate found it necessary to burn Pete Schmidt's Beverly Hills Club near Newport to get him in a cooperative frame of mind. That alone didn't do the trick. Some stickups and other incidents—the process was called "dingdonging" locally—were necessary before Pete finally gave the syndicate the million-dollar Beverly Hills Club in 1940.

Before the conquest of Kentucky began, however, the syndicate had business elsewhere.

4.

The date of the invasion of Arizona by organized crime is usually placed at 1945 and is tied to the purchase of the Grace Ranch by Peter Licavoli. Actually, it began earlier when Moe Dalitz allegedly developed sinus trouble and "Big Al" Polizzi wanted to go big-game hunting near Nogales, Mexico.

In the latter part of 1936, after Coney Island had been acquired, Dalitz went to Arizona. He remained there for several months in 1937, and, by his own admission, visited Mexico with Polizzi.

While Dalitz was there, the "sand and lizards" of the area around Tucson attracted a strange collection of Eastern Syndicate gangsters. Joe Zucker, alias Baker, and lieutenant of Frank Costello, became Dalitz' shadow. "Trigger Mike" Coppola, Mafia boss of the numbers in New York and elsewhere, arrived. Lepke sent out two close associates.

Dalitz, of course, had "Big Al" Polizzi along for the Ohio Mafia as represented by the Mayfield Road Mob. This was important, for over in Mexico at the time was another expatriate of Mayfield Road—Frank Milano.

Frank, along with brother Antonio and assorted relatives by blood and marriage—including Al Polizzi—grew wealthy during Prohibition. Like many of their friends they were given a boost up the ladder by Mickey McBride in the days when he was "circulator" for Hanna's newspapers. Mickey invested in the Brotherhood Loan Company which became a dominating influence, socially and economically, in the world of Mayfield Road.

It was in Frank's restaurant on Mayfield Road that Joe Porello, would-be corn-sugar baron, and his aide, Sam Tilocca, were blasted in 1930. Police at the time found evidence of gambling at the place along with a high-powered rifle, two automatic shotguns, a Luger, and other weapons. Milano explained he used them to hunt rabbits.

Later, Frank and Tony created the Mayfield Importing Company, which allegedly imported olive oil and tomato paste, but was suspected of handling livelier things as well. It had links with Joe Profaci in New York. Out of Brotherhood Loan came such things as the Brotherhood Club. It owned, among other things, a plush gambling joint which the Cleveland Syndicate operated for years as the Ohio Villa. Later, it was turned back to the Brotherhood and became the Richmond Country Club.

The "Brotherhood," it should be noted, was the word used to refer to the Unione Siciliano, and it, in turn, was the polite name for the Mafia. As recognized head of the Unione Siciliano, the Milano boys ruled the Mayfield Road area. Bob Bridges, the federal agent who had difficulty with his own organization, knew how to handle the problems that arose along Mayfield Road.

When he arrived in Cleveland, he said, it was customary for federal agents who had business along Mayfield Road to go together in groups of three or four—for protection. "These young punks would spit on the car, and curse and threaten." One day it happened to him, he said, and he lost his temper. "I grabbed one of them by the neck and told him the next time it happened I would pistol-whip one of them. I was conducting myself officially in the proper manner and I'd stand no more insults."

The crowd was moving in when a local attorney came along and spoke to the youths in Italian. They dispersed in a hurry. "I don't know what he said," Bridges continued, "but I told him to tell the Milanos since they seem to be kings up here that I wanted to see them."

Apparently the message wasn't delivered, and Bridges decided he'd do it personally. He drove up to the Brotherhood Club one night. The door was locked, but Bridges shouted he'd drive the car through a window if someone didn't come out.

> Frank Milano came out and wanted to know what was going on. I identified myself and told him that when I came to Mayfield Road I came on legitimate business and I wouldn't stand for any more rocks being thrown or pistols being fired. I said I was pretty good at that sort of thing myself, and I expected to hold him accountable. He wanted to know why him. And I said, "Well, you're reported to be the boss up here and if you're not you know who is. I'll stand for no more of this. I'm not being intimidated and I'm not being paid off."
>
> Milano gave me a telephone number to call [Bridges added] and told me to call it if I was insulted any more. I never had occasion to call it. I went up there many a night and many a day after that and I went alone and they stood on

the other corner. They muttered, but they called me "Mister" when they talked to me. I had the same experience over in the Hill district. It was another Italian settlement about four or five miles away. . . .

Another agent confirmed Bridges' account and added a detail. At one point Milano declared the "Hill" area around 116 and Kinsman, a heavily populated Italian district, off limits to federal agents. A meeting was called in downtown Cleveland with Milano and his attorney. At the meeting the agents placed submachine guns on the conference table and told Milano they would go into the area whenever they desired and would shoot anyone who tried to stop them.

By 1934 Frank Milano decided the United States Government was becoming too tough. Newspapers reported it was even checking to see if he had paid his income taxes. In any case, Milano removed himself to Vera Cruz, Mexico, and constructed on the coast a new empire based on coffee plantations and lumber.

Tony Milano remained in Cleveland to run the various Brotherhood enterprises, although the newspapers speculated hopefully that enough hoods would follow Frank "to establish a new Mayfield Road in old Mexico."

The hope was a vain one. In fact, when a Kefauver Committee witness was asked what Frank was doing in Mexico, he replied:

"He has a coffee plantation, and he is suspected of a number of operations, helping to smuggle in various individuals that have been deported, dope, hop, and so forth."

One man who re-entered the country illegally was Frank Cammerata, brother-in-law of Pete Licavoli. He had been deported in 1937, but came back in 1939 and hid in Cleveland until 1946. When the Immigration and Naturalization Service tried to re-deport him, Representative Michael Kirwan of Youngstown, Ohio, managed to block them by getting the Congress of the United States to pass a "private bill." That delayed things awhile and Teamster President James Hoffa admittedly came to the rescue of the old bank robber and tried to arrange for the governor of Michigan to pardon Cammerata. That would have effectively removed the legal basis of the deportation order. Considerable delay was gained, but after the Kefauver Committee publicized the affair Cammerata was re-deported. As far as is known, he has not re-re-entered the country—but who can be sure?

The important thing—when Cammerata first re-entered back in 1939, he came by way of Vera Cruz, Mexico, and Arizona. A lot of so-called "wet Italians" entered about the same time, and followed the same route. So did a vast amount of narcotics in which Lucky Luciano was directly interested.

Thus it is that the strange gathering on the sands of Arizona near the Mexican border in 1937 of representatives of Lucky and Lepke, of Coppola, of Cleveland lads, such as Moe Dalitz and Al Polizzi, takes on added meaning.

Long before Cammerata's brother-in-law, Pete Licavoli, took over the Grace Ranch near Tucson, law-enforcement agents knew the Cleveland Syndicate had a ranch located "in Arizona near the Mexican border." And when Licavoli did go to the Southwest, he found Dalitz had prepared the way by various discreet investments.

The 1937 visit obviously convinced Dalitz that—aside from whatever international arrangements might be made—the territory of Arizona was not yet ready for exploitation. And when the time came, after World War II, he gave the job to Licavoli —his old pal from Detroit. However, just to make sure he was protected, he provided Pete with a partner from the Yorkshire Club back in Kentucky—a gentleman who wore a ring in his nose literally as well as figuratively.

CHAPTER ELEVEN

An honest Jew hasn't got a chance.
Leon "Honest Frenchie" Gips, 1951

HE WAS a little man and he couldn't speak English very well, but he had come by Paris on his way from Russia and had picked up a certain Continental air. In Miami Beach, where he arrived in 1925, he also picked up a reputation for honesty—a quality not often found in the sucker traps of that city, then or now.

So it was in 1937, when Thomas Jefferson McGinty completed a muscle job, he remembered "Honest Frenchie" Gips and dispatched a telegram to Boston.

"I took a plane and come fast to Miami Beach," Gips recalled, "and five minutes later I was in the ring managing six roulette wheels and we never have a losing day."

The casino was at the Hickory House, on which McGinty had a ninety-nine-year lease, at Twenty-third Street and Liberty Avenue. Frenchie recalled his first day there:

"That's the day when the governor was setting in front having dinner—no right to interfere with gambling. Beautiful dinner out front and in back we had six crap tables and eight roulette tables and Bill Burbridge [Miami Beach city councilman] was there every day for protection and nobody touched it."

The joint was officially in the name of George R. K. Carter, who for many years had operated a huge "sawdust joint" at South Miami Beach. Newspapers in Miami said the old "Carter's" was "the biggest gambling establishment from a standpoint of money handled that had ever been operated in the United States since the days of the Gold Rush." But in Florida things sometimes seem larger than life. In any case, McGinty made the new "Carter's" into an equally large "rug" joint.

Exactly how much of the new Miami Beach casino belonged to McGinty and how much to other members of the Cleveland Syndicate, whom he represented, is uncertain. Since Miami belonged, casinowise, to Meyer Lansky, all major gambling operations there were joint ventures. Individual action on a big scale was not permitted. The names appearing on official records were those of nominees who represented not individuals, but syndicates.

Thus the new "Carter's" was divided 65-25-10. McGinty had the 65 per cent for the Cleveland Syndicate. Moe "Dimples" Wolinsky held 25 per cent for the Eastern Syndicate, and Carter, the local man, was left with 10 per cent. He almost lost that when McGinty, a sometimes impulsive man, tried to kill him one night.

Such a division in Miami Beach was not unique. The files of the Miami Crime Commission reveal that at the same time McGinty was operating at Carter's, Gameboy Miller was running the Frolics Club nearby. Partners there reflected the same co-operative spirit—Wolinsky for the Eastern Syndicate, Moe Dalitz for the Cleveland boys.

Cooperation between the Cleveland Syndicate and McGinty was not easily obtained. As leader of the Irish faction of the Cleveland underworld, McGinty built up quite an empire after his Prohibition era conviction. He turned to gambling early, leaving the O'Boyles to represent him in the liquor business.

This worked well enough so long as the syndicate was concentrating on rumrunning and alcohol. McGinty, with a little help from the ever-helpful Sammy Haas, became general manager of the Bainbridge Breeders and Racing Association and owner of Bainbridge Park. To avoid the technicality that horse betting was illegal, McGinty made use of the so-called contribution system. Under it, patrons didn't bet, they "contributed" their money, and occasionally they shared a "dividend" if they were lucky enough to pick a winning horse.

The system had been thrown out at three tracks in Cuyahoga County, so McGinty went next door to Geauga County and Bainbridge Township. Not only did both legal entities share the profits, but the farmer found a market for his hay. In fact, when at last McGinty was taken into court on a charge of gambling, a delegation of farmers appeared at the courthouse and told him: "The price of hay is going down every minute since you closed your track. If the hay isn't eaten pretty soon, we'll have to let it rot."

On September 27, 1929, McGinty was acquitted and the so-called system upheld. In 1933, Ohio legalized pari-mutuel betting and the suckers could quit calling their bets *contributions*.

With a race track established, it was not long until McGinty got off-track betting—if not legalized—at least protected by another contribution system. The bookies contributed a percentage of their take to McGinty, and he passed on a percentage of their contributions to the proper parties at various levels of official life. In his spare time, he promoted fights, bicycle races, and roller derbies.

McGinty dressed the part of "sportsman" as well as he acted it. A reporter interviewed him in March, 1930, shortly after he had been voted one of Cleveland's five best-dressed men. He found "Tommy dressed in a stunning grey striped suit, pink shirt with collar to match, and a rose and grey tie."

As the handbooks got bigger, it became easy to add dice and blackjack tables, and in some the casino overshadowed the book. Thus the upstairs room at the Hotel Hermitage developed into quite an operation. A reporter who visited it in 1934, right after Mayor Davis announced the town as closed, passed by a lookout on the street, another in the lobby of the hotel, went up a stairs to a locked door which opened when a concealed button was pushed, down a narrow corridor to another locked door, then to another where a third man frisked visitors for whiskey and/or weapons, and finally was admitted into a "room which looked like a huge attic with white-washed brick walls. . . ."

After Eliot Ness took office as safety director, the joint gave him a considerable headache. Several raids failed because of the elaborate security arrangements. It was July 22, 1936, before he achieved his goal and he did it by planting six plainclothesmen in the joint in advance of the raid. A vast amount of records were seized, as well as stationery bearing the name T. J. McGinty.

Yet long before reformers took office, McGinty had come to an understanding with the syndicate. It had muscled in on his bookie-protection racket after first taking the local wire service away from a McGinty lieutenant, William Swarts. The syndicate-owned Thistle Downs Race Track was cutting into his track revenue, and syndicate casinos, such as the Thomas Club, were competing as well. Being a realist, McGinty offered a compromise. Always willing to use local talent, even in Cleveland, the syndicate accepted. In return for pieces of some McGinty properties, they helped him finance a new and plush casino over in Lake County—the Mounds Club. It was for Cleveland and Ohio what the Beverly Hills Club became for Cincinnati and Kentucky—a "rug" joint offering "big-name" entertainment and the best in food and drink. McGinty was also rewarded with a piece of the Beverly Hills and, later, the Desert Inn at Las Vegas. In time he achieved a special relationship—not so much a junior partner in the syndicate as an associate member.

The decision to cooperate with the syndicate made possible McGinty's operations in Miami Beach. Indeed, in April, 1936, he announced plans to conduct racing at Oriental Park in Havana. Meyer Lansky was in Havana at the time, working with his friend "Sergeant" Batista. It was Lansky's territory, and without Cleveland Syndicate connections McGinty couldn't have promoted a stableboy's job there. Havana, like Arizona, was not quite ready for development, however.

The manner in which McGinty operated in Florida during the winter season and moved north with the horses when spring arrived was well illustrated by the murder of Harry "Champ" Joyce in May, 1936.

William Swarts, ex-wire-service operator and manager of the

Mounds Club for McGinty, shot Joyce on Vincent Street in view of hundreds of pedestrians. The trial established this background:

Swarts, then forty-nine, had lived at the Hollenden Hotel, along with many other syndicate hoods, for six years prior to the shooting. He had formed the habit of going south to Miami during the winter season. During the 1935–36 season just ended, he had worked at Carter's and Joyce served as his bodyguard. Swarts needed a guard because he handled much of the cash for McGinty, but whether the guard was protecting Swarts or protecting the cash wasn't made clear.

In any case, when the season ended, McGinty and Company moved to Jeffersonville, Indiana, across the Ohio from Louisville, for the Kentucky Derby. It seemed McGinty, in addition to bringing down the suckers from Cleveland by the train load, felt it necessary to provide them with familiar faces with whom to gamble. Jeffersonville was a wide-open town in those days, but a syndicate gambling operation somewhere in the Louisville suburbs has continued to be part of Derby tradition.

The McGinty operation at Jeffersonville lasted nine days, and then moved on to Cleveland where the Mounds Club was scheduled to open for its spring run. (For many years, the syndicate closed plush places, such as the Mounds and the Beverly Hills, in the belief, apparently, that everyone with money went to Florida during the winter months.)

Joyce had showed up at Jeffersonville, Swarts said, and now he appeared at Cleveland and asked for a job. Presumably, Swarts didn't need a bodyguard in his home town and he refused to hire the applicant.

The shooting occurred the day before the Mounds Club opened. Swarts said he had gone to the Hollenden where McGinty maintained an office in Room 380 to get the weekly payroll. With the cash in his pocket, he had gone out the rear door and started down Vincent Street toward Mushy Wexler's Theatrical Grill—social headquarters of the syndicate—when Joyce grabbed him from the rear. It was assumed Joyce wanted to ask about that job, but, said Swarts, "I naturally thought I was being robbed and I went for my gun. I didn't recognize Joyce until after I had shot him."

Someone put Joyce in a taxi and took him to the hospital. Swarts went back to the Hollenden and up to McGinty's room. They decided to find a mouthpiece, one Richard Moriarty, before Swarts surrendered. It was next day before he did. Newspapers noted that Swarts then shared the hospital ward of the county jail with a convicted police captain. The two "old friends" smoked "fat cigars" furnished by a businessman who was "serving time for killing two persons with his automobile." Meanwhile Joyce died at the hospital with his brother, a Cleveland cop, at his bedside.

Justice triumphed, and Swarts received a one-to-twenty-year sentence for manslaughter. He was paroled in 1938, and ultimately was given a new assignment for the syndicate at Chesapeake, Ohio.

"Honest Frenchie" Gips drifted north to Cleveland too, and found work with Gameboy Miller. He didn't like Gameboy—and he didn't mind telling why:

> Every time he catch somebody stealing a penny he knock his finger off. He took a blackjack and hit 'em over the hand. Everybody must be honest with Gameboy Miller; the only man crooked is himself. He done all the cheating. No help can do cheating with him. That was Gameboy Miller.
>
> [But jobs were scarce] and I went to work in a dirty, dirty gambling place where we rob them poor working men working in a factory. Half-dollar place, and I worked hard to get $12 a day. There was no other jobs open and I worked for the dope fiend Gameboy Miller, for his fifty-cent crap games and his ten-cent roulette wheels.
>
> [In contrast, Frenchie noted,] the Mounds Club was operated by big people, where society have a little place to entertain themselves—roulette wheels and dice tables. The same people worked with me in Miami Beach worked over there. Mr. Tom McGinty was the big boss. . . .

"Honest Frenchie," who got into gambling because he couldn't see "any difference in being a head waiter in a gambling place or a head waiter in a restaurant," quit the business in 1950 after talking freely to the Kefauver Committee about the S & G Syndicate at Miami Beach. Fourteen years later he was working as a cook in a little Daytona Beach restaurant. In his shabby hotel room hung the full-dress suit he had worn as a head waiter. There was also a scrapbook of pictures, many autographed by notables. . . . "Honest Frenchie" had his memories—many too bitter to enjoy.

2.

The arrangement with McGinty was unique insofar as the syndicate was concerned only because of its scope. McGinty was a big man, as Frenchie put it, and had many and big interests. As the syndicate expanded its area of activity and grew in wealth, it became more and more necessary to depend upon associates to handle supervisory details. The four equals—Dalitz, Kleinman, Rothkopf, and Tucker—had time to do little more than approve a proposal, put up the cash in one way or another, and turn it over to lieutenants or local men recruited for the purpose.

In many of their enterprises, years passed before their names were mentioned. Under the circumstances, it seems fair to assume that in others they have yet to be identified. Thistle Downs Race Track was thought to be the property of those old allies, E. P. Strong and Sammy Haas, for example, but after years of operation the company owning it was liquidated in 1951, and the real owners revealed.

Robert Kaye had 40 per cent, and Kleinman, Rothkopf, Dalitz, and Tucker, 15 per cent each. It also was revealed that Kaye had advanced the money used by the other stockholders. In other words, the syndicate cut itself in for free.

As sometimes happens, however, when men cooperate, Kaye didn't lose anything. He was a one-third partner with Mushy

Wexler and Gameboy Miller in Empire News, the Ohio branch of Continental Press, and a member of the Ess-Kay-Gee Company with Gilbert Smollin and Abe Goodman. It provided a lay-off betting service for bookies around the country. Anyone who received a bet too large to handle could always lay it off with Ess-Kay-Gee. The partnership broke up in 1950 when Kaye moved to the Desert Inn at Las Vegas to act as credit manager. By then, however, the lay-off betting business had become centered in Newport, Kentucky.

But with all the attention being devoted to gambling, the Cleveland Syndicate still had time to listen to a proposition from an old friend from Detroit. Not unnaturally, coming from Abe Moss, it concerned liquor. Moss had represented the syndicate during Prohibition in smuggling vast amounts of booze from Canada. Now, according to Moss, the time had come to smuggle it back.

As Moss explained it, the idea made good financial sense. Untaxpaid alcohol, as the "feds" called it, could be purchased in quantity in Chicago, for about $1.10 a gallon in five-gallon cans. Prices had indeed dropped since Molaska quit the business. In Toronto a five-gallon can would bring as much as $45, or $9.00 a gallon.

Moss got the idea while working with Allied Sales Company in Toronto, and his second thought was of his old friend Moe Dalitz.

The syndicate decided to back the venture but left all the details to Moss. He contacted Hyman Frank and Louis Schneiderman in Chicago. The two had operated illicit distilleries for many years and, when called upon in August, 1939, were operating one on West Lawrence Avenue. Its output was considered insufficient, so arrangements were made to set up a second distillery on North Kilpatrick.

Moss bought a truck and car and hired Jack Jolly to drive on the American side and Nat Levitt and Harold Barron to handle the Canadian driving. Arrangements were made to hire boats, and in the course of the operation four were used. Operations were first centered at Ecourse, Michigan, just down the Detroit River from Detroit, and the alcohol was taken across to LaSalle, Ontario. Later, headquarters was shifted to Grosse Ile, Michigan, and the booze was taken into that old export center, Amherstburg, Ontario. It was a classic case of send your booze out upon the water and it shall be returned to you.

Whereas Moss, in earlier days, had been part of what the syndicate liked to hear called "the Combination," meaning that Mafia members played active roles along with men of Jewish descent, the new smuggling operation consisted almost entirely of people with Jewish backgrounds. There were Louis Moss, Nathan Rosen, David Rothman, Bernard Schneiderman, Ben Sert, Harry Steiner, George Lessowitz, William Koury, Sam Mindell, and Jack Isenberg. The one exception was Matthew Walker, a Negro from Arkansas.

Moss soon realized the economic loss involved in sending loaded boats to Canada and letting them return empty, so he arranged with his Canadian connections to smuggle in merchandise on the return trip. Barron was given the job of purchasing furs in Canada for resale in the United States.

The idea impressed Nat Levitt. Before he could do much with it he was caught at Toronto in 1939 with 118 gallons of illicit alcohol. When he got out of jail, however, he pursued the thought and found pure gold.

When at last the ring was captured, Moss was sentenced to ten years in prison and a $10,000 fine. Years before he had boasted of paying $100,000 to officials to avoid prosecution, but in July, 1941, his luck ran out for the first time. His wife, who was placed on probation, had to be carried from the courtroom when she fainted upon hearing sentence passed.

Moe Dalitz and the boys could feel sorry for their old aide, but they had no time for tears. In 1940 they had invaded Kentucky and established a base in the Beverly Hills. Now it was time to expand those holdings. The Canadian venture had been profitable, but Moss had made the mistake of trying old tricks in a new era.

3.

As a historian, Kenton County Circuit Judge Joseph P. Goodenough had one virtue—he was eloquent. Asked by the Kefauver Committee to tell of certain events in his county in 1941, the judge began by telling of his home town:

> Covington, second largest city in Kentucky, lies on a flood plain of the Ohio River at the foot of suburban hills that reach back to a high plain of the Bluegrass. The Licking River separates Covington from Newport. In this setting, Covington looks like a city on the Rhine. The impression is heightened by the spires of many churches that taper up from among the compact business buildings.
>
> In the Panic of 1873, the genius of Covington flowered. John G. Carlisle and William Goebel grew to national stature politically. Bishop Maes inaugurated the construction of beautiful St. Mary's Cathedral. Frank Duveneck painted murals in it and in our Covington homes.
>
> Since then we have grown and prospered. We have many churches—of all denominations. Our citizens are God-fearing, churchgoing people. We are morally sound. We have excellent schools and two fine hospitals. Our crime rate is low.
>
> Yes, we have had occasion to do some housecleaning of the gambling situation. No doubt there is room for more cleaning. We never did have and do not have hoodlums or gangsters. The assassination of a community's good name is as debase [sic] and vile as the assassination of an individual's name. . . ."

Then Kefauver pressed Judge Goodenough into an admission that a 1938 injunction prohibited certain individuals, including James Brink, from permitting gambling at the Lookout House in Kenton County. The Judge also confirmed that thirteen years later Brink was still permitting gambling at the Lookout House.

> You must remember, [explained Judge Goodenough] that we have had gambling in Kenton County for many, many years. Up to 1910 we had about six large casinos that existed

within the shadow of the city hall, and these were handbook clubs—poolrooms, they called them in those days, and they were literally licensed. They would come into the police court every day and pay a $25 fine. . . .

Now, Senator, we live in a community which is the home of the old Latonia Race Track. Most of our people were born on the back stretch of that race track. We live within 110 miles of Churchill Downs, which vies with your great race, the Preakness. [He was apparently addressing Senator Herbert O'Connor of Maryland.] Now, when you have folks born and raised and educated in an environment like that, you are not going to convert them in one day. . . .

Nor in several days, as the history of James H. "Jimmie" Brink made clear.

Brink was in the "whiskey business" with his father during Prohibition. "I bought it locally and sold it." Born in 1904 in Cincinnati, he followed the pattern of other bootleggers and went into the gambling business after Repeal. In 1933 he bought the Lookout House, a huge, barnlike structure on the hill overlooking Covington and the road to Louisville.

The life of a gambler even in the environment of Kenton County had its problems. On June 13, 1936, Brink was indicted along with two of Kentucky's most famous names in gambling—"Sleep Out" Louis Levinson and Ed Curd of Lexington. Curd was to become a nationally known lay-off betting "commissioner," who fled to Canada to avoid prosecution for income-tax evasions. Levinson won his fame in Newport. All were eventually acquitted in the 1936 case.

On April 5, 1938, a "blue-ribbon" grand jury indicted Brink on forty-five counts. Brink was reported to be in Hot Springs, Arkansas, but four leading businessmen, including a bank president, arrived with $50,000 to go on his bond.

The jury declared there was "a laxity in law enforcement," and Circuit Judge Johnst Northcutt—predecessor to Judge Goodenough—called a new grand jury to investigate officials. At Attorney General Hubert Meredith's suggestion, an injunction was sought and obtained forbidding Brink and others from gambling or permitting anyone else to gamble at the Lookout House.

No more effort to enforce the injunction was made in Kenton than was made later when similar injunctions against Cleveland Syndicate casinos in adjoining Campbell County were obtained. Before the injunction was issued, however, Judge Northcutt had to order Brink and Sheriff Henry Berndt from his home. A grand jury witness was blackjacked and ammonia was squirted into the eyes of another. Meanwhile, gambling continued at the Lookout House.

In 1941 Brink bowed to pressure from another source and became a junior partner in the Kentucky operations of the Cleveland Syndicate. He made no effort to fight the inevitable, having had a ringside seat for the battle of the Beverly Hills. In that long-drawn struggle, Peter Schmidt, a tough old former bootlegger, turned down a cash offer from the syndicate in 1936, and had fought for four years. The battle ended in 1940 with Pete begging the syndicate to take the plush casino off his hands. According to Sam Tucker, Schmidt "just wasn't man enough to run it."

The syndicate wanted the Lookout House for several reasons. For one thing, it made possible a two-county operation. If, for example, the "heat" went on in Campbell County, the bulk of operations could be shifted to Kenton County—or vice versa. That way the folks who came to Cincinnati's conventions would never have to go home disappointed. The same thing could be done during routine grand jury sessions in each county where native custom required that respect for law and order be demonstrated during the few days a year grand juries were convened. By having a staggered schedule for the respective juries, it would be possible to keep casinos going in one county while the jury met in the other.

A second reason for taking over the Lookout House was nothing more or less than a natural desire to corner the market. Kenton County was just as much a part of the metropolitan area of Cincinnati as Campbell County, and just as attractive to suckers. Either there had to be no major gambling in Kenton, or it had to be controlled by, and synchronized with, Campbell.

Brink told the Kefauver Committee that he dealt with Sam Tucker,

> the gentlemen of the boys. There was some negotiations about it, asking me to set a price, and eventually I did set a price. I think if I remember right, it is a matter of record, I believe it was around $125,000, something, and I also remember I came out with an interest in Beverly Hills, a 10 per cent interest in Beverly Hills. I bought in on the Beverly Hills deal and kept a 20 per cent interest in the Lookout House, of which 5 per cent went to my father and 5 per cent went to the Carrs, and I retained 10 per cent.

Brink added that Alvin Giesey was brought in by the syndicate "after the price was set." Also brought in to run the Lookout House was Gameboy Miller, the casino troubleshooter of the syndicate. "They wasn't doing much business," Gameboy explained, "and I was pretty well known."

A pattern perfected at the Beverly resulted in the creation of three separate organizations: Lookout House, Inc., operated the nightclub, restaurant, and bar; Jimmie Brink, Inc., held title to the land and building; and a partnership, the Lookout Club, ran the casino. Giesey was secretary of the corporations.

Business was bad during the war years, but in the first six months of 1944, the gross receipts at the Lookout House were listed for tax purposes as $117, 719. The net income of $62,770.69 was divided among partners as follows:

Jimmy Brink and Samuel Miller, $9,123.10; Charles V. Carr and Mitchell Meyer, $3,041.03; John Croft, $1,520.53; Samuel Schraeder, $5,777.96; Louis Rothkopf, Morris Kleinman, M. B. Davis [Dalitz], and Louise K. Tucker, wife of Samuel Tucker, $6,082.07 each; and Charles Polizzi, $4,865.65.

In addition, Miller received $1,950 in salary for the six-months period.

By 1946, business was improving. Gross receipts that year were listed for tax purposes as $506,795. Net income of $148,844.29 was divided:

Marion Brink [wife of James Brink], $14,884.43; Sam Miller got nothing; Carr, $7,442.21; Meyer, $9,168.81; Croft, $4,584.40; Schraeder, $17,399.90; Rothkopf, Kleinman, Dalitz, and Tucker, $18,315.29 each; Chuck Polizzi, $14,661.17; and B. W. Brink, father of James, $7,442.21.

Brink said he was "given a piece" of the Yorkshire Club in downtown Newport when the syndicate acquired that plush casino handbook in 1944. Others having "pieces" were those old Mayfield Road boys, Chuck Polizzi and John "King" Angersola, as well as George Gordon, John Croft, Ruby Kolod, and Alfred Goltsman, all of Cleveland. Local partners included Red "the Enforcer" Masterson and E. R. "Butts" Lowe. Also represented was George Bear of Detroit.

Kefauver Committee counsel Joseph Nellis commented to Brink, "This is a very curious combination of the Cleveland Syndicate plus a lot of local people."

"It was satisfying a lot of people," Brink replied.

But of all that the eloquent Judge Goodenough was unaware. He boasted to the committee, "We don't have any Costellos or 'Greasy Thumb' Guziks in our community."

Senator Kefauver inquired, "What do you call McGinty, Dalitz, and Rothkopf?"

"That is a Cleveland group, is it not, Senator?" replied Goodenough.

Nothing was said of Tucker. The Kentucky operations had become so large that "Sambo" was assigned the over-all management of the division. He moved to Southgate outside Newport, where the Beverly Hills was located. Eventually, expansion would force his partners to leave Cleveland, too. The syndicate was becoming national. When it became international, Tucker would move once more.

CHAPTER TWELVE

Is this community helpless against crooked cops?
The Cleveland Press, 1953

CLEVELAND SAFETY DIRECTOR Eliot Ness, assisted by his ace investigator, Lieutenant Ernest Molnar, climaxed a long investigation of the numbers racket in 1939 by presenting evidence to a grand jury.

The jury voted indictments immediately, but decided to seal them to permit additional investigation.

Lieutenant Molnar promptly tipped off some of those named in the still-secret indictments and thus launched the yacht *Wood Duck* on an epic voyage to Florida.

Why Ness didn't know Molnar was a crook is one of those minor mysteries of law enforcement—almost everyone else did. A federal agent who worked with Ness before the "Untouchable" became safety director said Molnar would come far out of his assigned district to interfere with raids on bootleggers—raids being conducted by Ness.

Alvin G. Sutton, one of Ness' successors as Cleveland safety director, told the Kefauver Committee that Molnar took advantage of the flight of the big boys in the numbers racket to make himself boss. Sutton conducted the investigation that nine years later resulted in Molnar being fired as a Cleveland cop. He entered the penitentiary on May 6, 1949, sentenced to serve sixty-six years on various bribery counts. In 1953 he was paroled, and released to "enjoy the fruits of his crime plus a $75 a month pension from the taxpayers," as the *Press* put it.

Among the twenty-three persons indicted in the numbers investigation were Chuck Polizzi, John and George "King" Angersola, Shondor Birns, Milton Rockman, Angelo Lonardo—a survivor of the corn-sugar wars—and Angelo Sciria. The latter fled south aboard the *Wood Duck* and kept going until he reached Frank Milano's plantation at Vera Cruz, Mexico. Ultimately he was captured in Mexico City.

The *Wood Duck*, at the time of its voyage, was owned by Arthur B. "Mickey" McBride, the old circulator of the Hanna newspapers, but McBride didn't make the trip. He was too busy establishing Continental Press to take over the wire service from Moses Annenberg.

The yacht was a forty-foot boat which McBride said he bought for $8,000 in 1937 or 1938. The *Wood Duck*, with six fugitives aboard, went across Lake Erie, through the Welland Canal to Lake Ontario, out the St. Lawrence River to the Atlantic, and down the east coast via the Inland Waterway to Miami Beach. The value of a St. Lawrence Seaway was demonstrated.

Once arrived, the Angersola boys went into the hotel business in a big way. They were aided financially by Big Al Polizzi, who, he said, decided to put his past behind him. In 1944 he too moved to Florida with between—he couldn't be sure—$300,000 and $500,000 profits from the past. In Florida, among other things, he invested in the Polkin Company—*Polizzi-king*, for now the Angersola boys called themselves King.

In conjunction with Mickey McBride, Big Al practically built the city of Coral Gables. He also built homes for racketeers, such as Joe Massei, and gave Tommy McGinty a hand in expanding Palm Beach.

Something of the involved nature of the relationships of the transplanted Clevelanders is shown in the history of the *Wood Duck*. Coast Guard records show that on July 23, 1940, McBride transferred title to Fred King Angersola. On August 15, 1941, Angersola transferred title to Charles K. Green, who held it exactly five days before presenting it to Amy King, wife of John

Angersola. On June 3, 1944, McBride's old boat became the property of his partner in Coral Gables, Big Al Polizzi. Al said he paid Amy King Angersola $5,000 for it.

Why did McBride sell it in the first place? "Well," he explained, "I had the boat in Miami and I was tired of it, and the war was coming on. . . ."

2.

The war was coming on . . . it brought changes. If, on the one hand it curtailed gambling by limiting travel, it also created opportunities in war contracts and the black market.

Tucker settled down outside Newport to mastermind the process by which the Cleveland Syndicate over a period of nine years was to get control of all major casinos in the area. There was enough to keep Kleinman busy in and around Cleveland, where the new Arrow Club was soon to become the fabulous Pettibone Club, and slots and numbers presented constant headaches. Rothkopf was active too, but he had learned caution. Black-market liquor deals might be profitable, but "Uncle Louie" preferred to let that lover of silk shirts from Detroit, Sam Stein, take the rap if a rap had to be taken.

The war was almost certain to make New York and Washington the economic and political centers of power. Dalitz, who didn't want the Cleveland Syndicate neglected in any important deals, decided he should go there. So on June 25, 1943, he enlisted in the Army at Fort Hayes, Ohio.

After six months of laundry school at Fort Lee, Petersburg, Virginia, which was as close as he could get to Washington, he was promoted to second lieutenant and assigned to Headquarters, Second Service Command, Governor's Island, New York. He was put in charge of a quartermaster laundry, and promoted to first lieutenant.

Military duties did not set too heavily upon Lieutenant Dalitz, it would appear. He lived while in New York at the Hotel Savoy-Plaza, where he met a choice collection of Eastern Syndicate hoods. For some years, associations formed at the Savoy-Plaza were developed in business deals.

It should not be assumed that Dalitz was unique in his desire to serve his country at the Savoy-Plaza. There was, for example, the mysterious "Operation Underworld" in which two of Dalitz' old associates played key roles.

The story as developed by the Kefauver Committee had Naval Intelligence needing help from the Mafia in protecting east coast shipping from sabotage. Charles "Lucky" Luciano was the man to provide it, if he would, but Luciano was in Dannemora Prison, where Tom Dewey had sent him some years before. And, conceivably, he might not be feeling patriotic.

The Navy turned to Luciano's attorney, Moses Polakoff. He promised to try, but suggested they also take along "one person with me in whom I had confidence." That person was Meyer Lansky.

Dannemora proved to be inconvenient, so Lucky was moved to a closer, and more comfortable, prison. Thereafter, at frequent intervals, Polakoff, Lansky, and whoever needed to get orders, would visit Luciano. This continued for many months. How much it contributed to the nation's welfare is still a military secret. There can be no doubt it contributed to Luciano's welfare. Lucky, who was serving a fifty-year sentence for compulsory prostitution, found himself paroled at war's end on condition he go home to Italy.

Among those having a long chat with Lucky at Ellis Island just before he sailed was Lansky. Perhaps he was saying goodbye. Perhaps he was rechecking plans for Lucky to visit Havana in the near future. At any rate, Lansky was in Cuba to greet him when Luciano, in violation of his parole agreement, came back to the Western Hemisphere. He stopped to pay his respects to Frank Milano at Vera Cruz on his way to Cuba.

Others who were active in the war effort didn't wear uniforms. Take Joe Zucker, alias Baker. Born in Poland in 1890, he came to New York at an early age and married Mabel

Schneider. They separated because of what was called "religious differences"—Joe had no religion and Mabel did—and were divorced in 1923.

After picking up some twenty arrests as a pickpocket, Joe became associated with Frank Costello and made the big time. Frank sent him to Cleveland as a liaison man shortly after the National Syndicate was formed. Joe served as an observer at Arrowhead and inspected Arizona with Dalitz and Big Al Polizzi, then went back to New York.

During the war Baker managed to get some contracts at Wright Field, Dayton, Ohio. Former New York District Attorney and later Ambassador to Mexico William O'Dwyer was in uniform doing his bit as an investigator. He heard, he testified, "all the way from Baltimore to Boston," that things were not "right at Wright Field." The rumor had it that Frank Costello and Baker were involved.

To find out, said O'Dwyer, he met with Costello in Costello's New York apartment. Some leading politicians were also present. O'Dwyer seemed unable to understand why the Kefauver Committee should later be skeptical of Costello's assurance that he was not in business at Wright Field. The Army threw Baker out just to be sure.

Typical of social life in those days was a meeting in a well-known New York café, Toots Shor's. Present were Baker, Costello, and Lansky. Baker was sent to the telephone to call Longie Zwillman, boss of the New Jersey rackets. Shortly thereafter, Zwillman appeared at the table. The subject under discussion was not reported.

Thus it was that Moe Dalitz felt right at home in New York. It was the place to be to have a finger on the pulse of affairs. The uniform didn't prohibit lending a hand when an old friend such as Sam Stein needed a little help. Sam had worked under Abe Moss back in the days of the "Combination," and he knew the smuggling racket pretty well. But unlike Moss, Sam could adjust to the demands of a new age. And in a world at war, what was more in demand than gold?

3.

Sam Stein was born in Bialystok, Russia (eastern Poland), in 1896, and entered the United States in 1913. He didn't bother to learn good English or to acquire citizenship, but by 1920 he indicated his familiarity with American culture by stealing an automobile and getting a two-to-five-year sentence at Detroit.

When released, it was but to be picked up on a succession of charges: armed robbery, 1923; forgery, 1924; liquor violation and armed robbery, 1925; grand larceny, 1928, etc. In each case, however, the charges were dismissed.

In 1933 he was arrested with Joe Massei in a famous case that went to the Supreme Court and aroused much newspaper ire. Police stopped a car in which the two were riding, and found a small arsenal. Since Massei had been suspected in several murders, the police charged them with carrying a concealed weapon. The court ruled, however, that the search was illegal, and police returned the weapons to the boys and sent them on their way. Shortly thereafter, Massei was arrested for the murder of Jimmy Hayes, erstwhile boss of Toledo gambling. The charges were soon dropped.

The Massei incident was enough to make Stein move to Cleveland, where he was rewarded for his services to the syndicate with a piece of Freddie's Club, 818 Vincent Street, near the Theatrical Grill, in partnership with Freddie Meyers. After a few years, Stein returned to Detroit and made his home at the Book-Cadillac Hotel. He was there when Abe Moss began rum-running to Canada, but, despite old friendships, he stayed out of it.

Nat Levitt slipped up early in the case and was arrested by the Royal Mounted Police. He served but a few months and took advantage of the opportunity to become a Canadian citizen. This helped when Moss and the rest of the crew were indicted. Nat was indicted too on fourteen counts, but his status as a Canadian citizen prevented his extradition.

Nevertheless, Levitt kept up with his Detroit associates.

Among them was a cousin who had a brother-in-law named Irving Wasserman. Irving had a brother, Morris Wasserman, who had a girl friend named Sally Izenberg. Sally was the widow of Jack Stein, a relative of Sam Stein, who had been murdered in Toledo in 1938.

With this lesson in international relations clear, it should be obvious how Nat Levitt set up his new smuggling operation, and how Sam Stein got involved.

The plan was to smuggle gold from Canada—this was long before anyone worried about the balance-of-payments problem that plagued the United States two decades later.

Canada ranked third, behind South Africa and Russia, in the production of raw gold. Much of its output came from Ontario, among which the mines at Timmins, north of Kirkland Lakes, ranked high. By June, 1942, the value of gold being stolen from the mines at Timmins was estimated at $3 million per year, and the Royal Mounted was ready to swear that none of it was being disposed of in Canada. It was going to the United States.

Levitt was a hard worker. The Foreign Exchange Control Board of Canada testified to that with an announcement that $75,000 in gold was being smuggled into the United States every week.

Sometimes it happens that crime doesn't always pay indefinately. Irving Wasserman was arrested in Milwaukee on April 30, 1942, and he put the finger on Levitt and a Toronto racketeer named Harry Perry. A co-defendant, Marlon Landau, offered to trap Stein. Plans had been made, he explained, for an outlet in Chicago to buy 2,000 ounces of gold from Stein. The report on what followed sounds like an Ian Fleming yarn.

Federal agents in Detroit received a telegram, alerting them to watch Stein, who was staying at the Book-Cadillac Hotel. It was September 13, 1942—a Sunday. At noon, Stein came down from his room, bought a newspaper, made a telephone call, kidded the cigar-counter girl, and went back to his room. Agents noted he was about forty-five, weighing 135 pounds, with sloping shoulders, slim face, big nose, hair neatly parted on the side.

He was wearing a brown pullover sweater and a yellow shirt.

About 1:35 P.M. Stein came down to the lobby again and had lunch with two men in the Cadillac Café off the lobby. One of the men was later identified as Charles Lipshitz, alias Charles Layton, who operated a distillery for whom Stein was nominally employed in a capacity made famous by Frank Costello—a "goodwill man." The other man proved to be a Benny Krell. Stein was overheard asking Krell to drive him to the airport, but Krell explained that since it was a Jewish holiday he wanted to have dinner with his mother. So Lipshitz acted as chauffeur. Upon arriving they found the 4 P.M. plane had already departed to Buffalo. Stein got a reservation on the 5:15 P.M. flight, and the agents discovered he already had a ticket on a Buffalo-to-Chicago flight under the name of Simons. When Stein checked his one suitcase, the agents examined and weighed it carefully. It contained nothing suspicious and weighed exactly twenty-six and a quarter pounds. When Stein took off, the agents watched him out of sight. When he landed in Buffalo, other agents were waiting.

The plane landed at 6:35 P.M. Stein got off and entered a telephone booth. An agent went into the booth beside him and listened to the conversation. Stein, still unsuspecting, retrieved his bag and took a bus to the Statler Hotel. He checked his bag at the baggage room, but instead of registering he went into the dining room. A man later identified as Michael Menneci joined him for dinner. They sat for two hours talking. Then Stein recovered his bag, gave it to the porter, and accompanied by Menneci, walked to the corner of Delaware and Mohawk where a 1938 Plymouth was parked. The two men entered the car, drove back to the Statler, where Stein obtained his bag from the porter and put it in the trunk of the car.

The next stop, after some aimless riding, was the New York Central Railroad Terminal. Menneci parked the car, opened the trunk, opened Stein's bag, put something inside it, and locked the bag once more. The agents assumed that whatever was put inside the bag was already in the trunk.

Continuing their evasive actions, Stein and Menneci walked to the entrance of the railroad terminal. Stein carried the bag and the invisible agents noted it now appeared to be very heavy. The men chatted a few minutes as people passed around them, and then they returned to the car. The bag was put back in the trunk, and now the companions headed for the airport.

Stein checked the bag once more—and the agents were pleased to note it now weighed forty-five pounds. While Stein was discussing his reservation to Chicago, the agents held a quick conference and decided to close in. Stein and Menneci were arrested at the information desk. The agents noted that Stein managed to discard the baggage check he had just been given, but they recovered it and the bag.

When the bag was searched, four gold buttons worth $8,900 were found. The buttons were almost three inches in diameter and one inch thick. It was the approved shape of illicit bullion.

Also found was a little black book containing numbers indicating the weights and fineness of the pieces of gold seized on Stein. When a little later the Royal Mounted raided an apartment in Toronto, they found another little black book containing identical numbers. Three brothers named Black were arrested.

On September 8, 1943, Stein and Menneci were sentenced to two years in prison. Stein also drew a $1,000 fine. But even before trial as well as while appealing the conviction, Stein kept busy. The agents who caught him once remained interested and occasionally checked him out. They discovered he was spending a lot of time at the Netherland-Plaza Hotel in Cincinnati and talking to a lot of Cleveland Syndicate people.

There was a record in April, 1943, of calls to the Lookout House outside Covington, and to Gameboy Miller. Other calls during April went to various jewelry dealers—this kept interest alive—to the outfit supplying slot machines in the Newport area, and in May to Gameboy again and to the Robert Gould Company, dealers in wholesale liquors.

Another flurry of interest developed in November, 1943, when it was learned Stein had made reservations to fly to Detroit. Instead, after an early call to Morris Kleinman in Cleveland, he changed plans and arranged to leave for Cleveland at 7:40 P.M.

At 11:50 A.M. Stein went to the hotel garage and secured a 1942 Buick registered in the name of Mrs. Sam Tucker. He drove to Tucker's home on Alexandria Pike, near Newport, and stayed there until 4 P.M. when Mrs. Tucker drove him back to the hotel at Cincinnati.

It was learned through "confidential sources," that Stein called a Mr. Simons in Detroit—apparently it was a favorite alias—and informed him that he was going to sell some "gin" to the Man in Cleveland that night, and would be in Detroit the following day. He noted that 17,000 cases were available.

Stein departed on a 7:40 P.M. flight to Cleveland, and one set of federal agents closed their report by noting:

"It is now definitely established that Stein is now engaged in the buying and selling of liquor and it was decided we would make no further checks unless information is again received that he is dealing in the smuggling of gold."

Another federal agency, meanwhile, assigned a jacket number to a new case file: Sam Stein, *et al.* Among the "*et al.*'s" was "Big Al."

4.

A man of many interests was "Big Al" Polizzi. Lubeck Distributing Company had not made him respectable but he kept trying. In 1940 he bought stock in the Sunrise Brewing Company, Cleveland. The name was changed to the Tip Top Brewing Company. Within a matter of a few months Polizzi was majority stockholder and president. Tip Top acquired Sunrise's former distributing company as well, and Polizzi shifted many of the officers of Lubeck to the new property. Among them was Fred W. Garmone, formerly an annual retainer to represent Lubeck's customers who violated city and state liquor laws.

Polizzi found a new use for Garmone. He set up an account in the Morris Plan Bank of Cleveland in Garmone's name. Its purpose was to guarantee repayment of loans by the bank to retail customers of Tip Top. This kind of arrangement made possible what was called the "tied-house system," and was in violation of federal law.

New opportunities developed early in 1943. Legal liquor in Ohio was a monopoly of the state and was sold under permits to dealers and retail outlets, such as taverns. But because of the war, there was a shortage of liquor. In an effort to keep its citizens happy, the state instituted what was called the "Consent System," whereby tavern owners were permitted to purchase liquor from out-of-state dealers and import it into Ohio. This importation was supposed to be strictly regulated, but so was Prohibition.

Polizzi and Garmone discovered that liquor was available but in a competitive situation. If the buyer was willing to pay prices in excess of the ceiling established by the Office of Price Administration, he could get all he wanted. The boys were willing and bought 1,501 cases from Peerless Liquors in Chicago. (As a matter of historical interest, it should be noted that back when Kleinman was trying to make a deal with the government, he named Peerless Carriers of Canada as the source of much of the syndicate's illicit booze.)

The 1,501 cases were resold to tavern owners at a price of $9.00 per case in excess of the legal ceiling. Of this added profit, $5.00 went to Peerless and $4.00 to Polizzi. Needless to say, the cooperating taverns were syndicate-connected places such as Freddie's Club and the Theatrical Grill.

When the liquor available from Peerless had been disposed of, Polizzi made a deal with Ulrich "Sonny" Vogt of Peerless whereby Peerless arranged with the Ohio Department of Liquor to act as an agent in selling and consigning liquor bought from out-of-state sources. Peerless received $1.00 a case for this service.

Thereupon all Polizzi needed were warehouse receipts—the wartime equivalent of Prohibition's "permit for withdrawal." It was in obtaining such receipts that Sam Stein proved valuable.

One episode brought the boys into contact with an international racketeer, Sergeant Batista of Cuba. The deal involved William "Billy" Weisman and his Cedar Valley Distillery at Wooster, Ohio, and the plan was to blend a little good bourbon with a lot of cheap Cuban rum and produce a new drink which would be sold as blended whiskey.

It was a scheme worthy of Prohibition, and the boys improved on it as they went along. Since whiskey barrels were hard to get in Cuba, a supply was shipped over. It was discovered that if the rum was put in the used whiskey barrels, left in the hot sunlight for a few days, and then rolled down a hill to the docks, it would take on some of the characteristics of whiskey.

Batista, who of course owned the rum, offered to help transport the finished product to Florida. What with the war, help was needed, and Batista made his yacht—an old American gunboat—available. First, after having learned of black-market prices, he demanded $10,000 more for the rum. And when the boat sailed, it never seemed to have an easy crossing to Key West. Batista's crew always reported the cargo was short because they had been forced to jettison some of the barrels to keep the old tub from sinking. The importers, of course, had to accept the loss as part of the penalty of doing business with Batista.

The bourbon-flavored rum was bottled at Weisman's plant. No one ever estimated how much of it was sold to the suckers at the Theatrical Grill and elsewhere, but eventually the government impounded all it could find on the grounds that it was not manufactured according to the label on the bottle. After all, rum could hardly be considered "neutral spirits."

Stein became an important part of the black-market operation through his ability to secure warehouse receipts. He was still awaiting trial on the gold-smuggling charge when he became involved. A Eugene Terenyi—an old friend of former days—met him in early April, 1943, and told him of the possibilities. All Terenyi needed, he said, was someone with capital. Stein knew plenty of people with capital. As he put it: "I knew a lot of people in Detroit and Cleveland, many of whom are respectable business people, and I was satisfied that if conditions were as represented I could get the necessary financing."

A few days later he met his friend in Cincinnati and went with him to Louisville. Among others, they talked to Sam Friedman, then manager of the Kentucky Hotel—one of Louisville's best. Friedman, who had many friends in the distilleries at Louisville, Bardstown, and Frankfort, Kentucky, had receipts for sale, Stein said, "but he wanted too much for them." Others in Louisville were more reasonable, and Stein arranged to buy several thousand dollars worth of receipts.

People were willing to sell receipts, not only because they brought good prices, but because they were useless to an individual who did not have an arrangement, such as Polizzi had with Peerless and Peerless had with the state of Ohio.

In other words, the receipt was prima facie evidence that the holder owned whiskey stored in barrels in a warehouse. Legitimate distilleries, whose business was primarily through government-regulated channels, had a self-policing agreement whereby they professed not to buy more bottles than they needed for their legitimate customers. Thus it was possible to own whiskey in a warehouse and have no way to get it bottled, labeled, and introduced into a monopoly state, such as Ohio.

That is why "middlemen," such as Stein and Friedman, could buy up a vast amount of whiskey receipts from people who could not move their liquor, and resell the receipts to people like Polizzi who could move it via the black market.

Stein, having located some receipts, had next to find someone with capital. He placed a collect call to Peter Licavoli, that old friend of the Cleveland Syndicate at Detroit and asked for some money. Pete responded promptly by wiring $7,000, and Stein was in business. He went over to the Fairfield Distillery at Bardstown and arranged for the bottling of his whiskey. Another $10,000 was needed, and Licavoli supplied it, but at the last moment the Fairfield Distillery withdrew and refunded the money. The whiskey was then sold in bulk to Garmone-Polizzi.

In early May, 1943, Stein continued, he was told by Garmone that much more whiskey was needed and "I entered an informal arrangement whereby it was understood that if I could locate some whiskey for him, I would receive something for my services. I made general inquiry and was told that Robert Gould, Cincinnati whiskey broker, had available warehouse receipts but that I would require an introduction to him and that he was a sharp trader. . . ."

Robert Gould was the George Remus of black-market whiskey. He lived at 26 Signal Hill, Cincinnati, was married but had no children. Born in 1897 of Jewish parents, he had built up an empire in legal liquor. He had controlling interest in the Pebbleford Distillery, valued at $373,316; controlling interest in Dowling Brothers Distillery, valued at $130,612; 60 per cent interest in Willow Spring Distillery, etc. He owned 12,057 barrels of Willow Springs Bourbon valued at $800,000; 7,498 barrels of Dowling Bourbon, and 4,380 barrels of Pebbleford with a total value of $651,530.

In 1943 alone, Alex Joasselson, liquor dealer of Ashland, Kentucky, and Edward Baumer, liquor dealer of Newport, paid $1,139,660 to Gould, and this amount was exactly $547,029 in excess of the OPA's ceiling price. But that was only part of Gould's business.

Stein managed an introduction to Gould through a Cleveland tavern owner whose brother was manager of the Netherland-Plaza Hotel in Cincinnati. Gould's office was in the Carew Tower, tallest building in the city, and it was there Stein offered to buy warehouse receipts. Gould seemed "indifferent," Stein reported, and "after asking who I knew" told him to come back later.

When Stein returned it was to discover just how sharp a trader Gould really was. He offered Stein receipts for 1,000 barrels at $4.00 per gallon. The ceiling price at the time was $1.15 per gallon. Stein told Gould the price was too high. Gould replied that "if I left the office without closing the deal the price would be $4.25 when I returned."

Stein left to confer with Garmone and was told to buy at $4.00. Garmone thought Gould was bluffing about increasing the price, but when Stein went back to the Carew Tower he was told the price had gone up as announced. Stein said he felt obliged to confer again with Garmone, but Gould warned that if he walked out the price would go up to $4.50.

Garmone wasn't happy about the price increase, Stein said, but he told him to buy. When Stein returned to Gould's office, he was told, however, that the deal was off. He had been "fooling around too long." It took considerable talk, but "I convinced him of my sincerity and he finally agreed to let me have the whiskey and quoted the price now at $4.50 per gallon. He told me if I left the office again, I would find the price at $5.00 a gallon on my return. I just held out my hand and asked him to shake on the deal, that he had just sold 1,000 barrels of whiskey. He said no, the deal only covered 500 barrels now because he had sold the other 500 originally offered.

Gould then advised Stein, who was to decide he was an amateur by comparison, to find a liquor dealer qualified to receive the receipts who could call the liquor in for bottling. Under plan, Gould was to invoice the warehouse receipts to the dealer and forward them to the bank in return for payment by check at ceiling prices. The extra or "overage" payment was to be made after the liquor was delivered.

The Marco Importing Company of Chicago was designated by Garmone as the liquor dealer to receive the receipts for a $1.00 per barrel fee. Stein could not recall how much the "overage" amounted to on the deal, but he said it was approximately $80,000, which he delivered in cash to Gould in his Cincinnati office. It later developed that Friedman at Louisville was a partner of Gould and owned a share in some of the whiskey.

Stein had occasion to use his contact with Fairfield Distillery at Bardstown on another occasion when Garmone was having trouble getting some liquor bottled. Stein introduced him to an official of the distillery and arrangements were made. The meeting took place in Garmone's car on a downtown Louisville street.

There were other deals involving Stein, Licavoli, Garmone-Polizzi, George Massu, Morris Margolis, etc. Eventually a slip-up occurred, and, after making fabulous profits, some men like Friedman, Gould, and "Big Al" Polizzi were convicted for short prison terms.

Friedman was killed in a wreck shortly thereafter. His widow became Keeper of the Great Seal of the Honorable Order of Kentucky Colonels—a development which recalled a statement by the federal agent who visited Newport during Prohibition and found a dead bootlegger in a chair.

"The punks all wore bulletproof vests," he said, "and all the big shots were Kentucky Colonels."

Chuck Polizzi's role in the black-market operations didn't become public knowledge until years later when it was revealed during a tax court hearing.

It was disclosed that Licavoli and Stein, together with Chuck Polizzi, invested $420,000 in a run-down Milwaukee distillery in order to get control of its bulk whiskey. The whiskey was bottled and sold through the usual black-market channels in Ohio. Polizzi, representing unnamed associates, put up $75,000 in the deal.

Stein was indicted December 17, 1943, in the black-market liquor case, but the charge was quashed on a technicality. He went on to prison, meanwhile, on the gold-smuggling conviction, and served nine months before being paroled early in 1945. Thereupon he married a relative of Mrs. Dalitz. Moe, trying to find his friend a "job in a legitimate business," introduced him to a representative of Consolidated Television—a company owned by the Eastern Syndicate. Some of the people associated with it had been fellow officers with Dalitz at the Savoy-Plaza.

5.

It should not be assumed that Dalitz was so preoccupied with running a laundry in New York that he didn't have time personally to handle a few good deals that came along. Among those, the most famous was the purchase of the Detroit Steel Company.

Max J. Zivian became president of Detroit Steel on July 1, 1943, at a time when a merger with Reliance Steel of Cleveland was under consideration. The merger failed when Sol Freedman of Reliance wanted to be president of the merged companies. Zivian set out to achieve the same goal by buying Freedman's stock in Reliance. An agreement was worked out whereby the stock was placed in escrow and Zivian put up a total of $176,000 of his own funds. His problem was to find investors who would provide $385,000 additional capital. Unless he secured the full amount by a specified time, the original $176,000 was lost, along with the opportunity to acquire Reliance.

With help from his wife and friends, Zivian obtained part of the money, but he was $200,000 short and getting desperate when in 1944 on the streets of Cleveland he "bumped into Moe Dalitz."

He had met Dalitz on the golf course some time before, and knew he had an interest in laundries in Detroit and Cleveland as well as an interest in race tracks.

Dalitz was in uniform when they met on the street. He asked Zivian what he was doing in Cleveland. Zivian said he was trying to close a deal, and Dalitz explained he was home "on leave or something." He then asked how the deal was coming along. Zivian, who estimated he could raise another $100,000 if he could find an equal amount somewhere else, replied that the deal was "pretty well settled, but I am short $100,000."

"I think I can arrange to get it for you," said Lieutenant Dalitz.

They agreed to meet an hour later at the office of Sammy Haas. An officer of the Morris Plan Bank was called on the telephone, and Haas explained the deal. It involved putting up 30,000 shares of Detroit Steel stock as collateral in return for a $200,000 loan. Haas and Dalitz were to be responsible for $100,000 of the loan and Zivian for the remainder.

The loan was approved. Dalitz and Haas received 10,000 shares of Detroit Steel stock for their investment which consisted of paying $100,000 to the bank. It was a little later when Lieutenant Dalitz, accompanied by his accountant, Alvin Giesey, called on Zivian at his office. Giesey was wearing the uniform of an Army major but he was taking orders from the lieutenant. Zivian, in obedience to instructions, issued the stock. Haas received 3,333 shares, and Dalitz, Kleinman, Rothkopf, and Tucker received 1,666 shares each.

It was still one for all and all for one with the Cleveland Syndicate. It added up to 9,997 shares. Perhaps Giesey got three shares as a fee. He later testified he bought 100 shares on four separate occasions. The stock was split at least twice in the next few years, and the 10,000 shares grew into 40,000.

Few lieutenants found such profitable ways to spend their furloughs. Only a few such afternoons would send a man back to the rigors of the Savoy-Plaza with morale restored.

On the other hand, why stay in New York with the war ending and such opportunities waiting on the streets of Cleveland for men with cash and credit?

In February, 1945, Lieutenant Dalitz received a letter from one of his Detroit attorneys, and a letter from a business associate, telling him he was needed at the Colonial Laundry. The War Manpower Commission obliged with a letter stating the Colonial Laundry was an essential agency. Thereupon, on March 1, 1945, Dalitz wrote to his commanding officer and asked to be relieved of duty.

He was relieved, and went home to marry the girl he left behind. To do so, of course, he had to divorce his first wife. But that was easily arranged. Moe was so pleased with his new wife, a former model, he named a boat after her, the *Toni Kid,* and found a job for Sam Stein, who married one of her relatives.

Love was wonderful, but insulation was safer. When next Stein was indicted in a smuggling case, Dalitz was a co-defendant. Long before he wiggled out of that mess, he sold the *Toni Kid,* and divorced Toni. Respectable married life was all right—the Dalitzes even adopted a son—but with all the action out West it was hard to concentrate.

CHAPTER THIRTEEN

Life is a game of chance.
Arthur B. McBride

According to a modern folk tale, World War II was followed by the Great Wire-Service War in which the Mafia defeated whatever it was fighting by surrendering, and Bugsy Siegel—a nice Jewish member—had to be "hit" because he was on the winning side and didn't understand the importance of letting the losers continue to control things.

Playing important roles in the "war" were those old "circulators" of the Hanna newspapers, James Ragen and Arthur B. "Mickey" McBride. Playing an important part in the "peace" that followed was "Uncle Louis" Rothkopf and one of his protégés, Mickey Cohen.

It was 1913 when Ragen and McBride went to Cleveland and employed many of the men who were to be associated in later years with the Mayfield Road division of the syndicate and with the Mafia. But Ragen remained only until 1922. He returned to Chicago to work as circulation manager of the Hearst newspaper, the *Journal-American.* Moses Annenberg was then circulation manager of all Hearst newspapers and magazines. When, ultimately, Annenberg branched out for himself to build a vast empire of newspapers, magazines, and racing publications, Ragen went with him. At the time of Annenberg's conviction on income tax charges, Ragen was general manager and vice-president of Annenberg's Nationwide News Service, the outfit supplying thousands of handbook operators across the country with data on races run and races coming up.

Annenberg took the wire service from Mont Tennes, who

called it General News. An associate of Tennes, one Jack Lynch, fought the takeover in and out of court, but was persuaded to accept $750,000 for his share, and get out. Ragen noted in an affidavit later, that on the day Lynch quit, he delivered one thousand $100 bills to Frank "the Enforcer" Nitti of the Chicago Syndicate for services rendered. He didn't say what those services were.

Annenberg's departure to federal prison in 1939 posed a problem of another kind. Ragen well knew the powder keg upon which he worked in Chicago. The possibility always existed that members of the Italian-Jewish-Irish underworld would follow the example in Cleveland and quit fighting among themselves long enough to realize the potentials for development.

Thus it was that Ragen wanted a friend with influence that he did not have—influence with the leaders of organized crime who, if a showdown came, would have power to protect. And Ragen knew where such a friend could be found. Back in Cleveland.

McBride had remained a circulation manager of the *News* until 1930. In that capacity he gave employment to such notables as "Big Al" Polizzi, John "King" Angersola and his brothers, Mushy Wexler, Gameboy Miller, etc. He became friends with Tommy McGinty and with Sammy Haas. He was even able by a well-timed investment to win the loyalty of Frank and Tony Milano when they were trying to start their Brotherhood Loan Company.

When McBride quit newspaper work, he went into another competitive situation—the taxicab business. As operating manager of a new company, McBride recruited another small army from Mayfield Road, including such men as "Muscle Tony" Civetta, and forced the Yellow Cab Company to the curb. The companies merged and McBride emerged as president.

Over the years McBride made other associations which were helpful. Cleveland Police Captain John Fleming was his partner in many real estate deals and was carried on the payroll of Yellow Cab in 1941. He represented McBride in a deal with the notorious Shondor Birns at the Alhambra Tavern, and in another tavern deal with Jimmy Dunn. When at last he resigned in 1949, he was put on the payroll of Continental Press. It was learned he owned $30,000 worth of real estate in Coral Gables—the city McBride and "Big Al" Polizzi built.

McBride was even able to get a cab company associate installed as a trustee of the short-lived Cleveland Crime Commission. He won public acclaim by building the Cleveland Browns professional football team to successive championships.

That Mickey had a soft heart was demonstrated when Ragen needed help with the wire service. As Mickey told it he was in Chicago to visit his mother, who was ill with cancer. Thomas Kelly, who worked for Annenberg, just happened to drop in. Kelly and McBride were brothers-in-law—a fact of no little importance.

It was November 10, 1939, McBride continued. His mother told him Annenberg was thinking of quitting the wire service, so when Kelly arrived he asked:

"Well, Tom, what do you think of it?"

"Well," replied Tom, "we are going to throw a lot of people out of work, including me."

Later, before he left for Cleveland, Mrs. McBride told her son, "You ought to try to do something. It is no use getting all them fellows thrown out of the job."

So, McBride related, "I said, 'All right.' "

Next week, McBride continued, he returned to Chicago and discussed the matter with Ragen, James Ragen, Jr., and Kelly. "They wanted me to go into it." He was willing, he said, but he wanted Ragen to run it. Ragen, who was also under indictment along with Annenberg, declined on the ground he was "in trouble." So Mickey persuaded "young Ragen" to take the management job, assisted, of course, by Kelly, and he announced:

"All right, I will take a chance at it and we will start off and we will see where we go."

Nationwide, Annenberg's service, went out of business on

November 15, 1939. Continental Press was born on November 20, 1939.

In its third interim report, the Kefauver Committee commented: "It is one of the amazing aspects of this whole story that without any break in the service, without any dislocation of the facilities used in the entire process of obtaining, legitimately or illegitimately, information from the race tracks and without any disruption in its distribution, one man stepped out of this complicated business and another man took it over without any formal transfer or without the passing of a single dollar."

The Kefauver Committee was puzzled as to why McBride was brought into the deal in the first place—but it suggested the answer when it noted McBride had "powerful connections" with "the Mafia leaders of Cleveland."

It now seems clear that Ragen and McBride had an unofficial understanding. For the weird shifts in management continued. On August 22, 1942, McBride "sold" Continental to "young Ragen." All he got back, he said, was the $20,000 he invested in the business. On October 31, 1943, the new owner added two partners—his father, James Ragen, Sr., and Eddie McBride, Mickey's son.

According to Mickey, the Ragen's really wanted him back in the business. They had discovered, apparently, that they still needed his influence "with the Mafia leaders of Cleveland." McBride said he told them he didn't want it. "I've got a lot of things to do."

But Ragen insisted, "I won't have it any other way but for one of the family to take an interest." And he won. Eddie was at Notre Dame at the time, and was soon drafted into the Army for three years and eleven months, but, on paper at least, he owned one-third of Continental Press.

It soon became obvious why Ragen wanted the power of the McBride name behind him. For he had determined to go on the offensive with the boys in Chicago. While they no longer threatened him, they apparently felt Ragen still owed something for helping drive Lynch out of the business. In any case, they were using the facilities of Continental without paying what Ragen thought they should pay.

In fact, shortly before he was shot, Ragen told the state attorney's office that Continental didn't "get any money from anybody in the northern district of Illinois for several years." According to Daniel Serritella, a member of the Chicago combine, not since Annenberg quit had the Chicago bookies paid for the wire service except to Hymie "Loud Mouth" Levin. And Levin got his service from Continental.

Ragen was pointing for a showdown. He demanded all the profits, agreeing in return to put Levin, a cripple, on salary. Levin offered 60 per cent of the Chicago profits to Ragen, but the old "circulator" thought he had muscle enough to take it all.

Out of Levin's offer to compromise grew the legend that the Mob or Mafia or the Capone Syndicate, or what have you, demanded 40 per cent of all Continental's continental operations.

Things moved rapidly toward a showdown in the latter part of 1945. Ragen gave Levin an ultimatum—get out of the wire-service business and stick to handbooks. When Levin refused, Ragen cut off the wire service to Levin.

It was the ultimate weapon—but it boomeranged. Levin had enough support in Chicago and elsewhere to attempt to keep going. He began stealing the essential data from Ragen's leased wires. And on March 20, 1946, the formation of Trans-American Publishing and News Service, Inc., was announced.

At that stage, it was still a threat. To service a single handbook in Chicago, in Louisville, in Biloxi, or in Paducah, data from all tracks in the country holding race meets are necessary. Thus an organization nationwide in scope is needed. The Chicago boys wanted to show Ragen they could set up the machinery to get that far-flung data—if they had to.

At this point the matter could have been resolved. Levin was willing to sell out to Ragen—for a price. But Ragen was angry, and perhaps arrogant. He obviously overestimated the value of a name—at least the name of a college boy. It is doubtful if even the senior McBride could have helped Ragen after his next action.

According to Virgil Peterson, long-time director of the Chicago Crime Commission, Ragen became angry enough to assume "the role of a knight in shining armor who was determined to rid the city of the evil Capone gang. His ire was particularly directed at Patrick J. Burns, who had deserted him for the rival company. Ragen suddenly remembered that his once-trusted lieutenant had been a fugitive from justice since April 7, 1916, when he escaped from a bailiff in a Chicago courtroom while he was on trial for assault and robbery."

Ragen "squealed," but suddenly realizing he had broken one of gangdom's most sacred commandments, he rushed to the F.B.I. for protection. He was in danger of his life, he said. The Capone mob was after him. Not because he was a "squealer," of course, but because they wanted Continental Press. And legend got another boost as Ragen got bodyguards who kept him alive for several weeks.

On April 29, 1946, Burns was lodged in the House of Correction to serve the sentence imposed thirty years before.

On June 24, 1946, Ragen was shot down on the streets of Chicago. The gunmen used shotguns and fired from a tarpaulin-covered truck. It was a revenge killing if ever there was one, but it was widely hailed as the first shot of the Great Wire-Service War. If, as reported, police officers across the country held their collective breaths in anticipation of the next volley, they had a rather strong lung capacity.

Meanwhile, Ragen provided a thriller. He lived for seven weeks. In the rather nervous interval, a few ambitious hoods across the country moved to improve their bargaining position with Ragen, should he live, or with his successor should he die.

Among the most ambitious was that old partner of the Bugs and Meyer mob, Benjamin Siegel. When the National Syndicate chopped up the country, Bugs wanted California. He thought its climate was better than Florida, which is what his pal, Meyer Lansky, wanted. The Bug waited until 1937 before moving out to Hollywood, but that wasn't unusual. Lansky waited until the 1950's before changing his voting address from New York to Hollywood, Florida. But he spent half his time there for years—there and in Havana.

Back when Molaska was being investigated, a federal agent wrote in an official report that "the Bug looks like Edward G. Robinson, the actor." Indeed, there were those who said the resemblance was not exactly a natural coincidence. Bugsy allegedly had ambitions to be a screen star. In any case, he found Hollywood to his liking and Hollywood responded warmly.

There is no need to tell here how Siegel shook down Hollywood stars and starlets, organized the rackets up and down the west coast, and, in general, developed things to the tastes of the National Syndicate. However, some of the credit should go to the syndicate, which in 1934 muscled in on a union with a long name: the International Alliance of Theatrical Stage Employees and Moving Picture Machine Operators of the United States and Canada. It was a joint operation, with Chicago hoods, such as Nitti, "Cherry Nose" Gioe, and the like, doing much of the muscle work. There can be no question that control of this key union was vital to Bugsy's success. Later, when in March, 1943, nine top gangsters in the takeover were indicted, Nitti killed himself. Seven survivors were convicted of extortion and sent to prison. Unfortunately for Ragen, they were quickly paroled.

It is possible the sacrifices made by Chicago hoods who had helped him was a factor in Bugsy's decision to assist the Chicago hoods in their battle against Ragen. More likely, however, is the fact that Siegel had painted himself into a corner with his old friends in the East and was looking for new allies.

The corner in which "the Bug" had trapped himself is known today as "the fabulous Flamingo." Siegel found Las Vegas a small, dusty little town with a few poker games in dirty saloons, but he saw it as a potential oasis in the desert to which the bored sophisticates of Beverly Hills would come to gamble amid palms, soft music, and name entertainment.

It was a dream, but Bugsy was an action man, and he had plenty of connections who had plenty of cash. The Flamingo was begun—not in downtown Las Vegas, but on what was to become famous as "the Strip." Bugsy and his friends had enough experience to prefer the suburbs—the "ice" is cheaper, for one thing.

The boys back east went along, and millions of dollars were invested. A pioneer, Bugsy paid the price pioneers must pay when breaking "new ground." He was willing to struggle but his friends began to grumble. When would the delays stop? When would the hotel open? When would it start paying off?

Comforted by the self-styled "world's best lay"—Virginia Hill—the Bug plowed on. Routine business on the coast was left to Mickey Cohen, a Brooklyn-Cleveland transplant, and to Jack Dragna, long-time Mafia boss who had greeted Bugsy when he first arrived in the West.

Two days after Siegel wrote a $12,000 check to help his Chicago pals, Ragen back in Chicago gasped, "Dragna is the Al Capone of Los Angeles." He also mentioned that "Big Al" Polizzi controlled the wire service in Cleveland. It was almost as if he was trying to balance a foe against a friend. But no one could be sure. For on that day, August 14, 1946, Ragen died.

The death was expected and brought no immediate change. Around the country, Continental forces stood their ground. Several revolts were reported, and Trans-American set up rival services in several cities. But the effort was costing far more than had been expected. Even the $12,000 Siegel could spare was needed. Income-tax returns filed by Trans-American listed losses of $122,958 in 1946, and $184,784 in 1947. Meanwhile, Continental was making money, although only half as much as it normally would have made.

It was fast becoming an impossible situation. Everybody was losing something. And the prospects of anyone winning appeared more and more doubtful as the months dragged on.

The end came abruptly. On May 29, 1947, James Ragen, Jr., sold Continental to Eddie McBride—both the one-third he owned and the one-third his father had owned. According to the contract, if one partner wanted to sell he had to offer his share first to the other partner. According to Mickey McBride:

"I said, 'Eddie, what do you think of it?' "

Eddie replied, "Well, I'll be getting out of school. I will have to have some place to go."

Less than two weeks later, Trans-American announced it was folding its tents and stealing softly away. By June 21, it was out of business and out of existence.

Many of those who had deserted Continental were now welcomed back. Some even profited by their revolt. The McBrides, backed by "the Mafia leaders of Cleveland," could afford to be generous.

And what of Chicago? For face-saving purposes a dummy, Illinois Sports News, was set up with the son and brother of Tom Kelly, manager of Continental, as owners. "Loud Mouth" Levin's company, R & H, bought—and paid for—service from Illinois Sports, which, in turn, passed the profits on to Continental.

And thus the Great Wire-Service War ended. But some shots remained to be fired.

Ragen had stepped beyond the pale when he squealed on Pat Burns. Bugsy Siegel had gone even further when he defied the established order and gave aid and comfort to the rebels in Chicago.

The rebels could be accepted back—but they were of a different level in the society of crime. Siegel was an overlord, a member, if you wish, of the board of directors.

When men such as Lansky, Siegel, Lepke, Luciano, Costello, Dalitz, Kleinman, etc., ally themselves, what force is there to bind the relationship? Only mutual confidence, mutual respect. To say there is no honor among thieves is to be right if you are speaking of ordinary crooks—but what was it that for forty years made Dalitz, Kleinman, Rothkopf, and Tucker share everything that came their way in equal proportions? And, if at any point along the way one of the four had violated that understanding, what would have happened to the organization?

For whatever reason—sentiment, fear, avarice—the Bug had done what no leader of organized crime can do—claimed a right to be independent.

Various sensational stories have been written about the Great Wire-Service War and its consequences for Siegel. But since the writers didn't bother to understand the war, they were at a loss to explain why Siegel should be on the spot. The usual answer is that the Bug decided to keep the wire service in California for himself.

With this theory to work with, much exciting fiction has been written which depicts the Bug, completely crazy, of course, flying to New York to defy the National Syndicate and/or to Havana to defy Lucky Luciano. Indeed, Lucky's presence in Havana is attributed to the crisis confronting the National Syndicate when Siegel allegedly refused to give back what, in reality, he never possessed.

There are two things wrong with this theory. Assume Siegel did have control of the wire service in California. What could he do with it? To make it useless to him, Continental would need to do no more than Ragen when "Loud Mouth" Levin refused to come to terms—cut off the service. Siegel would have had no alternative but to form another Trans-American and build from scratch the machinery needed to get racing data from every track in the country. The Chicago hoods had just discovered how expensive that could be.

As to the second thing wrong with the theory—Luciano's presence in Havana in violation of his parole was discovered in February, 1957. But investigation proved he had been there four months.

It doesn't take four months to conduct a court martial—not even for a Bugsy Siegel.

There is little doubt Bugsy's fate was discussed and even decided in Havana. Practically every top hood in the country beat a path to Luciano's door. A lot of things were discussed. But Luciano came back with every intention of staying. He resisted bitterly when forced at last to return to Italy. With a little luck, he might have made his headquarters "just ninety miles off the coast of Florida."

The question then arises—why did the National Syndicate wait until the "war" was over to dispose of the Siegel problem? The answer is the Flamingo Club. Individual gang members had hundreds of thousands invested in the hotel-casino, and they wanted their money back if possible. They knew that Siegel, with his drive and ambition, would make a success of it if anyone could. So they waited.

On December 26, 1946, the half-finished Flamingo opened. Bad weather, bad luck in general, cut attendance and casino revenue. Two weeks later, the hotel closed.

The syndicate waited.

Siegel drove himself night and day. The wire-service war was the last thing he worried about. On March 27, 1947, the Flamingo reopened. There were several nervous days, but Siegel played it cool. This time he had it made. Within three weeks, the Flamingo was in the black. It cleared $300,000 in May.

As Siegel reviewed the balance sheets, he could feel elation. His dream had come true. The fabulous Flamingo was a reality. But now there was no longer any need to wait.

Allan Smiley, son of a Russian named Smihoff, was sitting on the couch by Siegel when the blast came through the window of Virginia Hill's home in Beverly Hills on June 20, 1947. Police agreed he was there for a purpose. They also say his purpose was achieved. Smiley was unhurt. The Bug was dead.

A very few minutes after the shooting, Moe Sedway, a native of Poland, took charge of the Flamingo Club for the National Syndicate. Sedway said he just happened to be in Las Vegas at the time. He had flown up the day before, he told the

Kefauver Committee, to arrange with Siegel for a United Jewish Appeal fund drive.

"I wanted to put a drive on at the Flamingo," Sedway said, "which eventually I did, after he died."

And shortly afterward, Mickey Cohen—another member of the Jewish Mafia—took over California for the syndicate. He was a friend of Mickey McBride, of "Big Al" Polizzi, of Tony Milano. He was a close friend of Louis Rothkopf.

Cohen's father was born in Russia. Mickey was the youngest of six children. When the father died in 1915, Mrs. Cohen took her brood from New York to Los Angeles. Mickey was only two years old at the time. At age fifteen he ran away to Cleveland, where his oldest brother managed a drugstore and promoted fights on the side. Mickey became a featherweight and attracted the attention of such old boxers as Tommy McGinty and Rothkopf. They tried to build him up and sent him on tour to Chicago and New York, but apparently not even influence could make a champion out of Mickey. He turned to gambling, and there his friends could help him.

Returning to Los Angeles in 1939, he gradually impressed himself on Siegel. He was available, he was ruthless, he was greedy, and he had some of the flashy characteristics the Bug himself possessed. The fact that they also had some mutual friends helped too.

Following Siegel's execution Mickey moved into a $125,000 house and prepared to live in the style his predecessor had demanded. It was some months before Mickey learned that Los Angeles police had anticipated his desires and thoroughly "bugged" his new home with concealed microphones attached to tape recorders.

The conversations were most interesting—the more so since it had become apparent that someone, somewhere, didn't like Mickey. People kept trying to kill him.

But police heard a lot of talk about the Milanos. Tony, who had always liked Mickey, moved to Los Angeles for a while.

His son was especially fond of Mickey, and was in the Cohen home constantly. In fact, guided by Cohen, young Pete Milano quit school and with help from Mickey invested in a used-car lot.

Others often in the Cohen home were "High Pockets" Farrinaci, a Mayfield Road boy who ran errands for Mickey, and Louis "Babe" Triscaro. Babe was to become an important Ohio lieutenant of teamster president James Hoffa.

Finally, when the "heat" became too intense—five attempts on his life failed and several of his associates died—Mickey entertained other visitors from Cleveland—Mr. and Mrs. Rothkopf. LaVonne Cohen and Blanche Rothkopf were as friendly as Lou and Mickey. Listening police heard a lot of intimate chatter. At one point, on October 27, 1947, Cohen blurted:

"Yeah, Lou, I'm afraid to show my face. . . . You have been so God-damned good to me."

The problem was to make Jack Dragna accept the situation. He had been closely identified with Siegel's revolt, and quite naturally had resented the National Syndicate's decision to eliminate the Bug. Perhaps he had also assumed the Mafia division of the syndicate would swing his appointment as Siegel's successor.

In any case, conditions were approaching civil war. Several efforts were made to convince Dragna that Cohen was the boss. Back in Italy, Lucky Luciano sent greetings to the new king of California. But Lucky was far away, and it now appeared he would never get much closer. Rothkopf talked to Dragna personally. Things improved only to get worse again.

Mickey stayed busy all the while: reorganizing the books, fixing fights, shaking down movie stars, setting up pipelines to Mexico. It was annoying to be always wondering if Dragna would try again. He kept the lines hot to the Hollenden Hotel in Cleveland, headquarters of the Cleveland Syndicate. He also called Milano often, causing Tony to comment to Forrest Allen of the Cleveland *Press:*

"Mickey gets himself in trouble—gets others into this mess by using the phones the way he does. He can't write so well, so he just grabs the phone all the time. I told my boys to stay away from him."

"Uncle Lou" decided stronger action was needed. He went to Oakland early in 1949—Mickey had begun an expansion program in the Bay area—and stayed at the Leemington Hotel. His guest there for several days was Frank Costello, the man everyone said was now boss of the Mafia in the absence of Luciano.

Costello made a deal with Dragna—and after that Cohen breathed easier. Or, at least, he kept on breathing. The deal provided that Cohen's successor would be Tom Dragna, Jack's nephew.

Yet things were never the same again after the Great Wire-Service War. Too much had happened. Siegel's discovery of Las Vegas, for one thing, ended the relative isolation the west coast had enjoyed. Other boys, and most especially the Cleveland Syndicate, were quick to capitalize on Bugsy's dream. Equally important were new laws inspired by the publicity the "war" received, new laws which restricted wire-service operations. Continental lived and made money until the Kefauver Committee put an end to it. Tom Kelly then carried on under the banner of the Illinois Sports News, but Continental died after being thoroughly exposed by the committee.

There was yet another development. In August, 1949, the Los Angeles Police Department set up the first police intelligence unit to function as a regular part of a major police department. A year later the men to go with the idea came into power. William H. Parker became chief of police and Captain James E. Hamilton became head of the intelligence squad. Between the two of them and with the help of picked men, they made organized crime activity impossible on the scale the late Bugsy Siegel had assumed was normal, natural, and desirable.

Mickey went to prison, got out, went back. Dragna, his chance come at last, tried to rule in his absence. But the good days were gone. Not even Uncle Louie could do anything about that.

2.

All western adventures were not as loudly dramatic as those of Bugsy Siegel. The Cleveland Syndicate operated for years in Arizona without anyone knowing it was there. And when at last Peter Licavoli arrived, everyone blamed the Mafia.

In the same period that Siegel went to Hollywood, Moe Dalitz and some friends inspected Arizona and decided that, while it had a future, the time was not yet ripe. They bought some land cheap, made discreet investments in both Tucson and Phoenix, and turned to other things.

As World War II neared its end, the syndicate's economists forecast a business boom. The situation was somewhat similar to the period at the bottom of the Depression. Then, after the "growth rate" had slowed because of economic factors, opportunities existed for those with cash to invest against the day when the economy would start catching up with the need. During the war, the civilian economy had lagged for military reasons. Few homes had been built, and even fewer home furnishings manufactured. With a "baby boom" expected, a period of expansion was inevitable. Furthermore, there was reason to hope that after years of self-denial and discipline, veteran and civilian alike would go on an emotional, anti-authority binge similar to the period after World War I.

Taking into account the fact that the unanticipated cold war came along as a brake on the release of inhibitions, syndicate planners were as right as they usually are. They counted on a demand for new homes, cars, and refrigerators on the one hand, and they made the proper investments. On the other hand they prepared for an equally strong interest in resort hotels, casinos, sex, and television sets.

While making such plans to help the consumer "escape" the problems of installment buying, it was decided the time had come at last for Arizona. Very quietly, a task force headed by Peter Licavoli and that old traveling man, Gameboy Miller, went to Tucson.

Licavoli, who had come a long way since he bribed Lawrence Fleishman to let him land some liquor, ruled a gambling empire with Joe Massei and others of the Brotherhood. They ruled it, of course, in cooperation with the Cleveland Syndicate. Even before the National Syndicate handed down the edict that "Moey Davis" was the Man in Cleveland, the Mafia had co-operated. Licavoli had long been associated in Detroit with Moe Dalitz. He was best man at Big Al Polizzi's wedding, and Big Al, as a member of the Mayfield Road Mob and Buckeye Enterprises, was associated with the syndicate from its beginning. Al had helped arrange the parole of James Licavoli, a cousin of Pete and co-boss of the Youngstown, Ohio, operations with Joe DiCarlo.

The Licavoli clan came from Sicily to St. Louis. There, with his older brother, Thomas "Yonnie" Licavoli, Peter lived in a tenement house which ultimately his parents bought. It was a red-brick building containing eleven flats, each with three rooms. Downstairs were two stores. One of the flats across the hall from the Licavolis was used as a Jewish synagogue. The standard pattern of immigration was represented—a wave of Irish had piled into the district, then Jews, then Italians, and later, Negroes. The Licavoli boys learned Yiddish at the same time they learned Italian with a Sicilian accent, and English.

One block east of the tenement house was the police station, and one block beyond that was the hangout of Egan's Rats, as nasty a pack of hoodlums as could be found. Quite early, Peter learned to earn a quarter by carrying a pail of beer for one of the rats. Another source of income was found by diving into the Mississippi for pennies thrown by tourists on boats.

It was a rough childhood, and the Licavoli boys had to fight their way. Their parents, hardworking and religious, sought to make Peter a doctor and Yonnie a priest. Yonnie was first to revolt. He ran away from Christian Brothers College, joined the Navy only to desert, began bootlegging, and found employment with the Purple Gang in Detroit. Then he sent for Pete and other relatives.

Yonnie was convicted and sent to prison for the killing of Jackie Kennedy during the takeover in Toledo. Not even Big Al Polizzi was able to win parole for him despite repeated efforts over the years. Pete became leader of the gang Yonnie had put together and in a triumph of irony soon found it dubbed the "Purple Gang." A long and bloody career followed. Estes Kefauver, a man who became somewhat hardened to criminals, said Pete was "one of the most cold-blooded and contemptuous characters to appear before our committee."

But by 1945 Pete was ready to expand. It had become rather fashionable in Mafia circles to move from the old home ground and run things from afar. Big Al had just moved to Coral Gables. Joe Massei went to Miami. Tony Milano had a mansion in Beverly Hills, and even "Trigger Mike" Coppola was deserting New York for Florida. Eventually he bought a Miami Beach home from John "King" Angersola, another Cleveland boy who had cruised south on the *Wood Duck*. So the desert air of Tucson was doubly attractive.

In some respects it was a typical Cleveland Syndicate ploy. When attention focused on gangsters in Tucson, it centered around Licavoli and the ranch he had renamed in honor of his wife, the former Grace Bommarito. Meanwhile, Gameboy took over the handbooks and set up small casino operations. When he had everything in order, he moved on to other fields and E. Rogers Lowe came out from Newport to keep them running.

Gameboy made his headquarters at the Santa Rita Hotel in Tucson. Assisting him was Jacob Lerner of Pittsburgh. Lerner had been associated with the syndicate in a dog track at Steubenville, Ohio, and he fronted for Miller in Tucson. They bought the wire service operating at 1604 South Sixth, a not too difficult operation in view of Miller's long association with Empire News and Mickey McBride. With that as a weapon, control of handbooks was secured.

Standard News, as Lerner's outfit was known, was supplanted by Stockman's News as operations expanded and the syndicate decided it needed a more reliable person in charge. Selected to replace Lerner was Edwin Rogers Lowenstein, known in Newport, Louisville, and eventually in Tucson, as "Butts" Lowe. A Cincinnati native, Lowe (he dropped the "enstein" early in life) associated himself with the Cleveland Syndicate when first it moved into the area at the Arrowhead Club. At one period he lived in Jeffersonville, Indiana. Long after Jeffersonville cleaned up, Lowe returned as a specialist to run the syndicate's "Derby week" operation. In 1953, when up from Tucson for the big race, he was arrested in a raid on the Chicken Trail Inn near Louisville.

In his youth, Lowe had been a merchant seaman and on a visit to a South American port followed the custom of the day by having a small, white-gold ring inserted in his nose. It was not conspicuous, fitting closely as it did to the flesh, and it was a mark of distinction rather unique in syndicate circles.

As a junior partner in the syndicate's Newport operations, Lowe in 1949, for example, picked up from the Yorkshire Club's handbook pocket change totaling $26,842, and from the Yorkshire's casino $10,043, for a total of $36,885.

When Lowe arrived in Tucson early in 1947, he set up the "big book" in the rear of Stockman's News to handle lay-off betting for the area, and the "little book" up front to take care of local bettors. Partners were Harold Fischer and Fred Kreisler, but Kreisler was soon forced out. The "big book" was listed as E. R. Lowe & Company, which ultimately, after other local partners came and went, was divided between Fischer with 20 per cent and Lowe with 80 per cent. Fischer claimed later he didn't know that Lowe's share was equally divided with Peter Licavoli.

This 20-40-40 ratio of stock was carried over in the formation of a legitimate corporation, the Tucson Printing Company, which opened in 1948. Tucson Printing bought land and a building at 1901 S. Fourth in 1950. The $20,000 it cost was taken from the "E. R. Lowe & Company Juarez Account." The account had been used to finance gambling operations in Juarez, Mexico, across from El Paso, Texas.

Lowe and Licavoli also had an operation at Albuquerque, New Mexico, known as Silver City News. Set up in 1949, it controlled handbooks in New Mexico. Licavoli's role in New Mexico as in Tucson, was simply to bankroll the handbooks. Personally, he was too busy developing ranches and making real estate deals. Operating from a base created years before, Licavoli made more than $600,000 in legitimate land deals in the Tucson area over a ten-year period.

Moe Dalitz and the boys back in Cleveland didn't overlook the legitimate end of business either. In 1947, Robert J. Brickman came down with money and instructions.

Brickman had for many years been a Cleveland sports promoter, following the well-marked footsteps of Tommy McGinty and Louis Rothkopf. He did rather well until he matched Jimmy Doyle against "Sugar Ray" Robinson on June 25, 1947.

Doyle had been badly beaten by Art Levine in a fight fifteen months before and such "sports" as Mike Jacobs in New York refused to let him fight again. But Brickman saw a chance to cash in on Sugar Ray's immense popularity, and put Doyle in against one of the hardest punchers in the business. Seventeen hours after Doyle was knocked out, he died.

One of those periodic uproars which boxing manages to survive followed. Cuyahoga County Coroner Dr. Samuel R. Gerber reported a "great deal of unholy pressure has been put on me to divert this investigation." Evidence was developed notwithstanding that proved Doyle should never have fought anyone, to say nothing of Robinson. Brickman decided the climate of Arizona would be more comfortable.

In seeking investments for the syndicate, what would be more logical than a laundry? After all, Moe Dalitz had been in the laundry business all his life. So the Tucson Steam Laundry, founded in 1911 by Moses Drachman, was purchased by Brickman for the syndicate. Heirs of Drachman, hero of the best-selling book *Chicken Every Sunday* received $450,000 for the laundry.

At the same time Brickman let it be known he also represented what was politely called a "Cleveland combine" in purchasing property for a 356-room hotel at North Stone Avenue and Drachman Street. Two blocks of land were purchased, Brickman said, but he wanted it understood the laundry had nothing to do with the hotel.

The Cleveland combine formed Tucson Motels, Inc., on August 8, 1947. Brickman and George R. Darnell were incorporators. The owners of record were Chuck Polizzi, who invested $14,000, Big Al Polizzi, who put in $35,000, and George Gordon, who allegedly put in $56,000.

Gordon was a front for Dalitz, Kleinman, Rothkopf, and Tucker. Their individual shares of the $56,000 matched the $14,000 put in by Chuck Polizzi.

Born in New York in 1911 as George C. Burslem, Gordon went to Cleveland late in the Prohibition era and worked in the syndicate's first gambling joints. Later, along with such men as Alfred Goltsman, Ruby Kolod, and John Croft, he graduated to better-paying positions at the plush Pettibone and Beverly Hills clubs.

Rejected by the Army as a "psychopathic personality," Gordon became known to police departments from Boston to Los Angeles under a score of aliases. But his chief function for some years was serving as a "front" for top syndicate people who, for one reason or another, wanted their names unmentioned. Thus, when the syndicate bought the Desert Inn, it was considered wise to give the impression that it had pulled out of the Beverly Hills in Newport. Gordon's income had been steady but not exactly astronomical; suddenly he was listed as a big partner in the Beverly and his income hit the six-figure mark. When Newport closed after a great reform battle, Gordon's income dropped to very low four figures. He was soon shifted to Miami, however, and given the task of supervising Hymie Martin in gaining control of the numbers racket in South Florida. When his role was exposed in 1965, Gordon, along with Kleinman, entered a Miami Beach hospital.

The use of fronts was developed by the syndicate into a fine art, and Gordon became quite an artist. Behind Gordon, Brickman, and others, the syndicate concealed its Arizona business interests. Behind Lowe, it concealed its gambling partnerships with Licavoli. Eventually, Police Chief Don Juan Hays exposed Licavoli's role in the economic life of Tucson, but very few people there ever knew the silent syndicate existed.

They could hardly be blamed. Back in Cleveland a shotgun blast caused citizens to credit once more that old whipping boy, the Mayfield Road Mob. While the Mafia got the glory, the syndicate got the remains of Nate Weisenberg's slot-machine empire.

CHAPTER FOURTEEN

It was the quietest place I ever saw.
Sheriff Walton Spahr

It was a long day and it began badly. First came the alarm and then the race to Chester Avenue. He won the race and when police appeared, he was able to greet them with a smile.

Lieutenant Peter Ulrich, a rather nosy individual, had a question: "What's up?"

The answer was easy. "Nothing to it. I don't want any report made on this. Might as well go on back to central and forget it."

The lieutenant left—but the basic problem remained. Someone had forced a window in the neighboring store and then chopped a five-foot hole in the interior wall. Whoever did the chopping knew where he was going for the hole was between two racks where twenty-four slot machines were stored. Someone had tripped the alarm while trying to move out the slots.

It was a problem. All day he worked on it, finding it necessary to visit Chief George J. Matowitz at police headquarters, see the prosecutor, and have some conferences over at the Hollenden, where the real bosses worked.

Late in the afternoon he relaxed with a steam bath and returned to the Hollenden to dine in the Flemish Room. A meeting followed upstairs in the Artists and Writers Club with Common Pleas Judge Frank J. Merrick.

By 10 P.M. he was ready for a few drinks with two friendly girls. In their report of the incident, police noted chivalrously that the girls didn't want their names mentioned. Although Betty Rayan and Emma Babcock, both familiar figures at the Hollenden, were the last to see their host alive, police respected their wishes.

At 11:45 P.M. it was time to go home. The girls asked for a lift to a suburban joint—business downtown was slow that night. Miss Babcock drove the car. She recalled looking in the rearview mirror repeatedly, she said, but was not conscious that anyone was following.

The girls got out at 107 and Euclid, and watched the car drive away.

At 1 A.M. Davis Doescher was returning from a high school dance to his home in Cleveland Heights. He was walking in the street because on that night of February 24, 1945, the sidewalks were icy. On Silsby Road, parked at the curb with its lights burning, was a Lincoln coupe.

The youth walked past the car, then turned back for a closer look. He noted there were two jagged holes in the left window, each about an inch in diameter. Peeping in, he saw a hand with a large diamond ring hanging limply through the steering wheel. A body was slumped in the seat.

A long day had ended for Nathan "Nate" Weisenberg as it had begun—badly.

Cleveland police learned of the killing and although Cleveland Heights was outside the city, they were interested enough to investigate. Their official report of the murder noted:

> The victim was shot in the back of the head and the charge almost took off the whole back of the head. The feet of the victim were resting on the clutch and brake pedals, and the upper part of the body had fallen over to the right of the steering wheel on the seat. There were two two-inch holes in the glass on the driver's side and ten holes in the glass on the right side. Evidently a shotgun was used at close range. . . .
>
> The Cleveland Heights police interviewed the victim's son, Francis, who stated he had seen his father for the last time at 3 P.M. on February 23, and he seemed in good spirits. The son stated his father had no enemies and he knows of no one who would take his life.

The attitude of the son could only be called "realistic." He knew his father had bought continued existence by making concessions to the Cleveland Syndicate, which, through Buckeye Enterprises, controlled the Buckeye Catering Company in which Weisenberg owned a smaller and smaller part. He knew what happened to two of his father's partners, Lawrence Lupo and, more recently, Frank Joiner, when they opposed what Joiner's girl friend called "the Muscle."

Police decided, under the circumstances, they'd better go back to 1706 Chester Avenue and check out that burglar alarm. They found the hole in the wall, and they found sixty-nine slot machines still in storage. Since there was now no one to tell them to forget it, they confiscated the machines. Herbert R. Gove, age sixty-six, who lived over on Rocky River, was questioned. The warehouse was listed in his name. He said he actually owned the place and received rent of $50 monthly for the huge warehouse. Much later, when Coroner Samuel R. Gerber insisted on holding an inquest, Gove mentioned that additional slot machines were stored at 1702 Chester. Police found them there and Dr. Gerber wanted to know why Gove had not mentioned the matter earlier.

"You didn't ask me," said the witness.

The girls from the Hollenden were questioned by police, but it was not until after they left town that their names were put in the record. Dr. Gerber wasn't happy with the anonymous statements presented by police at the inquest, and demanded to know who made them.

It should not be supposed, however, that Cleveland police were incompetent or inactive. City Safety Director Frank Celebreeze received information that among those talking to Weisenberg on his last day were Lou Rhody (one of Lou Rothkopf's favorite aliases), Morris Kleinman, George Gordon, and Frank Rosen.

Two detectives immediately checked out the information and reported:

"Frank Rosen said he did see him [Weisenberg] some time

before he was shot, but can't remember what the date was. Lou Rhody is supposed to be in Florida at the present time and has been there for some time as far as we can learn. Morris Kleinman is supposed to have returned to Cleveland last Monday night [after the killing]. We were unable to locate George Gordon but heard rumors that he has been sick over a week."

Later, after the inquest, Lieutenant Martin Cooney took note of some of the names that had been dropped—Kleinman, Chuck Polizzi, Louis Rothkopf, Frank Rosen—and in an official report commented:

"These men can be found in the afternoon and night in and around Vincent Avenue and the lobby of the Hollenden Hotel, and in Room 281 of the Hollenden Hotel, a gambling place operated by Frank Rosen. I have had several telephone calls that Nathan Weisenberg was in this room the night he was killed. Nearly all the abovementioned men live outside Cleveland and have no legitimate businesses in Cleveland."

Dr. Gerber's inquest produced 62,700 words of testimony and if it did not officially answer who pulled the triggers of the double-barreled shotgun that blasted Weisenberg, it made the motives clear.

Weisenberg's once powerful empire had been cut up into little pieces and parceled out to sons, daughters, in-laws, and nephews of the big shots.

Edward Kleinman, nephew of Morris, had taken over two slot machine routes. Joe Polizzi, brother of Big Al had a piece, as did Joe's son, Alphonso. Jerry Milano, a relative of Tony, had taken his cut, and Regis Duddy, son-in-law of Tommy McGinty, had a share. Others who had been rewarded included Gladys Giesey, wife of Alvin; John and William McGinty, sons of Tommy; Richard Moriarty, long-time McGinty attorney; Samuel T. Haas, long-time mystery figure; and many others.

The empire had been larger than many supposed. Not only were there vast holdings in Ohio, such as the Skill Amusement Company, but Weisenberg and his partners owned the Century Music Company in Denver, Colorado; the Modern Music Company in Colorado Springs; and the Melodee Music Company in Phoenix, Arizona, with a branch office in Tucson. His various companies, while concentrating upon slots, also offered juke boxes and pinball machines.

Francis Weisenberg, the man who couldn't think of why anyone should kill his father, shared with his mother what remained of the estate. But before it could be divided young Francis had what was called an "unexplained accident." While driving down the street one day, his car hit a traffic island and came to a stop. Francis was found dead at the wheel. A heart attack was blamed. The various partners in the various companies paid his estate $22,139, and the long association of Weisenbergs and slot machines came to an end. It had begun in 1922 when Fred Kohler was mayor of Cleveland.

In Weisenberg's files was found a letter dated October 8, 1944. A former associate, Thomas Gerak, had gone to Seattle and was reporting a good business prospect. He suggested Weisenberg should come out.

> You never saw so many people, [Gerak wrote] soldiers and sailors, as well as civilians, in a town of this size in your life. And they're out on the streets at all hours of the day and night. It's a seaport town. Its lumber, canning, and trading industries are not affected by depressions. It's the Gateway to Alaska, and it's a young, growing town. . . . The important thing is that there is plenty of action and money in circulation here so let me know if you're interested. You have nothing to live for in Cleveland now—since your old pal Frank Noonan died. Let me hear from you.

Alas, poor Nathan! Had he heeded the invitation, a meeting of the junior-league Mafia might never had been held on the night of February 14, 1945, at the Ohio Villa, that Cleveland Syndicate gambling joint of which Tony Milano was landlord. Mafia lieutenants from all over Ohio attended with "Cadillac Charley" Cavallaro presiding.

The business on hand was simple. The "big boys" had taken

what they wanted from Weisenberg. The "little boys" could now help themselves to the remains. And when Weisenberg unexpectedly showed resentment at the attempted hijacking of his slots a few days later, the Mafia hoods reacted in the same direct manner that years later made Youngstown famous as a happy hunting ground.

Ironically enough, among those who died in Youngstown was Cadillac Charley.

2.

During the postwar period a Cleveland newspaper reporter in a memo to his editor commented:

"Sammy Haas and Morris Kleinman have so much money they are asking real estate agents they know, 'Have you got anything good?' Kleinman offers to make deals in currency so capital gains can escape taxation. . . ."

The land-buying spree actually began before the war ended. The syndicate expected a boom, it had the cash, so it bought while prices were still relatively low. So great was the boom, it continued buying and still made money at higher prices.

In 1953 a rather sad little story related how State Auditor, and later, Governor, James A. Rhodes, held up payment of rent for some state offices because he had discovered the building which housed them was owned by Morris Kleinman, *et al.*

The building was at 2034 East 105 Street, and the rent was $505 monthly. In the same building was a branch office of the Internal Revenue Service.

According to the news story, Alvin E. Giesey, president of the holding company which owned the building, said a charge by Rhodes that the building was owned by "racket money" was, in his words, "a ridiculous statement." Giesey noted the boys had owned the building for nine years. "There is nothing new about this," added Giesey.

Gangsters often cite a theory that because nothing has been done for years about an illegal situation, it somehow becomes legal by default. Thus presumably the "racket money" that bought the building had become clean over the years. But to bolster his argument, Giesey noted that the same "fellows also own the apartment house on East Thirtieth Street between Chester and Euclid. Governor [Frank] Lausche lived there several years and paid rent to these fellows."

The story well illustrates how the syndicate bought its way into the nooks and crannies of Cleveland's economic life. The process had, of course, begun back in the early thirties after banks dependent upon the Van Sweringen railroad empire failed and left a financial void which bootleggers' cash could and did fill.

United States Tax Court records and other sources only hint at the vast and complex web of investments made by syndicate members, acting together or as individuals. A top-ranking syndicate member finding a good opportunity had an obligation to present it to his partners and allow them to share equally. If any member was not interested, the others could go along without him in strictly legitimate enterprises. In the illegal ones it was still all for one and one for all.

The Pioneer Linen and Laundry Company, for example, was organized in Cleveland about 1938. The syndicate owned 75 per cent of the stock which was divided equally between Dalitz, Kleinman, Tucker, Rothkopf, and Chuck Polizzi. Maurice Maschke, Jr., son of the Republican leader of Cleveland, owned the rest and acted as president and manager. Polizzi sold his interest to Tucker and Dalitz in 1943. In 1945 Kleinman and Rothkopf sold their shares to Tucker and Dalitz, and in 1949 Tucker sold his share to Dalitz for $120,000.

Some of the problems involved in remaining fluid enough financially to take advantage of opportunities were once described by Mrs. Angela Polizzi, wife of Chuck. She said that from the day she married in 1930 they kept large amounts of cash at home. Polizzi had a two-foot wide safe bolted to the floor of the clothes closet in which as much as $75,000 was kept. In addition, he had two safe deposit boxes.

Polizzi's tax court attorneys commented on this practice, explaining: "His good fortune in having cash in 1929 and the early 1930's when cash was at a premium and script in vogue, enabled him to operate most profitably. . . . In his own words he expressed the impression this experience had upon him when he said, 'From there on I realized the value of cash and I just never did have a personal bank account.' "

In most syndicate deals, Sammy Haas was somewhere in the background pulling strings. And he always got his cut. A partial list of his holdings gives some indication of the varied nature of syndicate business interests. Haas at one time or another bought stock in the following:

Detroit Steel Company, 1944; Kaiser-Frazier Corporation, 1945; Warner Brothers Corporation, 1945; Illinois Producing Corporation, 1940; Mammoth Producing Corporation, 1942; Standard Cap and Seal Corporation, 1945; Corday-Gross Company, 1945; McKay Realty Company, 1942; Boston Stores, 1946; Sanford Libraries, 1944; Burroughs Brothers Corporation, 1944; Angerman Company, 1939 and 1945; Elevator Safety Corporation, 1950; Kinetic Manufacturing Company, 1942; Morgan Steel Products Company, 1943; San Diego Bowling Building Company, 1941–42; Larchmere-Moreland Company, 1939; Engineers Public Service Company, 1944; Speigel, Inc., 1944; Chicago-Rock Island Railroad, 1943; Bark Controller, 1939; Acquarius Porcupine, 1942; Para Bowling and Recreation, Inc., 1941.

Consolidated Retail Stores, 1944; Sigfried-Lowenthael Company, 1941; Glass Fibers, Inc., 1948; Central Railroad of New Jersey, 1948; Northern Natural Gas Company, 1947; Verney Corporation, 1948; Missouri Cap & Seal Corporation, 1947; G. L. K. Products, Inc., 1948; Cleveland Ring Theater Company, 1950; Midwest Chemical Development Company, 1950; Towne Shop, 1948; Capital Breast Company, 1947; Modern Music Company, 1946; Century Music Company, 1946; 2525 Kemper Company, 1949; Kinsman-Warrensville Center Company, 1949; and drive-in theaters, such as the Dayton, Cuyahoga, Miami, Toledo, Pittsburgh, McKnight's, and Allegheny, as well as a long list of theater management and land companies.

As noted, this is a partial list. But it is impressive in view of the fact that Haas was bankrupt in 1932 and listed his total assets as worth $400. As of December 31, 1950, his net assets were valued at $2,473,179.

Morris Kleinman was another man who made a remarkable financial comeback. When released from prison and paroled in 1937, he filed a pauper's oath to escape paying the fine imposed. Ten years later his total assets were valued at $423,443. By 1949 they had increased to $663,880, and the process continued. In 1954, for example, his assets were valued at $1,047,884.

Kleinman's 1947 income from gambling alone was better than $138,000, and a report noted: "His other investments include apartment buildings, commercial properties, unimproved land, investments in listed stocks, investments in race tracks, investments in closely held businesses, loans received, investments in oil wells, and investments in U.S. Government bonds. . . ."

Similar figures, and similar statements, could be quoted about all syndicate members.

Some investments were short-term affairs, made to meet the needs of the moment. At the end of the war, for example, automobiles were in great demand and hard to get. The syndicate organized Church Motor Company, Inc., at Sharon, Pennsylvania, late in 1946. The company got a Lincoln-Mercury dealership, and all members of the syndicate, their relatives and friends, got new cars at wholesale prices. Sam Tucker purchased two for his children in 1949, just before the syndicate turned the company over to Giesey to squeeze out the last drop for himself.

The Crown Investment Company was organized by the syndicate to purchase the stock of the Cleveland Hockey Company, Inc. Later, the company's name was changed to Cleveland Arena, Inc. A $200,000 loan from the Fidelity Trust Company in Indianapolis was useful in this investment.

Years before that loan was obtained, the syndicate incorporated the Prudential Finance Company to hold money for later investment and to "loan" it out in such a way as to avoid identification of the syndicate with a legitimate business. It also made "loans" to such companies as Bradey Lake Amusements, one of several organizations set up to control its huge Bradey Lake gambling enterprise. Skill Amusement Company, one of the companies allegedly owned by Nate Weisenberg also "borrowed" from Prudential.

In 1946 the syndicate purchased Pierre's Restaurant, 85111 Euclid Avenue, and renamed it Lindy's. Another restaurant which was also used for gambling, at Fifty-fifth and Lexington, was called Hatton's Corners. Warfield Drug Company began as one store under the direction of Allen Kleinman, and grew into four. It too was a syndicate operation. The 2925 Euclid Corporation owned a building. Fred Meyers of Freddie's Club was nominee for Lou Rothkopf in that investment.

Not only did the syndicate members take care of themselves and each other, they also provided for relatives and friends. Kleinman, for example, had a nephew by marriage, Joe Gould. The syndicate "loaned" Gould at least $80,000 to build Hotel Gould, a motel, at North Miami Beach in 1949.

The Liberty Ice Cream Company, an early syndicate investment, became a home for relatives. Dean Rothkopf, brother of Lou, managed it until 1945, when Leo Kirkell, brother-in-law of Morris Kleinman's nephew, Edward Kleinman, took over the management. Edward's wife, Edna Kleinman, was principal owner of Roxy's, a burlesque house in the Ninth-Chester Building. The building also housed the Chester-Ninth Ticket Office, often described as a "ticketless ticket office." For years it was headquarters of Mushy Wexler–Gameboy Miller's wire service. Max Marmorstein, who came from Hungary in 1913 and went bankrupt in 1926, owned the building. He also took title to the old Thomas Club in 1940 and converted it into a bingo hall.

Syndicate members didn't forget their old friendship for Lake Erie and Canada. One enterprise involved the good ship *Alabama*, an excursion boat. Tommy McGinty masterminded the deal, but Moe Dalitz later admitted it was a syndicate operation. The boat cruised Lake Erie with fifty slot machines aboard in 1946. When winter came, the liquor license and the slots were transferred to the Wayside Tavern, 17801 Euclid Avenue, where Regis Duddy, McGinty's son-in-law, made use of them during the off-season.

Lou Rothkopf, meanwhile, bought land and a six-bedroom "cottage" on Sheep Island, approximately 100 miles from Portland, Ontario, in the Riebeau Lakes. The transaction was one of those strange deals designed, apparently, to frustrate investigators. Benjamin Rothkopf bought the property in 1946, sold it in 1947 to Morris Kleinman, who, on the same day, sold it to Mrs. Lou Rothkopf.

The place was used for conferences and to entertain useful guests. Boxer Billy Conn was there for a week in 1947, recovering no doubt from his fight with Joe Louis which drew a $1,925,564 gate, largest since the 1927 Dempsey–Tunney bout. Frank Costello spent a week there in 1949, the same year Rothkopf was his host in Oakland, California.

"Uncle Louie" also took over the old Maple Club which McGinty started back in the twenties. Located some twenty-four miles from downtown Cleveland near Chagrin Falls, it was an elaborate place. Rothkopf added paneling, ceramic tile, and a fancy stairway to the second floor. Asked if he was planning to operate it, he explained he was fixing it up for the tenant farmer who cared for his thirty-six-acre farm.

It was plausible—after all, the syndicate had enough new casinos going not to need the old ones. When in 1951 the "heat" went on the Pettibone Club, the syndicate turned it into a film studio.

3.

The Oak Grove Country Club in Greene County near Dayton, Ohio, was in some respects the spiritual heir of the old Arrowhead Club a few miles to the south near Cincinnati. It was opened in May, 1947, to service those citizens of southern Ohio who believed in keeping their dollars in the state instead of losing them across the Ohio River at the Lookout House or the Beverly Hills Club.

The club encountered problems from the start—not from the sheriff who suffered from the same eye trouble that afflicted his Kentucky colleagues, but from reporters of the Dayton *Daily News* and Dayton *Journal-Herald.* The club had hardly opened before the reporters described the action and the sheriff was assailed by editorial writers for inactivity. Sheriff Walton Spahr had an answer for his critics:

"I am not a magician. I cannot walk through a stone wall or a steel door, but I am ready to go at any time of the day or night where any body of citizens may desire."

The sheriff did visit the club eventually and reported it was a quiet place with "about fifty people sitting around . . . playing euchre. They were very nice and courteous to us."

The Greene County Grand Jury didn't agree, however, and in the wake of its probe the club shut down until the "heat" passed. It soon reopened and managed to operate for quite a while before the Dayton newspapers again mounted an offensive.

Reporter Carl V. Roberts and Michael Boeke visited the club in 1950 and their reports indicate it was a rather small casino being operated cautiously. The sucker went up a long drive after passing through a gate. A yardman checked him before he got out of the car. At the door, another check was given through a peephole. Still another check was made inside the door. If the sucker passed the various inspections, he was allowed into the casino. Three dice tables, assorted blackjack and poker tables were the only games offered, but patrons could win a television set as a door prize.

The operation was related to the Kentucky casinos through the Osborn Realty Company in Cincinnati. Jack Kuresman, accountant, and Sol Goodman, an attorney, were among the officers of Osborn Realty which owned the land, and among the incorporators of Oak Grove. They also performed similar services on occasion in Kentucky. Goodman was also attorney for the Chesapeake operation of the syndicate.

Principal operator of the club was Paul Dennis, an Ohio "cattle breeder" who also owned a small piece of the Beverly Hills Club in Newport. The Kefauver Committee established that the real owner was the Cleveland Syndicate. Following the publicity, Governor Frank Lausche put pressure on local officials and forced the club to close in 1951.

The Continental Club up the Ohio River at Chesapeake was a far larger and plusher operation than Oak Grove.

Named after a short-lived Cleveland casino, the Continental Club was on the left side of U.S. 52 as the highway approached the bridge across the Ohio River to Huntington, West Virginia. While many of the patrons came from Huntington—cocktails as well as casinos were illegal in West Virginia—others came from Ashland, Kentucky, just down the road on the south bank of the Ohio, and from Ironton, county seat of Lawrence County, Ohio, on the north bank.

Living space is constricted. Tall mountains rise sharply from the river, and the cities have difficulty expanding. Only Huntington had much level area in which to grow. For many years the region was something of a no-man's land as far as law enforcement was concerned. Operators could skip from one state to another to another in fifteen minutes. State officials were inclined to ignore the problem, and local officials were happy to do so.

James "Shimmy" Patton, the ex-Harvard Club operator who gave Eliot Ness headaches in the thirties, claimed credit for discovering the unique advantages of the area. He founded the Continental Club, and brought in William Swarts and his brother, Howard, to operate it. William Swarts was the McGinty aide who killed Champ Joyce on Vincent Street in 1936. They operated for several years before the Cleveland Syndicate took an official interest in the place.

After the syndicate came in, the usual three-headed setup it favored was organized. The Lawrence Union Company held title to the property. The Chesapeake Operating Company, Inc., ran the restaurant. Union Enterprises Company, Inc., ran the casino. And as usual the syndicate let local operators share in the profits.

The syndicate had 37.334 per cent, divided equally between Dalitz, Kleinman, Rothkopf, Tucker, and Chuck Polizzi. Swarts, who bought out Patton, had 25 per cent. William V. Potee, a local gambler and fixer, had 25 per cent. Sam Schraeder, an old rumrunner and junior partner in the Newport operations, had 6.666 per cent. The remaining 6 per cent was held by Mitchell Meyer, another Newport lieutenant.

The Newport boys had no reason to feel anything but at home when they visited Chesapeake. Conditions there were very similar to those in Kentucky. Sheriff Peter A. Burke, for example, guaranteed the water bill for the Continental Club. The gas bill for the club was in his name as well. A deputy sheriff, Maxine Lentz, who had worked for Burke since 1924, was married to Clarence Lentz, who was employed at the club.

Sheriff Burke ran the Ironton *News* on the side, and accepted advertisements from the gamblers. Under the circumstances, it isn't surprising there was no newspaper crusade comparable to the one at Dayton.

The Cleveland Syndicate did encounter something unusual in Chesapeake in the person of a man known improbably as Dustin "Ducky" Corn. The real "political boss" of the area, Ducky had for years promoted and hustled as best he could. Born in Ironton in 1906, he completed the eighth grade. After some years as a salesman with Ashland Oil & Refining Company, he was fired because of "his sharp practices and glib tongue." Apparently he had not fared too badly for he immediately opened his own oil business on a large scale. That got him into trucking and led to the restaurant business, which opened his eyes to opportunities in pinball and slot machines. From there it was a short step to gambling joints.

Corn built the Hickory Club along the river and brought in Potee from Cincinnati to operate it. He added other joints, all of the "sawdust" variety. The Ritzy Ray Club became notorious as a place for free-for-all fights, and eventually Corn remodeled it and called it the Riviera.

When the syndicate took over the Continental Club, Corn secretly bought an old mansion and spread the word that soon the Plantation Club would open to compete with Continental. Whether or not the syndicate members knew what was going on—in view of Corn's reputation the local lieutenants should have guessed—they responded when Corn announced that for $60,000 they could buy Plantation and end the threat. The money was paid. Chuck Polizzi later admitted that his share was taken out of his "Kentucky earnings."

The Plantation Club opened briefly before Corn got his money. Duncan W. Daugherty, Sr., a former United States Attorney in Huntington, told of a group of women from a Huntington church who met there for lunch. One of the women put a coin in a slot machine in the belief it was a gum machine. She learned her mistake when a handful of coins gushed out.

Corn had too much political influence for the syndicate to resent an occasional shakedown. He was essential to keeping the area corrupt, but syndicate members didn't trust him. Few people did. He boasted his influence extended to Washington, and once he almost "stopped" a federal tax investigation. When he couldn't resist bragging about it, the case was reopened. He was ultimately found guilty on eight felony counts—and got a $5,000 fine and a number of concurrent one-year sentences. But a doctor said his health was bad, the sentences were suspended, and he was put on probation. However, he did pay $160,000 in back taxes, penalties, and interest.

In 1949, the Colony Club, next door to the Continental, was raided by Ohio liquor agents led by Anthony A. Rutkowski. It was part of a drive against gambling ordered by Governor Lausche which ultimately closed most of the major casinos in Ohio. The raids gave rise to the legend that Lausche drove the syndicate into other states, such as Kentucky. In reality, the shift began in 1936.

A few days before the raid, Continental shifted gambling into the Colony Club. By thus separating the bar and the roulette wheel, it hoped to frustrate the state's liquor agents. But Rutkowski maintained it was still one operation, and he made it stick. Many years later, the abandoned buildings were torn down to make way for a shopping center. Workmen uncovered bullet-proof glass portholes in the walls, armor plating inside concrete blocks, and gun slits.

The syndicate, true to its record of not being caught unprepared, had already sent the Swarts brothers across the Ohio to Huntington. There they bought an old hotel for $100,000.

Daugherty, who represented the owners of the hotel, said a crisis arose when the wife, a co-owner, refused to sign the papers upon learning the hotel was to be used for gambling. Daugherty got her into his office, told her what the Swarts did with the hotel was none of her business, and persuaded her to sign.

The Swarts boys spent three times as much remodeling the hotel as they paid to buy it, Daugherty said. They achieved a plush three-story joint called the Huntington Athletic Club. But part of the program which Swarts and the syndicate had planned, a change in the state's liquor laws to permit sale by the drink, failed to pass. Liquor by the drink could be served only in private clubs. Hotels in Huntington today have "private clubs" which patrons can join by paying a small membership fee and signing a card. It is similar to the problem in Texas. Such a system, however, was not what the syndicate had in mind when it invested in the Huntington Athletic Club. The club continued to operate—offering liquor, good food, and gambling to its members. While it was not the wide-open operation anticipated by the syndicate, it provided a good living for the Swarts boys. In time they became as respectable in Huntington as Mushy Wexler became in Cleveland. Good food can sometimes buy more than money.

If Huntington did not provide as much return as expected, the syndicate compensated for it in White Sulphur Springs, West Virginia.

White Sulphur is on the east side of West Virginia from Huntington. For many years it has been famous for the Greenbriar. Originally it was famous for its sulphur water, and the Greenbriar was built to provide accommodations for patrons of the watering place. Gradually, as faith in water decreased somewhat, the magnificence of Greenbriar became an attraction in its own right.

The Cleveland Syndicate was well acquainted with the potentials of a watering place. Its members had been going to Hot Springs, Arkansas, for many years to meet with top gangsters who came there to get advice from Owney "the Killer" Madden and to relax in hot baths. Gameboy Miller even installed his father-in-law there, and occasionally promoted a little action. But it was Madden's town, and no serious poaching was permitted. The syndicate decided it would be better to develop White Sulphur Springs.

Property was acquired in April, 1948. Abe Goodman, a relative of Sam Tucker's wife and member of Ess-Kay-Gee, served as the front man. Tommy McGinty was invited by Kleinman, Dalitz, Rothkopf, and Tucker to join the project and he put up one-fifth of the first $40,000 invested.

Plans were to build a resort hotel along the order of the 650-room Greenbriar. Nothing less would be equal to the task, for the Greenbriar was in fact a city in itself. It had every facility for recreation and relaxation, including the Old White Club where guests could become instant members and buy cocktails.

Despite the propaganda gamblers shovel out at every opportunity, the more intelligent ones know that gambling is not in itself sufficient to attract tourists. The syndicate's experience at the Beverly Hills Club, and later in Las Vegas, made it plain that a sucker may be hooked by cheap, good food and name entertainment or a magnificent golf course, but that something extra is required. In Hot Springs people bathe and then cross Central Avenue to the Southern Club. That was proved when they continued to come to bathe after gambling closed during a reform movement.

The Greenbriar dominated White Sulphur Springs. Its owner,

the Chesapeake & Ohio Railroad, was not eager for competition. Headquarters of the C. & O. had been moved years before to Cleveland by the Van Sweringen brothers. Indeed, the Cleveland Syndicate had shipped a lot of alcohol over the railroad, thus proving cooperation on some levels, at least, was possible.

The Cleveland Syndicate switched signals. Instead of building its giant resort hotel and casino in White Sulphur Springs, where technically, at least, gambling was illegal, it built the Desert Inn in Las Vegas. Greenbriar patrons who felt an urge to gamble were encouraged to patronize a small but very plush casino the syndicate operated at a location near the hotel.

The condition continued for many years. One such location was the Clover Club just beyond the "nineteenth hole" of the Greenbriar's famous golf course on land acquired in 1952 from the Chesapeake & Ohio. Despite the fact that the Greenbriar was on the American plan, the Clover Club served "Delicious Food at Moderate Prices." Behind a door marked PRIVATE was a small but lavish casino offering dice, roulette, blackjack, and slot machines. Free drinks were served by a uniformed maid. A lack of action was explained by a dealer—a professional to the tips of his fingers—on the fact that the Greenbriar had a special program that night and wouldn't release its guests until midnight.

Greenbriar County Court records showed the syndicate held its land until 1955 before selling it to Latelle M. LaFollette, a Charleston, West Virginia, attorney. By then it was apparent White Sulphur Springs would never become much more than the site of the Greenbriar, and a casino such as the Clover Club was adequate for the action Greenbriar patrons could provide.

4.

Action of another kind came to plague the syndicate's plush Mounds Club in Lake County outside Cleveland on September 23, 1947.

At 12:15 A.M. the second show of the evening began in the

green and yellow dining room. A big crowd was on hand. The attraction was Mary Healy and Peter Lind Hayes.

Miss Healy, staging an impersonation of Hildegarde, was dragging Hayes from a ringside table when a masked man wearing a green GI fatigue uniform entered from the kitchen.

The masked man was carrying a machine-pistol, and he fired a volley into the ceiling. The audience roared with laughter at this "realistic" bit of play-acting. Miss Healy, realizing the shooting wasn't part of the act, ran into the rest room and remained there.

Three more hooded men entered. One wore a gray hat and appeared to be the leader. The audience applauded, still assuming it was part of the entertainment that made the loss of their money less painful. Another volley into the ceiling ended the laughter.

"This is no joke," said the man with the machine-pistol. "Everybody sit down," ordered Gray Hat.

One of the masked men who held a submachine gun in his arms walked to the rear of the room, climbed a radiator, and sat there. His gun moved back and forth, on the ready.

Six other men entered and went into the casino where the dice had been more interesting than Healy-Hayes for about twenty patrons. These gamblers were lined up against the wall and searched, diamond rings were taken from fingers, wallets from pockets; nothing was missed. Money was scooped from the gambling tables and from the boxes underneath the tables.

Buck Schaffner, club manager, was forced at gunpoint into the office. On command, he opened the safe. It was heavily loaded, containing as it did the weekend "take" as well as Monday's receipts. Monday had been a legal holiday and the banks had been closed.

While the syndicate declined to estimate the loss, first estimates ranged from $250,000 to $500,000. Later, investigators placed it unofficially at $300,000. The figure included the contents of the safe as well as money and jewels taken from the patrons.

Peter Lind Hayes didn't have a dime in the pockets of his floor-show clothes. He "borrowed" $40 from a man who was putting $1,500 on the table, telling the man, "I'm afraid they'll paste me for holding out on them."

Hayes' fear was inspired by the "example" made of a man who seemed slow unloading his pockets. He was taken into another room where a shot was fired. A gunman returned alone. Later the frightened patrons learned the "victim" had not been hurt.

The upstairs dressing rooms were looted, and the raiders left by the kitchen door. They roared away in cars selected from those parked around the club. The cars were later recovered.

Five guards outside the club said they had been surprised by the raiders who slipped into the rear yard from a wooded area. During the robbery the guards were locked in a small shed.

Newspapers that day noted "it was the first robbery at the Mounds in its seventeen years of existence."

The official investigation received no cooperation from syndicate officials and soon reached a dead end.

A similar robbery occurred a few days later in Chesapeake at the Continental Club, but it received even less publicity. Six men got inside disguised as customers and took $60,000.

It was a challenge the syndicate could not ignore. Federal agents said they learned by the grapevine that the syndicate conducted its own probe of both robberies and its own trial. The men who pulled the daring raids were dead within six months.

There were no appeals when the syndicate passed sentence. Nor were there any more armed robberies of syndicate casinos.

CHAPTER FIFTEEN

> If I forget thee, O Jerusalem, let
> my right hand forget her cunning . . .
> *Hebrew Prayer*

On a day in May, 1945, Robert Gould stood in the tiny courtroom of the Federal Building in Covington, Kentucky, and heard sentence passed. For his company, Dowling Brothers Distillery, the penalty for black-market liquor activities was a fine of $240,000. For Gould, the man, the penalty was another $240,000 fine and six years in prison.

There was a moment of silence before marshals moved in to take their prisoner. Gould turned, and his eyes met those of a federal agent who had directed the complicated investigation. Gould smiled faintly, and his lips moved:

"Six years—six million dollars. Not so bad at that."

It was not so bad as that. October, 1946, came before the Supreme Court turned down his appeal and he went to prison. In December, 1948, he was released on parole.

On February 1, 1949, the New York *Times* carried a front-page story about Major General Harry H. Vaughan, military aide to President Harry Truman. In the course of the so-called deep-freeze probe by a Senate subcommittee, Vaughan admitted three things regarding Robert Gould:

1. Gould's attorney, William H. Neblett, former law partner of the late Senator William H. McAdoo, approached Vaughan in 1947 about a parole for Gould.

2. In 1948, Neblett made a "campaign contribution" to the Democratic Party through Vaughan. "I was the conduit," he explained.

3. Shortly after the "contribution" was received, Gould was paroled.

But, said Vaughan, it was all a coincidence. From Cincinnati, Gould agreed. He had no knowledge, he said, that Neblett made a political contribution. Neblett was "one of several" attorneys he employed from November, 1947, to March, 1948.

The Cleveland Syndicate, along with others in organized crime, had anticipated a revolt against authority, a decline in morality, in the years following World War II. They based the prediction on first-hand knowledge of a similar period after World War I.

While the "revolt" and "decline" were not as strong, perhaps, as in the days of Prohibition and the Ohio Gang, the so-called Truman scandals were evidence that the gangsters had not greatly misjudged human nature. If anything, it was the crooks who were less dishonest. Jess Smith took money from George Remus—and left him in prison. Robert Gould got out. Crooks in the Justice and Treasury departments under Harding sometimes double-crossed the bootleggers, but the boys of Gotham Liquor Corporation got what they wanted in the 1940's.

Had Harding lived, he might have escaped the influence of the Ohio Gang and cleaned up his administration. No one can say he would not have done so. But the record of Harry Truman is clear—when at last he realized what government-by-crony was doing to the country and to his reputation, he took effective action. The Internal Revenue Service was reorganized, and many of the veteran civil servants who had been shoved aside were allowed to resume their duties.

Older I.R.S. agents tell strange stories about those days. Some even have kind words for their crooked superiors. One, for example, always warned the "regulars" to neglect nothing even though the case under investigation would be pigeonholed. "Someday we'll be gone and you and the case will still be here," the political appointee advised.

Then there was the high-ranking official who traveled constantly on official business and never turned in an expense account—to his office. His expenses were being paid by the men who put him in office to do a job, an agent explained, and he didn't try to cheat the government twice.

A series of congressional hearings which continued until 1954 exposed many of the crooks and helped bring their removal. The hearings, however, could not bring back the honest men who quit in disgust, or reactivate criminal cases that had gone out the window.

One case involved Gotham Liquor Corporation, which came into the world on October 4, 1946. It could trace its ancestry back to Molaska Corporation and, in fact, it gave as its corporate address that old home of Molaska, 500 Fifth Avenue.

Key man in Gotham was Louis I. Pokrass. Born in Russia in 1898 he came to the United States in 1915 and joined the Navy. Upon his discharge in 1919, he married and entered the dress business. Prohibition's opportunities were more attractive. Pokrass was arrested four times for liquor law violations between 1925 and 1931. He became connected with Capitol Wine & Spirits as its general manager in 1934. In obtaining the basic permits needed to operate a liquor business, he neglected to mention his criminal record as required. He also failed to identify to the Alcohol Tax Unit all persons having a financial interest in the business. He didn't, for example, say a word about Meyer Lansky, Joe Adonis, Bugsy Siegel, or even Frank Costello.

Several other violations occurred, bringing an official investigation which was climaxed in 1942 when Pokrass offered $100,000 as a compromise settlement of civil and criminal liabilities. The offer was accepted, but Capitol's basic permits were revoked. A stubborn man, Pokrass carried an appeal to the Supreme Court, but the revocation stood. The appeals delayed it until July 16, 1945, however.

Capitol's assets were sold to Atlantic Liquors & Wholesalers, and the funds received were invested in Bugsy Siegel's Flamingo Hotel under construction in Las Vegas. It was syndicate money, part of the several million the syndicate gave to Siegel for the Flamingo.

Pokrass, meanwhile, tried to get back into the liquor business. He made application for new permits under the name of the Fairmont Liquor Corporation. The application was disapproved on the official grounds that "in view of the criminal record of the applicant the revenue of the country would be in jeopardy."

Upon receiving notice that the application would be rejected, Pokrass tried again under the name Central Liquors. When this application was rejected, he appealed but the denial was upheld.

Meanwhile, Roosevelt died, Truman took over as President, the war ended.

Pokrass formed Gotham Liquor and filed a new application for the essential permits. He listed his legal residence on the application as 115 Central Park West. By another strange coincidence that proved to be the address of Frank Costello when later he was questioned by the Kefauver Committee.

Despite all the past rejections, the new application went through established channels. And an inspector reached this conclusion:

"Recommend disapproval of the application. Applicant [Gotham] is not entitled to confidence of the Department and will not conduct operations in conformity with federal law by reason of its association with Louis I. Pokrass, principal stockholder, president and director."

Before formal action could be taken, Carroll Mealey, deputy commissioner of the Internal Revenue Service in charge of the Alcohol Tax Unit, intervened. He called James A. Wright, an A.T.U. official in New York, and told Wright that Pokrass should be given the permits.

There was some delay, however, and Mealey called Wright from Washington on November 19, 1946. A transcript of the conversation was made—the veteran agents who remained in the belief that better days would come took no chances. The transcript reveals that Mealey asked if the "Gotham thing" had been issued. When told it was still being processed, Mealey said, "The commissioner asked me yesterday if the permit had been issued yet."

"You know the background," Wright replied. "I want something in our files to show we actually went through the regular routine so if anything ever comes up in the future they will know we did give it consideration. I think that is the way to do on this sort of thing."

Two days later the permit was issued.

The commissioner at the time was Joseph D. Nunan. It was he who hired Mealey. When asked, he said Mealey's name was submitted by the Democratic organization in New York.

Later investigation revealed that Pokrass arranged for Mealey to buy a fur coat "cheap." Pokrass also bought a new Buick and gave it to Mealey. Still later, when Pokrass went into the television business with Frank Costello, *et al.*, Mealey received two $1,000 checks written by Pokrass and said to be for "legal services."

Nunan was fired in 1947—and was promptly retained by Joseph Reinfeld. It was learned that at the time he ordered Mealey to give Pokrass a permit, he also ordered one for Somerset Liquor Company, an outfit owned by Reinfeld, who was still working closely with the New York boys. The whole thing was now the Eastern Syndicate, of course.

Pokrass, who by now was vice-president of the Flamingo Hotel in Las Vegas, stayed busy on other fronts. Consolidated Television was formed. Partners of record included Pokrass, Meyer Lansky, Joe Adonis, Frank Costello, and several others. Accountant was George Goldstein—the Alvin Giesey of the Eastern Syndicate.

The idea behind Consolidated Television was a theory that the big market for television sets would be bars and taverns—not homes. Meyer Lansky said the syndicate was approached about the idea because "we had knowledge of distribution of juke boxes. We knew every place that had a juke box and that would be a good place to have television."

One of the men hired to place the television sets in taverns was Sam Stein. And out of that association grew a tale of international intrigue—a tale of action that ranged from the Theatrical Grill in Cleveland to Casablanca and Cairo.

2.

Principal character in the new saga of Sam Stein was a soldier-of-fortune straight out of Richard Harding Davis. Lieutenant Colonel Terrill J. Murrell, U.S.A.R., had served his country in various parts of the world during the war, but most especially in Italy and the Near East. In the process, making full use of his rank and authority, he made many valuable contacts.

His active service ended in May, 1947, and Colonel Murrell returned to his native land and, logically enough, set up camp in the Savoy-Plaza in New York. There he met one of his former contacts, Joseph "Joe Bananas" Bonanno, a well-known narcotics peddler who had connections with that new giant of American industry, Consolidated Television Corporation, 601 West Twenty-sixth Street.

Through this narcotics peddler—the term is used here to imply a man of international stature in contrast to a back-alley "pusher"—Colonel Murrell soon found himself a vice-president of Consolidated in charge of sales.

The scene now shifts to the Theatrical Grill in Cleveland. A warm and friendly place it was, with Mushy Wexler as host, and Miss Bessie Miller, sister of Gameboy, as cashier. Next door to the rear entrance of the Hollenden, it was almost an extension of the syndicate's offices there.

Colonel Murrell visited the Theatrical Grill one day during a tour of the better Middle Western syndicate restaurants and taverns, arranging, among other things, to install Consolidated's television sets. He could point out, if the point needed elaboration, how busy syndicate executives could drop in for a drink and watch the fights on television to make sure the loser dropped in the prearranged round.

While in the Grill that night he just happened to find himself talking to Moe Dalitz, who was over from his new home in Detroit to check up on things. Murrell explained his problems in finding the right man to contact tavern owners and, he said, Dalitz told him he knew just the fellow he needed—Sam Stein.

Dalitz in a statement much later said he knew that Sam had been involved in some "shady deals in the past," but he was trying to go straight, and since Stein had married into Mrs. Dalitz' family, Moe wanted to help him. He had known Sam for twenty years, he added, and knew he was just the man for Consolidated. He would be especially valuable in dealing with tavern owners in Detroit.

About a week later, Colonel Murrell called on Stein and offered him the Detroit distributorship. Sam accepted, but the connection didn't last long. For reasons of policy no one has bothered to explain, Consolidated underwent a reorganization and emerged under a new name, Tele-King, Inc. Pokrass was still head of it, but Colonel Murrell decided to strike out on his own. And he wanted Stein with him—possibly because he knew how sentimental Dalitz had become.

After a trip to Europe to line up prospects, Colonel Murrell returned with a new idea. He would export war-surplus items to Europe, sell the merchandise there, buy European merchandise, and import it into the United States. This procedure would be good for the country in that it would avoid the usual losses on foreign exchange which ordinarily accompany the purchase or sale of a single item. It would have eliminated the balance-of-payment problems that became acute years later.

Colonel Murrell got in touch with Dalitz and Stein. In the interests of finding Sam an honest job, Dalitz agreed to discuss the plan with some friends in New York. Among his friends was Robert Goldstein, one of those warriors he had met at the Savoy-Plaza during the war.

Goldstein had connections with Universal Pictures, and the Cleveland Syndicate—always on the lookout for something to do with its gambling profits—wanted to discuss with Goldstein the possibility of making "soundies," short films for use in Tele-

King's bar-size TV sets. Apparently some kind of agreement was achieved, for eventually the syndicate converted the Pettibone Club near Cleveland into a studio for making film shorts.

During the discussion, Dalitz also mentioned the ideas Murrell had conceived, and Goldstein was interested. Dalitz sent Stein and Murrell around to talk to Goldstein, who checked details with his attorney, Sam Becker, who concurred. Becker had served on Governor's Island as a lieutenant colonel and had been billeted with Lieutenant Dalitz at the Savoy-Plaza. So a meeting of minds was easily achieved.

On April 26, 1948, a new company was registered with the Secretary of State at Albany, New York. It was called Masthead Export Corporation, and its officers were Robert Goldstein, president; Sam Stein and Moe B. Dalitz, vice-presidents; and Jack M. Kramer, secretary-treasurer. For some reason, Colonel Murrell was not given a title, but he soon compensated for the oversight. Kramer was a certified public accountant, brought in at the suggestion of Stein, to sign checks and keep the books.

Proof that an outside accountant was needed came when Masthead, as its first act, paid a $15,000 debt incurred earlier by Colonel Murrell. With that out of the way Murrell dashed off to Europe—on expense account. Word received by Kramer had him arranging to sell tires, sugar, auto parts, bricks, and, of special interest to Stein, currency.

Apparently annoyed at not having a title, Murrell in Paris formed Terrill J. Murrell & Company, with a branch office at 30 rue Murdock, Casablanca, Morocco. He used the name Masthead and the new company indiscriminately in future business deals.

During a trip to London, Colonel Murrell met V. Cochrane Hervey, director of Empire Film Productions, Ltd. Despite the title, Hervey had a criminal record which included convictions for housebreaking and larceny. Scotland Yard knew him as a suspected arms trafficker. He enjoyed very good relations with high Arab leaders, and he had a proposition for Colonel Murrell.

In brief it involved smuggling airplanes from the United

States to Egypt, which was then engaged, as were other Arab nations, in trying to defeat stubborn little Israel. They weren't making much progress, and were willing to pay high prices for planes.

As a result of the discussions with Hervey, Colonel Murrell returned to the United States and in September, 1948, met with Sam Hanna in Washington. Hanna was of Egyptian birth. Before becoming a naturalized citizen of the United States, he had been known as Sami R. Salim. He lived in Cairo and was a partner in the Middle East Commercial and Transport Company.

Apparently an agreement was reached. Colonel Murrell, who enjoyed flitting around the world, dashed back to Europe to return late in October with an order given in Egypt through Empire Films for twenty AT-6 airplanes and one B-25-J bomber.

The AT-6 was a single-engine craft designed by the United States Army as an advance trainer for fighter pilots. It ordinarily would be armed, but war-surplus planes available to the public had been stripped. The B-25 was, of course, the famous Mitchell bomber. It had carried General Doolittle and his men to the first bombing of Tokyo, and had become a workhorse in Europe. The "J" version of the B-25 was designed specifically for precision bombardment—something the Arabs needed when trying to hit a tiny country like Israel.

Colonel Murrell hastened to Detroit, where, at the Book-Cadillac, he told some of his partners of the venture. Apparently Dalitz and Stein decided insulation was needed. After all, Stein had a reputation as a smuggler, and Dalitz was beginning certain discussions in Nevada that unfavorable publicity could jeopardize.

Dalitz, Stein, and Kramer resigned from Masthead Corporation on November 1, 1948. Goldstein quit on November 19. As far as investigators could learn, Goldstein and Kramer had nothing more to do with Masthead, although Kramer still held the corporation's records.

Two new men had been interested in Murrell's proposals.

Arthur Leebove, an old friend of Stein in the jewelry business in Detroit and owner of the El Dorado Club in Las Vegas, was one addition, and his friend George Wilson, who owned some machine shops, was another.

Leebove introduced Murrell to a flight instructor who knew where a B-25 could be bought, and together they flew down to Lambert Field, St. Louis, and looked it over. Murrell asked for additional gasoline tanks and for the removal of military color. The plane was available for $22,500, and an option was obtained for $500.

Colonel Murrell hurried back to the Savoy-Plaza, and after some problems arranged to buy twenty AT-6 planes from Fred Ayer at Princeton, New Jersey. Wilson was sent to London to represent Murrell from that end. Ayer began assembling the training planes. On November 12, 1948, Murrell cabled Wilson that the planes would soon be ready and he needed a crew to ferry over the bomber. Wilson contacted four men who previously had flown a Halifax bomber from London to Egypt for Murrell. That plane actually saw action against the Israelis. The crew was willing to come to the United States so Murrell told Wilson to arrange passports, etc.

All kinds of red tape were involved. Murrell had to get an export permit. His crew had to have a license to fly planes in the United States. He got what he needed by swearing the B-25 was to be used as a freighter to fly between New York, Paris, and Casablanca. The Civil Aeronautics Administration had some doubts as to the suitability of using a B-25 as a freighter, and asked the State Department to investigate. Murrell explained he really intended to use the bomber as an executive-type plane to carry him about the world in connection with his far-flung interests.

Not entirely satisfied, the officials told Murrell that before the B-25 could depart, he would have to file with the collector of customs at the port of departure an Affidavit of Temporary Sojourn. He would also have to comply with all existing customs regulations.

This didn't alarm the colonel, who promptly cabled Empire

Films that all was ready. As quickly as the cash was supplied, delivery could be made. A weird mixup resulted when the Egyptians got Murrell's name wrong on a cable to the bank. He straightened it out and, after cabling "Nothing can move until solde received," got the *solde* (Italian for "money") in the amount of $28,108.40 on December 7, 1948.

One day before, December 6, Dalitz, Stein, and Art Leebove came to New York, and stayed at the Savoy-Plaza. Sam Hanna checked in from Cairo, and was introduced to the hotel as Murrell's personal pilot. In order that a full-scale conference could be held, a cable was sent to Wilson in London:

"RETURN IMMEDIATELY. STOPPING SAVOY-PLAZA."

The cable was signed "Art, Moe, and Sam."

Things were moving fast. The English crew, headed by David Bond, arrived December 7, and were sent to an airport in Ohio where the company owning the B-25 familiarized them with the controls. Three days later they were in St. Louis, ready to take over the plane. Some engine adjustments were necessary, however.

To avoid difficulty in moving the bomber and the twenty trainers, Colonel Murrell called upon a former sergeant under his command, Leonard DePippo. Murrell had helped DePippo in 1947 by arranging a job hauling Consolidated Television's products. Now, in this emergency, DePippo was asked to act in the capacity of owner and shipper of the AT-6 planes. It was decided additional insulation would be useful so DePippo assumed the name John A. Romano. He registered himself as doing business under the trade name of Acme Photo Geodetic Company.

The papers were drawn up. Address of Acme Photo was the address of a warehouse owned by the company for which DePippo drove a truck. Arrangements were easily made to ship the AT-6 planes aboard the *S. S. Mohammed Ali El Kabir,* a steamship which operated between New York and Alexandria, Egypt. DePippo, posing as Romano, signed an Export Declaration.

Meanwhile, the B-25 had been put in order and the crew

flew it up to Newark, New Jersey. An auto mechanic, Leonard LaBella, agreed to pose as its owner and to execute the necessary forms and affidavits. On December 27, with the newly born John A. Romano aboard as a passenger, the B-25 was given clearance by Customs Inspector Harold Butler and took off for Montreal on the first leg of its flight to Egypt.

It was here that chance—the thing gamblers try to avoid as much as possible—took a hand. Bad weather boiled up, and Captain Bond was forced to land at Albany, New York. Next day he tried to take off again, but the inspector at Albany refused to honor the Newark clearance for the flight to Montreal. Bond decided to return to Newark and start all over.

Meanwhile, Inspector Butler in Newark had some second thoughts about the whole business. To please him, Colonel Murrell produced the auto mechanic who signed a second affidavit, and again Butler cleared the flight. But at the same time he notified his superiors. Before Bond could get into the air, the clearance was rescinded. The export of the training planes was also blocked.

Murrell gave up. The planes remained on the ground. After an investigation, all were seized on January 14, 1949. It had been a weird effort that had almost succeeded. What followed was also weird—and it succeeded.

3.

Almost a year after the planes were seized, a federal grand jury indicted Murrell, DePippo, and LaBella on charges of violating Title 18 of the United States Code—making false statements to an agency of the United States. They were also indicted, along with Hanna, Wilson, Leebove, and Stein, on charges of conspiracy to violate Title 18 charges.

In June, 1950, the first three pleaded nolo contendere (no contest) to the indictments charging violations. Sentence was suspended pending disposal of the remaining indictments, and in December, 1951—eighteen months later—the conspiracy indictments were superseded by new indictments. They differed from the old in that Colonel Murrell was not included, and Moe B. Dalitz was added as a conspirator.

These developments were made possible by a decision of Colonel Murrell to cooperate. In plain words—he made a deal with someone who knew enough about organized crime to realize Moe Dalitz was a bigger fish than Terrill J. Murrell.

The long delay had enabled Dalitz to get the Desert Inn under control in Las Vegas. It had also enabled him to keep the matter from the prying eyes of Kefauver Committee investigators. The committee had ceased to exist by the time Dalitz was linked to the conspiracy.

How had the delay been achieved? D. F. Cardoza, supervising customs agent in New York, gave a hint as well as added insight into the personality of Colonel Murrell. In a statement long after the case was settled, he said:

> One day early in the Murrell Case, when it began to look as though we would have some evidence, I received a call from Colonel Murrell inviting me to come to the Savoy-Plaza Hotel. He said he had something very hot to tell me.
>
> Another agent and I went to the hotel. He had insisted on meeting us in the main dining room, and he ordered drinks immediately without asking whether we wanted them. We refused to drink them because we felt this was probably some way of easing us into something.
>
> He then began telling us about some big racket that existed in exporting rubber tires to North Africa. It had no connection whatever with the matter we were investigating, but he said it was a very lucrative proposition. He could set us up in a rubber exporting business in which we wouldn't even have to leave our jobs. There wouldn't be any investment on our part either. The thing he was most interested in was that we establish a better relationship with each other than what we had at this time.
>
> We told him we were so deeply involved in the case that establishing any relationship other than what we had would be impossible. Furthermore, we told him we would not be

interested in any rubber tire exporting business. Several times later on in meetings, he mentioned the fact that the offer he had made was still possible, and each time, of course, we gave him the same answer.

Years later, Inspector Cardoza was still angry about the case. So, apparently, had been his superiors. In the fashion of the day, they prepared a memorandum setting out details of the case. It was a protective gesture, but something more. Mention was made, for example, of a statement by Murrell "that he had paid a $10,000 bribe to an official of the Department of Justice." The official was not named.

Still the case dragged on. It was March 10, 1953, before H. M. Goldschein, special assistant to the Attorney General, came to Newark with instructions to prosecute. He quickly decided the evidence against Dalitz consisted largely of statements by Murrell and the record of his travels, cables, etc., which, in a legal sense, was largely circumstantial. Goldschein ordered additional investigation into Dalitz' financial affairs—an ambitious project in itself—but nothing conclusive was found in two weeks.

Sam Hanna had been out of the United States since 1949, so only three conspiracy-case defendants other than Dalitz remained. These three—Leebove, Wilson, and Stein—suddenly announced they would withdraw their not guilty pleas and plead nolo contendere if, and only if, the charges against Dalitz were dropped.

Dalitz once explained why he was concerned about the case. He refused to make a written statement, but he talked to agents. Repeating that his sole interest had been in helping Sam Stein "go straight," Dalitz insisted he knew nothing about shipping planes to Egypt. The memo about the interview continued:

"He further stated that he was a large contributor to Jewish charities and is very active in soliciting funds for these charities as well as for the new Jewish government in Palestine [Israel]. He said it would be very embarrassing for him if his name became implicated in a deal whereby planes were exported to the Egyptian government."

Embarrassing, perhaps, but it must have provided a topic of conversation for Dalitz and the publicity director of the Desert Inn. The director, Hank Greenspun, had been indicted on charges of conspiracy to smuggle arms to Israel—to use against Egypt.

But speculation aside, the fact remained that on April 7, 1953, the case ended. Charges against Dalitz were dropped on motion of United States Attorney Goldschein. Wilson, Stein, and Lee-bove changed their pleas and were fined $1,000 each. DePippo and LaBella, who had allowed their names to be used, were fined $100 each.

Murrell, the acknowledged mastermind, if the word applies, of the entire scheme, was fined $1,000. The judge noted he was taking into consideration the fact Murrell had been "very co-operative" with the government.

Exactly what had been achieved by that cooperation, the judge didn't say.

Murrell paid his fine and went to Florida to operate a Ca-ribbean flying service. Some years later the Cleveland Syndicate had need of him again.

CHAPTER SIXTEEN

Well, you can never make enough.
Henry W. Grunewald

JACK DRAGNA was in a bad humor when the telephone rang that midsummer evening. As he told his caller, he was "having trouble with Immigration again," and, if that wasn't enough, "I'm starving as all I'm doing is settling things."

The "Al Capone of Los Angeles" would have been in an even worse humor had he known Los Angeles police were hearing everything he said in the apartment. According Dragna equal treatment with his colleague, Mickey Cohen, the police installed hidden microphones. Later the news got out, and the underworld found it funny. Everywhere Jack moved, the cops with their "bugs" were there ahead of him. It ruined Dragna.

In 1950, however, he assured his caller, Al Smiley in New Orleans, that "I'm in a good place where I can talk."

Unhappily for historians, the telephone line was not tapped and Smiley's conversation was not recorded. Dragna's side of the conversation was revealing, however.

The Desert Inn, even more plush than the Fabulous Flamingo, had opened a short time before, and, as Dragna put it to Smiley, "that damn place is going like a house afire." Smiley, who had rendered some services to the syndicate, expected a reward. But in New Orleans he had heard disquieting rumors, and had called Dragna for the truth. Dragna's side of the conversation went like this:

"I don't know what in the hell they've got to do with it. After all, you got in here. . . . It's for you to say and them to.

. . . All you've got to say is that whatever you've got there is no special name and that is enough. . . . Them dirty bastards. . . . Ya . . . I was plenty. . . . There is plenty that goes out with the dishwater in there. . . . No, I was told they were supposed to give you five and now they're going to give you money instead. . . . That's what I was told. . . . Well, he didn't specify what he was going to give you. . . . He didn't specify. . . . I mean Lou himself. . . . That is a lot of crap. . . . He didn't go in there because. . . . People work like that. . . . He didn't go because of business. . . . Because he's too good natured for that, you understand. . . . So he sent the other guys out to do it. . . . I know how them people work. . . . I know how they work. . . . I could tell you a mouthful. . . . You know how to deal with the lousy . . ."

To understand what Dragna is saying requires a slight knowledge of the events and personalities involved.

First, the Mafia leader tries to discount the source of Smiley's information, but then acknowledges that sometimes the little crumbs get thrown out with the dishwater. That isn't very reassuring, so Dragna hastily repeats that Smiley was originally to have 5 per cent of the Desert Inn, but the partners now want to give him money. When Smiley questions this statement, Dragna says "Lou himself" made the promise. Lou is of course the "good-natured" Uncle Louie Rothkopf who had been in California the year before with Frank Costello attempting to straighten out problems arising from Siegel's death.

At this point Smiley becomes cynical. He suggest that Rothkopf's promises can't mean much because Rothkopf is not an owner of the Desert Inn. Dragna attempts to explain that business reasons prevented Lou from taking a cut of the D. I., and touts himself as an expert on "how them people work"—meaning the Jewish members of the Cleveland Syndicate. Then, apparently remembering Smiley's ancestry, he says, "You know how to deal with the lousy . . .

In other conversations, Dragna was overheard telling Smiley to settle for 2½ per cent of the Desert Inn.

"If you can get in there why take the money? . . . You and I could live it up here instead of there." Again he expressed disgust with the Cleveland boys: "I don't know when in the hell they start putting out of their own pockets . . ." Finally he told Smiley, "I'd show them people whether you could face it or if I could face it. . . . We're as clean as them anytime. . . . What? . . . Well, don't settle with them. . . . All you have to do is tell them you're splitting up with me, and that would end it. . . ."

The Desert Inn, which opened April 24, 1950, symbolized the fulfillment of assorted dreams. Characteristically, the name in lights above the $5 million casino was not that of any member of the Cleveland Syndicate. Indeed, if the Kefauver Committee had not come to Cleveland and Los Angeles, the part the Cleveland boys played might never have become general knowledge. The name in lights, the front man, was Wilbur Clark. It was Wilbur Clark's Desert Inn.

A native of Illinois, Wilbur Ivern Clark left home as a youth and hitchhiked to San Diego, where in 1928 he worked as a bus boy in Leighton's Cafeteria. By 1930 he had gone up to elevator operator and then bellman at the Knickerbocker Hotel. From 1931 to 1934 he worked as crap dealer at the Bank Club in Reno, Nevada, and graduated to the gambling ship *Monte Carlo* off Long Beach.

When California cracked down on offshore gambling, Clark wandered East in search of employment. He found a job as dealer at the Beverly Hills Club in Newport, Kentucky, in 1937. But the Cleveland Syndicate was even then applying pressure against the owner, Peter Schmidt, and working conditions were not the best. The club had just reopened after its earlier home had been burned by the syndicate as part of the effort to make Schmidt quit. Clark worked a month and moved on to Piping Rock Club, Saratoga, New York. Two months later he returned to San Diego and took over management of the Barbara Worth Hotel.

It was 1942 before Clark reached Las Vegas. He invested in

the El Rancho Vegas and served as manager of it. A Miami gambler reported the joint was a "hop-head's paradise." It ultimately went into receivership. After a trip East to scout the prospects, Clark returned to Vegas early in 1947 and took over the Players, a bar and casino on the main highway to Los Angeles. It seemed to have potential, so Clark formed the Desert Inn, Inc., and bought the property.

In late summer Clark began construction of a large hotel on land adjoining his club. Work proceeded in spurts. Construction would cease. Clark would go East—and East in Las Vegas is a vague term meaning anywhere on the other side of the Mississippi. When he returned from his mysterious trips, construction would resume.

It was not until February, 1950, that the source of Clark's capital became known—and only then because certain members of the Cleveland Syndicate applied to the Nevada Tax Commission for license to operate gambling.

No syndicate member doubted that, if necessary, proper arrangements could be made in West Virginia, or anywhere else, to operate illegally. But the very concept of legal gambling had a fascination. For a quarter of a century the leaders of the syndicate had operated in the shadows. They had made plenty of money, and perhaps had a lot of fun in the process, but they were getting up toward middle age now. There was an increasing yen for respectability.

True, any member of the syndicate could have retired at short notice and devoted himself to the legitimate investments his illicit enterprises had made possible. But that would have been dull. Gambling was still the fastest way of making a buck, and despite all the profits over the years, the making of money still was important. Henry W. Grunewald, the mysterious "Dutchman" of Washington influence peddlers, told a Senate subcommitte that a man never made enough money. Syndicate members shared his feelings. They wanted the easy money *and* the respectability of legalized gambling.

But there were problems. The Nevada Tax Commission, while

eager to attract investments to Las Vegas, had not yet been swallowed by the boom. It was yet free to act and still naïve enough to believe its action would be effective in keeping Nevada gambling "clean." Complicating the situation was the shadow early in 1950 of the Kefauver Committee. No one could tell how deeply it might dig, how much it might expose.

The Newport gambling empire was most obvious. It was too large to conceal. And Nevada officials made it clear they would not issue licenses to persons operating illegal gambling casinos in other states—not when they knew about them, anyway. Yet the Beverly Hills, the Latin Quarter, the Yorkshire, and Merchants Clubs, to mention a few, were gold mines. To give them up was to pay too high a price for respectability.

There was also the question of criminal records. Of the Big Four, Kleinman, Dalitz, Rothkopf, and Tucker, two had been convicted. But Kleinman had taken the fall for income-tax evasion, and in the eyes of many businessmen his only crime there was in getting caught. Rothkopf's conviction was another matter. It came after Prohibition, and while there was "no ultimate conviction," there was no question as to his guilt. While McGinty's conviction in 1925 could be dismissed as a boyish prank —no one regarded Prohibition violations very seriously—the Nevada Tax Commission couldn't stomach Rothkopf.

One answer was found to both problems. Lou Rothkopf "loaned" the Desert Inn $112,500 on March 1, 1950, and $30,000 more on April 30. But he did not buy capital stock as did Dalitz, Tucker, and Kleinman. Each made similar "loans" to the Desert Inn, and each bought $26,000 worth of stock on March 1.

Tommy McGinty was invited to participate on a large scale. He made large "loans" in March, and bought $20,000 worth of stock. Various junior partners in the syndicate were given a chance to "go legit"—Robert Kaye, Ruby Kolod, whose real name was Reubin Koloditsky, and Gilbert Smollin were among those making "loans" as the syndicate raised several million dollars for the Desert Inn.

Meanwhile, the Beverly Hills corporations underwent a drastic reorganization. The old partnerships were officially terminated. Kleinman, Rothkopf, Tucker, and McGinty "sold" their shares to Lou Rothkopf, to Chuck Polizzi, to Harry Potter, and to John Croft.

The word was spread in Las Vegas, and in certain circles in Newport. Indeed, local spokesmen repeated for years the Cleveland Syndicate had left town and that illegal gambling was now, somehow, morally sound since local men were operating it. Rothkopf helped the illusion along by allowing Harry Potter to pay his state income tax. As an official report put it: "This method was used to keep from authorities the fact that individuals other than native Kentuckians were operating the gambling clubs." Polizzi did the same thing, but even on the face of it, the assumption was untrue. Croft and Potter were not natives. They had come from Cleveland where, years before, they worked in the syndicate's first gambling joints.

Where the syndicate is concerned, the face of things seldom reflects the situation as it really is. The boys had pulled a fast one. Rothkopf's money was in the Desert Inn and his partners were owners of record. Dalitz, Kleinman, Tucker, and McGinty had pulled out of the Beverly Hills—and the other gambling partnerships in Newport—but their money remained as well as a senior partner of the syndicate. A final refinement was the continued legal presence in Newport of men such as Potter, George Gordon, E. Rogers Lowe, Alfred Goltsman, and John Licini—all nominees or "fronts" for the absent syndicate members.

This arrangement was what Jack Dragna was talking about when he tried to reassure Smiley that Lou was still a power whose promises were still valid. As Dragna boasted, he knew how "them people" worked, and he knew the "business" reasons that made it necessary for Lou Rothkopf's name not to appear on record in Las Vegas. He even knew that Lou was "good natured" enough to accept the situation, secure in the knowledge that whatever the force that bound top members of the syndicate together it would continue to protect his interests.

In Newport, the syndicate surrendered nothing of value. In

Las Vegas it gained the Desert Inn and all it symbolized. For with Rothkopf's name out, the Nevada Tax Commission took a deep breath and accepted his partners. Respectability had been achieved at last. Shortly thereafter, a Rothkopf appeared. Lou was to be represented by name. His nephew, Bernard Rothkopf, along with Allard Roen, also represented the second generation, college-trained and clean.

Bernard had attended Ohio Wesleyan University. While he had obtained solid experience working in syndicate clubs around Cleveland, he had never been arrested. Married, the father of two daughters, he was the personification of respectability. Given minor administrative duties at first, he advanced to a position of responsibility in the Desert Inn complex.

Roen was even more representative of the second generation than Rothkopf. His real name was Rosen. His father was Frank Rosen, office manager for the syndicate at the Hollenden Hotel for many years. When police investigated the Weisenberg murder, they went to Rosen for information about the dead man's day at the Hollenden.

An old bootlegger and gambler, the elder Rosen wanted something better for his son. He sent him to Duke University at Durham, North Carolina. Allard majored in business administration and graduated in 1943. Friends of his father helped his career. Tommy McGinty, then building some hotels and casinos at Palm Beach, Florida, gave him work as a building contractor. Sam Garfield, an old Detroit friend of Moe Dalitz, invested some gambling profits in oil wells and Roen worked in the fields. Garfield had no children, and more or less adopted Rosen-Roen.

The first evidence the Cleveland Syndicate was supplying funds to Wilbur Clark came in 1949 when Roen went out to Las Vegas to oversee construction. Upon completion of the Desert Inn, he remained as general manager and was allowed a small piece of the club and some related projects. Ultimately, Roen's friendship with Garfield was to get everyone into trouble.

Many legends have come into being about the birth of the

Desert Inn, almost as many as about the death of Bugsy Siegel. One of the most persistent has the Mafia coming to the aid of the Cleveland boys in getting Nevada licenses. Accept this report, and it is easy to believe the follow-up legend that the Mafia is the real power-behind-the-desk at the D.I.

Like most legends, a few facts cause this one to vanish. One might be cited here.

Ruby Kolod, who had been associated with the Cleveland Syndicate since 1939, and had worked his way up through the Thomas Club to the Pettibone, was one of the junior partners allowed to buy a small piece of respectability at the Desert Inn.

While working his way up, Kolod invested with May Katz and Max Stein in the Garfield Hotel, Cleveland. Room 504 was a casino. On the payroll of this syndicate junior lieutenant was John T. Scalish, who sometimes complained because Kolod didn't always pay him the full $100 a week he was due. The McClellan Committee identified Scalish in 1963 as a long-time member of the Mafia "Grand Council."

The "Grand Councilman" also worked for many years at the Cleveland Syndicate's Pettibone Club, and was paid $20 a day in cash. On opening night at the Desert Inn, Scalish was not present, but such old friends and business associates of the syndicate as Peter Licavoli, Joe Massei, and Frank Milano were present. They had the right, as the boys say.

In fact Milano had loaned the Desert Inn and his old Cleveland associates $500,000. The money came up from Mexico via certain friendly interests in Palm Beach, Florida, a place where Tommy McGinty had many friends. Fronting for Milano was a citizen of Haiti, then living in Mexico, who called himself George Francis. He was to figure soon in other international deals.

Had the legend makers known about Milano's investment, they would have gone wild. It was just as well they didn't—the silent syndicate finds legends useful. Nice things to hide behind.

2.

The approval of the Nevada Tax Commission and the opening of the Desert Inn came none too soon for the syndicate. Hot on the heels of organized crime stormed Senator Estes Kefauver and his crack crew of investigators. Around the country the "smart" boys went into hiding. Sammy Haas, for example, took off for his $100,000 home in Jamaica, and stayed there. For the first time in history, intelligence information on every level of law enforcement was studied and coordinated.

Unfortunately the task was too large for the committee. It lacked the time and the manpower to do the job it tried to do. But in the space of a few months, it uncovered more information about crime in America than any other group, before or afterward. Only a fraction of its data was made public. The files, after being "looted" by gangsters, went into restricted quarters at the National Archives to remain for fifty years unstudied. The official reason—the records contain tax information about the crooks and their associates in business.

When investigators arrived in Cleveland, they had to do much of their own digging. As one preliminary report noted:

"The records of the United States Attorney for the Northern District of Ohio, and those of the Revenue Agent, Intelligence Unit and Collector's Office, do not disclose any investigative material or summaries of investigations with respect to *any* of the known characters around Cleveland and Ohio."

The United States Attorney in Cleveland at the time was Don Miller, formerly one of Notre Dame's Four Horsemen and brother of Ray Miller, former mayor. Ray Miller, the investigators learned, represented the Cleveland Browns, a professional football team then owned by Mickey McBride.

Also barren were the files of the Cleveland Police Department. The local cops had no record and no information about such notables as Moe Dalitz or Sam Tucker. One of the Kefauver investigators, John McCormick, later became Cleveland safety director, but even then he continued to have difficulty getting information on syndicate members from police.

Nevertheless, the preliminary probe uncovered enough for one investigator to report: "Because of the enormous wealth that passes through the hands of the Ohio gambling syndicate . . . I have become more or less convinced that if Ohio is not the financial capital of gangsterdom, it is surely one of the best sources of easy money."

It was January, 1951, before the committee reached Cleveland and found many witnesses it wanted to hear were missing. But Tommy McGinty was available, as well as Alvin Giesey, Big Al Polizzi, Tony Milano, and Mickey McBride.

The pattern organized crime had followed from rum-running days was clearly outlined, but great hunks were missing. Giesey supplied some detail and a note of candor. When asked by Committee Counsel Rudolph Halley, "What is the inducement? Why do you do these things?" the former I.R.S. agent replied:

"For the almighty dollar."

It was February 28, 1951, in Los Angeles, when Dalitz and Tucker appeared. Their combined testimony filled thirty pages, of which Dalitz supplied twenty-two. Both witnesses told a few outright lies, evaded many questions, and escaped relatively unscathed.

Their admissions, such as they were, only scratched the surface, but this can be said only in light of knowledge since acquired. At that time, the revelation that a Cleveland syndicate existed astounded many. That it operated in Newport was a shock to good citizens in Kentucky. And that it had expanded to Nevada was a surprise to many people in Cleveland who had been assured the Mayfield Road Mob ran things.

Dalitz and Tucker proved the value of delay. By the time the committee caught up with them, the dramatic climax of the entire investigation had come and gone in New York. There Frank Costello and Ambassador William O'Dwyer had performed before fascinated millions on television. Anything else had to be anticlimatic. Committee members seemed to sense it, and they hurried through the hearing as if doing little more than winding up loose ends. Thus, when asked about Dixie Davis' old statement that "Moey Davis became the power in Cleveland . . ." Dalitz could reply:

"He had been reading dime novels, that fellow."

The schedule was even more crowded when at last Kleinman and Rothkopf were located and served with subpoenas. It was March 26, 1951, and the committee was attempting to wind up its work. It was to get a renewed lease on life and continue under the chairmanship of Senator Herbert R. O'Connor, but at the time it assumed the end was near. Thus Kleinman and Rothkopf could have gambled on receiving even more casual treatment than Dalitz and Tucker—but they didn't believe in gambling. Both had been convicted. The same easy evasions or outright lies their colleagues got away with would have left them subject to perjury charges. For certain facts were on the record and would have to be admitted.

Rather than face perjury charges, Kleinman and Rothkopf decided on contempt charges. Rothkopf had once blazed a trail in legal precedent and escaped a prison sentence. He had confidence his attorneys could repeat if necessary.

Abner "Longie" Zwillman, that old associate from the days of the Reinfeld Syndicate, stepped down from the witness chair in Washington, and Morris Kleinman stepped up. Represented by William J. Corrigan and Timothy McMahon of Cleveland, he gave his name and address, and demanded permission to read a statement. It was granted. The statement objected to the proceedings being televised. Kleinman noted:

"I feel this way: If the television industry wants me to aid in boosting the sale of TV sets, and the sponsors, saloons, and restaurants want my aid in boosting their business, I am entitled to be consulted just the same as any other American amusement industry. . . ."

Kefauver interrupted to say, "Well, Mr. Kleinman, if we had

been able to find you in Cleveland, where we tried very hard to get you in, you wouldn't have had this difficulty, because that hearing, I don't think, was televised."

The television lights were turned off, but Kleinman refused to talk because the radio broadcast was continuing. Senator Charles W. Tobey lost his temper. He told Kleinman:

"You skulked away somewhere and you won't tell us where you were, but I am telling you something: The people of this country are outraged at the likes of you, and when we all get through you will come up to the bar of justice. I promise you that. You wait and see. This is 'only the beginning' as they say in the Showboat."

Kleinman replied by refusing to open his mouth. No Fifth Amendment plea of self-incrimination here. He sat mute.

Rothkopf followed Kleinman to the stand—and put on an identical act. Even the statement he read was identical. When finished he, too, sat mute.

Both men were ordered arrested and held on bond of $10,000 each. The case went to court. Rothkopf's confidence in his attorneys rather than Tobey's faith in an outraged people seemed most justified when, on October 6, 1952, District Court Judge H. A. Schweinhaut ruled the refusal to testify was "justifiable disobedience."

The judge added, "It is said that these are hardened criminals who were not, and could not have been, affected by the paraphernalia and atmosphere to which they were exposed. That may be so, but the court cannot take judicial notice that it is so. Moreover, it cannot be said that for John, who is a good man, one rule applies, but for Jack, who is not a good man, another rule applies."

Courts now hold that freedom of speech does not include the right to shout "fire" in a crowded theater, but the "right" of the individual to set fire to the theater has not been seriously curtailed.

3.

The interstate nature of organized crime was illustrated in Arizona as well as Nevada. Butts Lowe provided one item when in April, 1953, he returned home to run the usual syndicate operation at the Kentucky Derby. Unfortunately for Lowe, he became caught up in the state's other favorite sport—politics.

The gentleman from Tucson, the gold of his ring showing white against the desert tan of his nose, set up operations in the Chicken Trail Inn near Louisville. The basement provided ample space for a full-sized dice table. Yellow chips cost $1.00 and red chips $5.00.

All would have been well had not Kentucky been undergoing an unusually bitter factional struggle that had caused repercussions even in Newport.

Former Governor A. B. "Happy" Chandler, a man who believed in the right, as he put it, "of the people to have it dirty," was preparing to return to power. To prove he didn't agree with Chandler, Governor Lawrence Wetherby had been forced to order state police to raid the Latin Quarter and the Lookout House near Newport.

Wetherby's problems were complicated by the fact that his elected attorney general was Jiggs Buckman, a Chandler supporter.

Unaware of the political climate, Lowe opened the temporary casino in the Chicken Trail Inn on April 24. He thought protection could be secured by having the brother-in-law of Governor Wetherby in the joint. But state police raided the place at 11:30 P.M. and arrested everyone.

The *Courier-Journal* was tipped in advance. Photographer Bud Kamenish's camera was broken, but other photographers got some pictures, and one of them showed the governor's brother-in-law. The evidence was important, for on the way to jail the in-law was "lost." After the picture was printed, he was rearrested on a warrant. Later, both pictures and the negatives vanished from separate files at the newspaper.

It was an interesting episode that cost Lowe a small fine and the money he might have made from Derby suckers. He went back to Arizona not knowing, however, that the complainant listed on the official report of the raid was "General" Buckman.

Something of Kentucky's interest in horse racing apparently was transmitted by Lowe to his partner, Peter Licavoli. Shortly after taking over the Grace Ranch, Licavoli organized Catalina Racing Stables and started acquiring thoroughbreds.

Finally, he even bought horses from James Brink, Cleveland Syndicate partner in the Lookout House and Beverly Hills Club in Newport. Brink, who liked to be called a "sportsman," owned Lookout Stud Farm. In 1950 Licavoli bought four horses from Brink for $25,000. Other Brink horses, such as Devil Red, were vanned to Tucson and put in stud there.

From owning race horses, it was only a short step to owning race tracks. The advantages had been apparent to gangsters since Owney "the Killer" Madden took over Tropical Park and Dutch Schultz operated what the syndicate called River Downs.

In September, 1953, Captain James Hamilton of the Los Angeles Police Department, Tucson Police Chief Don Juan Hays, and Lieutenant Joseph Sheridan of the Michigan State Police got together at the International Association of Chiefs of Police convention in Detroit and exchanged information. Their talk centered around a meeting of top gangsters at Licavoli's ranch. Informants had whispered the purpose of the meeting was to plan a new race track. A former governor of Michigan was mentioned as having attended the meeting.

Investigation began in the three cities. First word was the track would be at Las Vegas, where Cleveland capital was said to be interested. In Los Angeles, Hamilton, head of the Intelligence Unit, sought more information. But when word came, it came not from Las Vegas but from downtown.

A George Bourke, chauffeur for Mr. and Mrs. Harry Illions, told a strange story. His employers, he said, asked him to go to a Los Angeles bank and endorse a check for $34,000. Mrs. Illions explained "the man who signed the check had a very jealous and suspicious wife and it would cause trouble if she [the wife] saw Mrs. Illions' name on the canceled check, or even Mr. Illions'. As that seemed logical and my employers had always treated me well, I saw nothing wrong in agreeing to it."

They went to the bank, waited around until a banker Mrs.
Illions'. As that seemed logical and my employers had always
conference and made several telephone calls to Tucson, Arizona."

The four—Illions, Mrs. Illions, the banker, and the chauffeur —finally went downstairs, "where the banker gave me the check which I signed in their presence. After I signed the check, the banker took it, went upstairs, and returned carrying the money which he gave to Mrs. Illions. She wrapped it in a piece of newspaper and put it in her pocketbook. Then we went upstairs and were let out by a guard as it was past banking hours. . . ."

The check, it was discovered later, was made out to "cash" by Peter Licavoli. The $34,000 in cash arrived next day—October 8, 1953, in Tucson. A messenger delivered it to the Southern Arizona Bank & Trust Company, and it was credited to the account of the Rillito Race Track.

A bank official later admitted that Mrs. Illions had called on October 7 from Los Angeles and promised to send the money next day. In return for the money, Mrs. Illions was issued paid-up stock in the race track.

This bit of intelligence led to a full-scale investigation of the long-established track. It was discovered the track had been sold in June to Rillito Race Track, Inc., an Arizona corporation. When the track applied for a permit to conduct races during the 1953–54 season, the stockholders of record were Mrs. Ruth Illions and several other well-known citizens. Mrs. Illions, a resident since 1930, was a person of moderate means. So the permit was granted.

The investigation revealed that while Mrs. Illions had made less than $10,000 in two years, she suddenly was able to acquire nearly $100,000 in stock. This happened after the new corporation got permission on October 13 to sell $150,000 of stock to the public. As a result, six groups ended up with control. When the groups were investigated, it became apparent that only one group, that headed by Peter Licavoli, had control. The others, including Mrs. Illions, were fronts for Licavoli.

Mrs. Illions turned up in Las Vegas in 1960. Her Cameron Concessions Company, with help from what Las Vegas police tactfully referred to as "a former powerful political figure," obtained concession rights at the new convention center. But someone recalled that Mrs. Illions was a front for Peter Licavoli. They asked her about it and she said rather than have publicity she would quit her business and go home.

But some folks in Arizona had better luck in establishing themselves in Las Vegas. The Goldwaters of Phoenix made a deal with Moe Dalitz at the Desert Inn, and installed a plush clothing store there. It was first called Goldwater's of Las Vegas, but after Barry became a serious contender for the office of President of the United States, its name was changed to D.I. Distinctive Apparel.

The Goldwaters apparently agreed with Jimmy Hoffa who once remarked, "Moe Dalitz is a respected citizen."

The investment in the Desert Inn had paid off.

CHAPTER SEVENTEEN

> I understand a very large amount of capital is going into Havana and building up in amusements, etc.
>
> *Jesse W. Smith, 1922*

THE DESERT INN was the opening wedge in Las Vegas, as the Beverly Hills had been in Kentucky, and the Thomas Club in Cleveland.

Within a relatively short period a bewildering group of related companies came into being. The same thing had happened in Cleveland and in Newport, but there the syndicate worked in shadows. In Las Vegas, where respectability ruled, the complicated structure was erected in the daylight and was all the more imposing for being so clearly visible.

The so-called Desert Inn complex grew rapidly, and as this is written, continues to grow. In the first years a partial list looked like this:

Wilbur Clark's Desert Inn; the Desert Inn Operating Company; the Desert Inn Annex; the Desert Inn Improvement Company; the Desert Inn Country Club, Inc.; Golf Course Properties, Inc.; Desert Inn Manor, Inc.; Desert Inn Lodge, Inc.; Karat, Inc.; Desert Showboat, Inc.; Three-O-One Corporation; Colonial House, Inc.; Desert Inn Associates; A & M Enterprises; B. C. Enterprises; Paramount Homes, Inc.; United Hotel Corporation; Saturn, Inc.; Mercury, Inc.; Jupiter, Inc.; Dayland Company; Desert Inn Country Club Estates; United Subsidiary, Inc.; United Resort Hotels, Inc.; Harbor Island Spa; Nevada Building Company; Las Vegas Bowl, Inc.; Bowling, Inc.; Bowl Amusement Company; and Stardust, Inc.

This, as mentioned, was only a partial list. It does not include, for example, the D.I. Ranch, Inc., located thirty miles north of St. George in the southwestern corner of Utah, two hours from Las Vegas by way of Hoover Dam. Dalitz bought it as a retreat, a place for conferences and a place to develop that taste for big-game hunting he acquired with Big Al Polizzi back in 1937 in Mexico. The ranch had a landing strip just like Licavoli's ranch in Arizona.

Dalitz became too busy making money to enjoy the ranch, so in 1959 he formed a partnership with Rodney Leavitt, a neighboring rancher. It was a profitable venture. Dalitz contributed his vast grazing rights, money for the development of the land and a breeding herd, and was to share all profits and bear all losses. A portion of the land was retained by Dalitz, and he rented it to the D.I. Ranch, Inc., for $100 a month. Against this income, he once boasted, he could claim $6,000 in expenses.

With cash in hand, as well as money borrowed from the Teamster Union's Pension Fund through the good graces of that old friend James Hoffa, the D.I. complex expanded in every direction. It built hospitals, golf courses, downtown office buildings, suburban housing projects, and shopping centers to go with them. Much of the story is told in Wallace Turner's book *Gamblers' Money*. Essentially, it was but a repetition of what the syndicate did in Cleveland. Other gamblers at other Las Vegas resorts failed to match the "D.I. Syndicate," as it was now being called, primarily because owners came and went so fast there was little opportunity. At the Desert Inn, there was stability. In time, men like Dalitz came to be regarded as pioneers, and with each new investment their backgrounds faded.

Dalitz, it should be noted, divorced Toni in May, 1951. Presumably she wanted to stay and be respectable in the laundry business in Detroit. He moved to Las Vegas and in 1953 married a much younger employee of the Desert Inn.

Sam Tucker quit Newport in 1949, leaving his brother Garson to keep an eye on the unofficial but no less real interest in Kentucky operations. Tucker moved to Surfside, just north of Miami Beach, and bought a house on Biscaya Island for $55,000.

Purchase was handled for him by a former Cleveland city councilman, Herman Kohen, who had moved to Miami Beach along with other Cleveland politicians.

Kleinman found a home in Bay Harbors, just north of Surfside. There on Broadview Drive, he invested an estimated $140,000. Part of the cost was to equip the huge house. Mrs. Kleinman had become an invalid. Closed-circuit television was installed so Mrs. Kleinman could see any part of the house or grounds by flicking a switch. The property was also "bugged," so she could talk to anyone in any part of the house without moving from her bed. If these conveniences also served as security precautions, Kleinman didn't mind. He bought the adjoining lot and converted it into a status symbol unique even in that town of wealth—a $35,000, if you count the cost of the lot, putting green. A pole with a red flag remained in the hole for years, waiting for someone to use it.

Lou Rothkopf remained at his farm near Chagrin Falls, outside Cleveland, but spent the winters in Florida. Slowly, but perceptibly, Rothkopf was withdrawing from the syndicate's affairs, although he kept an eye on Cleveland investments. Mrs. Rothkopf was responsible. Blanche Rothkopf had been a good organization wife, traveling with Uncle Louie, sharing his adventures, enduring his show girls. Perhaps she resented his exclusion from the respectability of the Desert Inn. Perhaps there were other reasons. But her feelings of depression came to a climax on June 5, 1955, and she killed herself.

The same forces that pulled down Blanche went to work on Lou. His partners tried to help, and he was given the usual chance to invest in a huge new project. But Lou turned it down. Havana had no appeal. Miami Beach didn't have much either when Rothkopf went there for the winter of 1955–56.

In February, Trigger Mike Coppola's new wife, Ann, whose first husband once worked for the Cleveland Syndicate at the old Lookout House in Kentucky, gave a party for Rothkopf. Dalitz and his third wife attended. But the party was a flop, so much so that Trigger Mike beat his bride up when they got home. The blowout had cost $300, and the money had been wasted.

On July 17, 1956, back home in Ohio, Rothkopf was found dead. The official verdict was accidental carbon monoxide poisoning, but unofficially everyone agreed Uncle Louie had killed himself. His estate was valued at $740,000. The United States slapped a $576,000 claim against the estate, but settled in 1960 for $70,560.

Even assuming Rothkopf had no cash stored away in hidden places, Swiss banks, and safe deposit boxes, he had not done too badly. The syndicate turned out for his funeral, and then went back to the business of making more money. Bernard Rothkopf, the nephew, received a large bequest from his uncle and continued the family tradition at Las Vegas, but was never accorded the same rank enjoyed by Lou Rothkopf. More and more, that honor was going to Tommy McGinty. Conceivably, Chuck Polizzi might have taken Rothkopf's place had he desired, but Chuck was in ill health and having marital difficulties as well. He remained in Cleveland, away from the Desert Inn merry-go-round which seemed to spin faster every day.

Suicide is rather rare among top gangsters. Some, like "Legs" Diamond, have invited others to kill them, but the act of self-destruction runs contrary to the deep-seated optimism that keeps each gangster, big or little, hoping that somehow he'll beat the odds and escape the fate of the squares. It is therefore worthy of comment that two top Jewish gangsters died by their own hands within a space of thirty months.

On February 27, 1959, "Longie" Zwillman used a plastic extension cord to hang himself at his home in West Orange, New Jersey. He ranked as high in the Eastern Syndicate as Rothkopf ranked in the Cleveland Syndicate, and perhaps higher than Rothkopf in the National Syndicate.

A little more than a year before his death, Zwillman participated in a final act of cooperation with his old associates of rum-running days. He arrived at the Desert Inn on January 10, 1958. Sam Garfield, whose real name was Garfinkle, an old school chum of Moe Dalitz, also turned up as did Joseph "Doc" Statcher, formerly an associate of Zwillman in New Jersey.

The purpose of the meeting was to lease to the Cleveland Syndicate, the Desert Inn, the casino of the giant Stardust Hotel just across and down the street. The hotel, with 1,300 rooms, was the biggest in Las Vegas. It had been the dream of Antonio Cornero Stralla, better known as Tony Cornero, another ex-rumrunner and gambling-ship operator, but after putting millions into it Tony died of a heart attack. John "Jake the Barber" Factor of Chicago fame took over and finished the hotel. But he wanted to lease it to the Desert Inn crew—they had stability. So Zwillman, etc., who knew them well from old days with the Reinfeld Syndicate, came out to help arrange the deal.

Agreement was reached. The Stardust casino soon ranked third in the state in profits, ahead even of the Desert Inn. Karat, Inc., was formed to handle it, and who should appear as a manager and owner of a small piece but a man calling himself John Drew. Some writers who have cited Drew's presence as evidence of Chicago influence at the casino never heard of Jacob Stein.

The Stardust became famous for its Lido de Paris stage show. People jam the dining room-theater, sitting elbow to elbow with strangers at long tables, to watch nudes drop out of the ceiling on swings and, on stage, a jungle scene complete with an exploding volcano. Even without the nudes the show is spectacular —and draws thousands to the casino just outside the dining room.

Ed Sullivan was one of the stars who preceded Lido de Paris. He contracted in 1958 to appear for four weeks at the Stardust for a mere $25,000 a week. But at the same time he sold his farm at Southbury, Connecticut, to a corporation controlled by the Cleveland Syndicate, and ended with a nice capital gain of some $70,000. Next year the syndicate resold the farm at a loss of $109,000. All it got for the deal, in addition to Sullivan's services and use of the facilities for ten days when Kleinman vacationed on the farm, was the benefit of substantial operating losses in 1958 and 1959. Plus, of course, the $109,000 it could claim as a capital loss. And when you're making millions, it's important to have some deductions to list.

Legality was wonderful. When the syndicate's old friend, Louis M. Jacobs, president of Sportservice, which operates concessions at various stadiums around the country, needed quick cash, he appealed to Moe Dalitz. Back when the boys were trying to get River Downs Race Track on its feet, Jacobs had helped, so Dalitz was agreeable. A D.I. Operating Company check for $250,000 was issued to Sportservice Corporation at Buffalo. Sammy Haas, back in Cleveland, wrote checks for $150,000 more. The checks were deposited on December 30, 1958. By January 10, 1959, the crisis—whatever it was—had passed, and the money was returned. Just a friendly little gesture.

But the syndicate, while never overlooking a sure bet, had its eye on the main chance. Sam Garfield is credited with producing the man with the *big* idea. His man was the "Mad Russian" of high finance, Alexander L. Guterma, who said he was born in Siberia. Guterma apparently fooled Garfield; he certainly fooled Allard Roen, and he thought he fooled Moe Dalitz and the rest. He intended to use the syndicate, and perhaps get control of its gambling empire. Instead, the syndicate used him.

In line with the plot devised by Guterma, a holding company calling itself United Hotels, Inc., was formed on April 5, 1956. Guterma was going to sell the stock to the public, he thought. The Desert Inn crowd was supposed to turn over the physical properties of the Desert Inn, as distinguished from the casino ownership, to the holding company. Guterma put the Isle d'Capri hotel in Bay Harbors—the same town where Kleinman lived—into the holding company. The Desert Inn's physical plant was valued at $4,500,000. Guterma's hotel was valued at $25,700.

Apparently Guterma hoped to use the little piece of stock he got in the holding company in exchange for his hotel as a spoon to gobble up the giant custard. The syndicate found a use for his hotel, but it had its eyes on other things too. Guterma gave some trouble when he discovered he was not going to make a financial killing. He even went so far as to put his 275,000 shares of 10-cent par value common stock—out of the 5,000,000 shares authorized—on the market. A few citizens snapped it up, and the syndicate had some difficulty recovering it. But, when the time was ready, Guterma and his schemes were dumped.

On May 9, 1959, United Resort Hotels, Inc., was formed. John A. Donnelly, attorney for the Desert Inn, held 30 per cent of the stock, and Roen and Bernard Rothkopf divided up the remaining 70 per cent. They entered into an agreement with stockholders of United Hotels to purchase all United Hotel stock. It was a complex transaction, involving another sale to a new partnership, Desert Inn Associates, lease-back agreements, and a lot of red tape. But in the end, Guterma and the people who bought his stock were washed out of the business, and everything was the same as before—almost.

The big problem the syndicate had hitherto been unable to beat derived from the fact that when you make a lot of money you pay higher taxes. The Desert Inn had made a lot of money, legally and above-board. If the usual business practice of paying a dividend were followed, the individual members would pay income taxes on their respective shares. Already they were in a high bracket, and a dividend would push them into a higher one.

The elaborate scheme involving United Hotels and United Resort Hotels served a purpose—to create a conduit to transfer dividend distribution into capital gains. The sham sale to United Resort Hotels allowed stockholders of the Desert Inn to increase the basis of depreciable assets from $3,600,000 to $9,800,000, thus reducing the amount of income to be taxed to the corporation in later years. They were able to withdraw $2,000,000 from the business in January, 1960, and lesser amounts in following years. Most of what they withdrew was taxable at the minimum rate of 25 per cent instead of the 52 per cent corporate rate.

Lawrence A. Wien, a New York attorney who later sold the Empire State Building, handled the deal. As Turner put it, "What Wien put together for the Desert Inn gamblers was a far better deal for them than the most flowery proposals that Guterma could offer. They not only have eaten their cake, they still have it, and each year the frosting gets sweeter."

All of which was true enough. But there was another cake as well. It might be called an upside-down off-the-top cake with a Latin flavor. While as modern as Lawrence Wien, its basic recipe was tested back in the days of the Molaska Corporation.

One of the men who helped bake it was Meyer Lansky.

2.

Meyer Lansky went to Havana about the time Bugsy Siegel went to California, and he kept going back at intervals. His first venture there in 1937 was the race track Tommy McGinty had been interested in. He also won the gambling concession at the Nacional Hotel. The casino was a huge place with more floor space for gambling than any joint in the Western Hemisphere. There was also a beautiful restaurant, but Lansky rented that to Cubans to avoid, in his words, "friction with labor."

The war broke up the party just as it seemed a gambling boom might develop. As Lansky put it:

"We stopped when the war broke out because after that there weren't any boats on the sea. And at that time you didn't have enough planes, and you couldn't live from the planes coming from Miami. You can't live from Cuban people themselves."

Much of Lansky's success in Cuba resulted from his friendship with Fulgencio Batista y Zaldivar, the sergeant who overthrew President Gerard Machado in 1933 and promoted himself to colonel. He ruled Cuba until 1944 when, to avoid a revolution, he gambled on a free election and was defeated.

Thus it was when the war ended that Lansky was not immediately able to pick up again in Cuba. Instead, with help from others in the Eastern Syndicate, he developed several elaborate casinos in Broward County, Florida, just north of Miami. Places like the Colonial Inn next door to the Gulfstream Race Track became famous. Meanwhile, back on the outskirts of Miami Beach, Gameboy Miller ran a joint operation called the Island Club. But the Kefauver blight closed the Florida joints, and Lansky cast longing eyes once more at Cuba.

During his exile, Batista found a home near Daytona Beach, and renewed his old friendship with Lansky, who lived down the coast at Hollywood, Florida. While the details are lacking, it can be safely said the shutdown of Lansky's Florida casinos in 1951, and the return to power of Sergeant Batista in 1952, was no mere coincidence.

The Eastern Syndicate bankrolled the coup by which Batista regained power with help from the Cuban Army on March 10, 1952.

Lansky knew too much about the Cuban people to follow his friend back to Cuba immediately. Batista had to be given time to establish himself. The investment planned was a huge one, and it could not be gambled lightly. Part of the process of establishing himself included restoring old ties with the Communists. The United States Department of State in an official publication, Number 7171, noted:

"The Cuban Communist Party has had a long and intricate history. For years it had a working agreement with the Batista government; indeed, Batista in 1943 appointed to his cabinet the first avowed Communist ever to serve in any cabinet of any American Republic."

And Robert F. Smith in his 1960 book, *The United States and Cuba*, put it this way:

"The Communists have had a foothold in Cuba for years, and Batista had working agreements with them at various times."

Economic conditions in Cuba were also favorable to Lansky's plans. As in other Caribbean countries and places such as the Virgin Islands, sugar and sugar cane no longer were king. Thus it was that Batista could raise the old shout that the tourist industry offered economic salvation, and to have tourists one must provide gambling.

Gambling had long been legal, but as Lansky had found in the thirties, there was too much competition and too many restrictions to permit operations Vegas style. So Lansky had Batista change the laws to permit a casino only in a nightclub or hotel worth $1 million or more. He also arranged tax advantages and other financial help wanted by Lansky. For as the Desert Inn crowd demonstrated repeatedly, no gambler wants to sink much of his own cash in a deal that might go sour. He puts in enough to demonstrate his faith and uses his credit for the rest. If necessary, he can always go bankrupt.

For Lansky, the $14 million Riviera was built, with government-controlled Cuban banks putting in at least $6 million of the total.

Other new rules enabled pit-bosses, stickmen, and dealers to be classed as "technicians"—which they surely were—who could be admitted under two-year visas instead of the six-month visas workmen obtained. Import duties were waived on building materials brought into Cuba, an important item in that the old duties were sometimes 70 per cent of the total cost. And, finally, the government taxes were set very low—a casino license cost only $25,000, and 20 per cent of the profit. In Cuba, that was low indeed.

On slot machines the cut was a bit different. They became the special province of Batista's brother-in-law, the Cuban sports director, and he took half.

Other big gamblers might have to wait awhile before they could cut in on the boom which now developed, but not Lansky's old partners from Cleveland. While Havana's skyline changed as towering new hotel-casinos were built, the Cleveland boys simply took over the old Nacional. They fixed it up, and using the knowledge gained in thirty years of experience, made it into the nicest place in Cuba. As Mary Hemingway wrote in an article describing the pre-Castro Cuba:

> Many North Americans who lived in the fashionable west end of Havana and amused themselves at the Yacht Club or the Country Club, seldom came further into town for festive

evenings than the Hotel Nacional, which was THE [emphasis hers] place for gambling, the house take being 1 or 2 per cent less than at other gaming places. It also had plenty of bars, a staff that never changed and always remembered you, good music, first-class entertainment, and that great terrace upstairs looking out to the gardens with their palms, the Malecon, the sea and the sky.

On August 25, 1955, a corporation known as Wilbur Clark's Casino Internacional was organized under the laws of Cuba. Stock was held equally by Dalitz, Kleinman, Tucker, McGinty, and Clark.

The original capital was $45,000, but, in addition, $450,000 was supplied in the name of that nonresident George Francis of Haiti and Mexico. He "loaned" the money with the understanding, it was said, that he would acquire 50 per cent in the holding company to be organized to operate the casino.

On November 3, 1955, the Casino Internacional entered into a sublease agreement with Inter-Continental Hotels Corporation of Cuba, a subsidiary of Pan-American World Airways, to operate a gambling casino at the Hotel Nacional in Havana. Actual casino operations started January 19, 1956.

It was at this point the Cleveland Syndicate began to use Alexander Guterma and his United Hotels in ways Guterma had not dreamed. One day after United Hotels was incorporated, Mohawk Securities Corporation was organized on April 6, 1956, under the laws of Panama. All of the issued stock of Wilbur Clark's Casino Internacional was transferred to Mohawk Securities.

One half of the stock was issued to George Francis, and the remainder was divided equally between Dalitz, Kleinman, Tucker, McGinty, and Clark. Since the stock ownership of the American citizens was not more than 50 per cent, Mohawk qualified as a foreign holding company, and, as such, its earnings were not subject to United States income taxes. Just as important, its income was not subject to audit.

Sam Tucker moved to Havana, retaining, however, his home

in Surfside, and managed the over-all operation as years before he had managed the Beverly Hills Club in Newport. Jake Lansky, brother of Meyer, was casino manager and represented his brother in the operation. Years before, Meyer had used his father-in-law, Moses Citron, to represent him in Molaska.

Mohawk set up two bank accounts within the continental United States. One was with the Bank of Miami Beach and the other with the Union National Bank in Newark, New Jersey. Deposits at each totaled about $1 million a year.

The Union National Bank funds were used primarily to invest in Morrell Park, a huge housing development in northeast Philadelphia. McGinty and Roen represented the syndicate in this use of a legitimate outlet for gambling funds.

The Bank of Miami Beach served other purposes, as the case of Meyer Binder, of Gary, Indiana, illustrated. Binder lost rather heavily gambling at the Desert Inn and the Stardust, and wrote several checks. Four of them were ultimately endorsed by Mohawk Securities Corporation.

The picture developed—and the use the syndicate had for Guterma's Isle d'Capri became obvious. It operated a small casino—and a small one was all that was needed. Its bank account was the important thing.

Into Mohawk's account at Miami Beach converged three streams of gambling profits—cash and checks—from Havana, from Las Vegas, from the Isle d'Capri. The check system made possible for the first time an organized off-the-top draining of cash.

A gambler loses $10,000. He does or doesn't have the cash. In any case, someone suggests he pay by check.

In the "drop-boxes" underneath the gambling tables are vast sums lost by other players. At the end of the shift, the money therein is taken into a counting room and counted. Nevada officials have the right to watch. The Internal Revenue Service, at the time of this writing, doesn't have a similar right. But, in any case, until that money is counted, its total is unknown. When it is counted, taxes must be paid on the total. The process known as taking it "off-the-top," means removing some of the cash before it is counted.

With the $10,000 check in hand, and except for the check itself there is as yet no record of its existence, a casino boss can take $10,000 from the still uncounted money in a drop box. That money is then turned in as a substitute for the check. It is counted, of course, and taxes are paid on it, but in the normal course of events it would have been counted anyway. The check, however, is home free, representing $10,000 in uncounted and, consequently, untaxed money.

It could be mailed to Mohawk Securities—or carried by courier. Mohawk, remember, is a foreign holding corporation whose income is neither taxed nor audited. It doesn't have to explain to anyone why a $10,000 check appears in its coffers. At the same time, checks and cash are coming in from Havana and from the Isle d'Capri, and they are mingling, and mixing, and forming one large pool of funds.

In September, 1958, Jake Lansky arrived in Miami from Cuba. Customs gave him a thorough search and found $200,000 in cash and more than $50,000 in checks made out to Mohawk Securities and/or Sam Tucker. Lansky said cash and checks were for deposit in Mohawk's account at the Bank of Miami Beach.

During the three years the casino in Havana operated, a total of $1,530,000 in checks was drawn against its account in Miami. The usual procedure, bank officials revealed, required a telephone request from Sam Tucker in advance. The bank would order the desired amount of currency from the First National Bank of Miami—usually in $100 bills. Tucker would come in and pick up the money. His reason for wanting it was said to be the need to replenish the casino's supply. Winners liked to be paid in dollars rather than Cuban pesos. While this explanation sounds good, it would seem rather foolish for Jake Lansky to carry over $200,000 in cash, just so Tucker could carry it back.

To complete the arrangement whereby the $10,000 check originally offered in payment of gambling losses at Las Vegas and sent to Mohawk made its untaxed way into the private vaults of the syndicate, Tucker would need only to cash a $10,000 check against Mohawk and divide the currency.

Officials know this type of thing happens every day. The Cleveland Syndicate, as well as every other group dealing in so-called "black money," employs couriers who carry fortunes about the country to the various persons getting a cut.

The couriers also take cash to numbered bank accounts in Switzerland, in Panama, and, more recently, in Nassau. It goes, this money off-the-top, to be returned in the form of legitimate investments by dummy corporations set up for the purpose.

Mohawk Securities, with both Havana and Las Vegas to draw upon, became so rich it had to set up its separate bank account in Newark and invest an estimated $1 million in Morrell Park, a housing development so large it was designed to contain 17,000 dwelling units and 68,000 people. The design was so unique the American Conservation Association, a nonprofit group supported by the Rockefeller Foundation, featured it in a book, *Cluster Development*. Laurance Rockefeller wrote the Foreword.

Guterma, who of course had reason to be unhappy because the syndicate members were not quite the suckers he thought, once told federal investigators he learned the off-the-top "skim" at the Desert Inn alone was $6 million a year.

An example of something was uncovered in an investigation which disclosed that on August 5, 1960, Morris Kleinman purchased a cashier's check at the Bank of Las Vegas, payable to himself, in the amount of $299,682.07. On November 30, 1960, the check was cashed by George Gordon after Kleinman endorsed it. Gordon, well known as a Newport "front" for the syndicate, has won for himself in recent years the reputation of a man on the move. He travels all over the United States, and once or twice a year to Europe. What he did with the almost $300,000 is not a matter of record. At the time he received the money he was on the payroll of the Desert Inn—his salary, $5,000 a year. In 1961, he got a $1,700 raise, and a new job in the South Florida numbers racket.

There was also the case of William Graham, who sold the Golden Hotel in Reno and received a promissory note for $500,-000. In 1956, the note had been paid down to $346,000, but Graham needed cash and he discounted the note for $200,000. He said he was paid by Moe Dalitz, and the note was assigned to the casino in Havana. The Desert Inn received $100,000 on the note prior to late 1958 when the Golden Hotel was refinanced and the balance of $246,000 was settled for $175,000. A profit to the syndicate on this bit of shylocking of a neat $75,000. The cashier's check for the balance was made payable to Graham, who endorsed it to the D.I. Operating Company. The check was sent by mail to the Bank of Miami Beach—the same route followed by other checks—but because of the error in endorsement it remained there unidentified until Sam Tucker came in and claimed it for Mohawk. The endorsement, "Pay to the order of the D.I. Operating Company," was scratched out, and "Pay to the order of the Mohawk Sec. Corp., Sam Tucker, Treasurer," was substituted. When Graham's attorney confirmed that this was all right, the bank gave Tucker the cash. And there, as usual, the trail stopped.

But, unlike the cake baked by Wien, which provided for long-term tax profits, the second cake could not be had and eaten too. It depended, primarily, on how long the Cuban operation could continue. In other cities the length of operation depended upon how long the "protection" lasted. And in Havana, where everything was legal, the old rule still applied. For the "protection" there depended upon Lansky's friend, the dictator named Batista. And as the months passed it became increasingly obvious that Batista might not hold his power.

There was a man named Castro.

3.

Mary Hemingway, in that same article describing pre-Castro Cuba, ended on this note:

"Only a myopic visitor to Havana in those days could fail to observe evidence of neglectful government and of the greeds of the haves. But that is another story."

It was a story few people bothered to tell. If anything, they were reporting just the reverse. Senator Allen J. Ellender of Louisiana went to Havana in 1958 and declared himself in favor of selling arms to Batista "for internal security reasons." He "hoped" civil war wouldn't break out. This was just a few months before Batista fled for his life—but then perhaps Senator Ellender was myopic. He had failed to see the huge Beverly Club which Frank Costello, "Dandy Phil" Kastel, and Meyer Lansky operated for years just outside New Orleans.

Ambassador Earl E. T. Smith, who arrived in Havana in July, 1957, was a bit myopic himself. He wrote later of his first meeting with Batista:

"He impressed me as being a tough guy with bull-like strength and exuding a forceful, agreeable personality. Here was an extraordinary example of a virile man of the soil and of mixed antecedents, who had projected himself from simple sergeant to the Presidency of his country."

Was Ambassador Smith as naïve as he sounds? The answer must be—yes. One episode reported by Smith is indicative. He told how Foreign Minister Gonzalo Guell feared Smith might be anti-Batista, and checked in the United States to learn his background. Guell "received word that my father was a gentleman and well thought of in the United States. Dr. Guell was convinced that I would see things the correct way."

Mrs. Ruby Hart Phillips, then New York *Times* bureau chief in Havana, shared the general admiration for Batista. She knew him well, and when she wanted something done she could move the machinery of Cuban bureaucracy by appealing directly to the dictator. Her admiration was shared by many United States officials on every level—and for the same reason. Batista got things done—the things an official needed to have done at any rate.

As Fidel Castro grew stronger in the mountains and pressures increased, reporters flocked to Havana. But little real information came back—either on Castro's real strength or on the activities of gamblers who had overrun Havana. After Batista fled, an article in *The Nation,* a national magazine for intellectual liberals, said that in February, 1958, nearly 27,000 Cubans lived on the proceeds of gambling; 11,500 lived by or on prostitution; 5,000 lived by begging. The figures were based on a report by the Cuban National Council of Economy in 1958.

Indeed, most reporters found the plush casinos and the "name" entertainment a wonderful place from which to cover the campaign. They wrote glowing words, for example, about "Colonel Barron," vice-president of the brand new Riviera. If they identified Barron any further, it was to mention he was in the Army Reserve and formerly had been an automobile dealer in Chicago. They could have added that, back in Chicago, the gangsters knew him as "Charles 'Babe' Barron," and the automobile business he boasted was similar to the dealership Joe Adonis had made famous. They could have, but they didn't.

But if the press didn't know what was going on, the wise old boys who ran the Cleveland Syndicate did. They had their own sources—and they didn't like to gamble.

The big problem was how to pull out of Havana without alarming anyone. For the Cleveland Syndicate didn't believe in giving anything away. It had to find a sucker to buy its Havana holdings, and to do that it had to have a nonalarming excuse for selling.

By one of those happy coincidences, the Nevada Tax Commission just "happened" to discover "the gambling element in Cuba, many of them ineligible to hold Nevada licenses, has become an issue between the revolutionary parties and the Cuban government, lending to the situation an international aspect which though incidental could have serious repercussions here."

The Desert Inn crew and some other owners of record were told to pull out of Cuba. The order was issued in April. It was September 30, 1958, before Mohawk Securities sold the stocks of Wilbur Clark's Casino Internacional to Michael McLaney, and the Cuban adventure was at an end.

Everyone felt sorry for the Desert Inn boys at being forced to sell such a gold mine, but, it was obvious, they had no choice. Exactly three months later, on January 1, 1959, Batista fled Havana by plane and the men who had been feeling sorry for the Cleveland Syndicate took to their heels behind him.

In those last days of September, while Tucker was busy getting records, cash, and what other souvenirs he wanted out of Cuba, he called upon an old friend of Dalitz. Colonel Terrill J. Murrell, who ten years before had been trying to smuggle planes to Egypt, began flying out of the Fort Lauderdale International Airport. Most of his flights were to Havana.

Murrell found his old record was a handicap in his new assignment for the syndicate. He had been put on a suspect list, and every time he flew out of the United States he was automatically checked upon his return. In an effort to stop the practice, he made a formal protest to the collector of customs at Port Everglades, Florida. After investigating the reasons why Murrell had been so listed—the airplane smuggling case—the customs men doubled their precautions. And one day Murrell flew away and never came back. Rumor circulated that on his last trip from Havana with a load of cash, he somehow got lost and veered far off course never to be seen again. But that kind of report is hard to confirm.

Down in Panama, meanwhile, Mohawk Securities began to liquidate in January, 1959, and vanished formally on June 6, 1959. By another strange coincidence, United Resort Hotels was formed a month earlier on May 9, 1959, and began its task of buying up all the stock of United Hotels, which Guterma had sold. The Isle d'Capri became the Harbor Islands Spa, a health center. The next order of business, establishing the new tax arrangements, could proceed.

It should not be thought that the syndicate gave up such an effective arrangement as Mohawk without first investigating all possibilities. A casino in Haiti seemed to offer a possible new home for Wilbur Clark's Casino Internacional. The casino was being operated by Clifford Jones, former lieutenant-governor of

Nevada, and Jake Kosloff, but they had made the mistake of buying the concession from the people who held it instead of rebuying it from "Papa" Duvalier, the dictator. Jones wanted to sell while he could.

Since it was still Meyer Lansky's territory, Meyer was asked to lead a delegation to Port au Prince and confer with authorities. Peter Abeille, then United States commercial attaché in Haiti, greeted the visitors and took them in to see the American ambassador. The terms of Duvalier's offer—$250,000 plus 30 per cent of the profits—were discussed, but the official representative of the United States warned the official representatives of the Cleveland Syndicate against accepting on the grounds that political conditions in Haiti were "unstable."

The boys knew what that meant—and they did withdraw.

Jones and Kosloff managed to unload the casino on two brothers from Tulsa and a New York man, then had to fight a four-year court battle to get their money when the casino closed because of political instability.

Meanwhile, some gamblers returned to Havana and for a few months hope flared. It seemed Castro might permit at least a limited operation, so everyone went all out to cooperate with the revolution. Mike McLaney, the man who took over the Nacional, received the officer Castro assigned to his casino with open arms. The bearded officer drove McLaney around Havana in a Cadillac surrounded by beautiful girls, and it seemed perhaps the good old days were coming back. McLaney repaid his "friend" by letting him win at the gaming tables—an old custom anyway. Months later, after Castro cracked down and all gambling ceased, McLaney learned his friend was a complete phony. He had grown a beard after Batista fled, and conned Castro as well as the gambler into thinking he had been a loyal comrade all along.

Back in Surfside, Sambo Tucker must have laughed out loud.

CHAPTER EIGHTEEN

Merry Christmas
Morris Kleinman, 1964

It was business as usual in the sixties. The men who had begun as rumrunners in the twenties never rested from their labors, never paused to savor their victories, and never brooded over their defeats.

For the sixties brought defeats. The major one was in Newport, where the syndicate had ruled for more than two decades. But times were changing, and the lieutenants who had been left to mind the store were unable to adjust to new conditions.

A revolt began brewing in 1957. Led by the Newport Ministerial Association, a reaction to gambling and the stagnant conditions it created grew slowly, almost imperceptibly. Until 1960, Sam Schraeder, John Croft, and their aides ignored the situation. They had seen reform movements bloom and die before in Newport, and this one seemed no different. When, at last, they decided action was called for, they used methods that had worked before. Much to their surprise they worked no longer.

By 1961 the Protestant ministers were joined by Catholic clergy and laymen. A political organization was formed. George Ratterman, who had played for the Cleveland Browns when they were owned by Mickey McBride, agreed to run for sheriff of Campbell County. He pledged to end gambling, and all reform elements rallied to his support—Protestant and Catholic, Democrat and Republican.

The gamblers still underestimated the seriousness of the situation. A nonsyndicate faction headed by Charles E. Lester saw an opportunity to gain some local advantages by taking command in the crisis. A trick that had worked well on several occasions was attempted again. Ratterman was drugged and taken to a bust-out joint in Newport. A photographer who had cooperated in the past was supposed to show up and take a compromising picture of Ratterman with a striptease dancer, but the photographer had changed with the times. He didn't show. An alternate plan was improvised. The Newport police cooperated, as usual, and Ratterman was arrested with the dancer and taken to police headquarters wearing a bedspread.

Gamblers, even the syndicate faction, were jubilant, but they had badly misread the temper of a community which had seen too many frame-ups to be fooled by another one. The stunt backfired. The entire county rose in anger. Ratterman had a pretty wife and eight children. He was a Catholic—a fact of importance in a community where many who had tolerated gambling in the past were Catholics.

One blunder led to another. The Cleveland Syndicate leaders dropped their varied affairs and for the first time in many years met in Newport to discuss the crisis. The veteran police chief, George Gugel, and his chief of detectives, Leroy Fredericks, resigned. But that only added to the flames.

The climax came when the striptease dancer changed her mind and told the whole story of the frame to a federal grand jury a week before the election. The jury indicted six people for violating Ratterman's civil rights. A special grand jury on the local level, with a special judge instructing it, returned indictments against officials and gamblers alike. In a last effort to change the public's mind by scaring them, the gamblers closed down completely, throwing as many people as possible out of work. For a while Newport took on the appearance of a ghost town and predictions were loud that without gambling it would become one.

But even that old trick didn't work. Ratterman won election by an overwhelming margin. The Beverly Hills, the Yorkshire, the Merchants Club, the Flamingo Club, the Belmont, the Latin Quarter, etc., remained closed. Eventually, they were offered for sale. Appearing as trustee for the Beverly Hills was Alvin Giesey.

After four years of Ratterman in office, Newport and Campbell County gave every indication they could recover from their long economic blight. New industry moved in. Much of the town was rebuilt under an urban renewal program. The "smart boys" who had not fled to the Bahamas or to Nevada still talked of the "good old days" but even they admitted those days would not return.

Garson Tucker, Sam's "kid brother," moved to Miami after the Beverly Hills closed, and Sam put him to work managing the huge Skyways Motel he controlled outside Miami International Airport.

Other problems arose when Alexander Guterma's personal empire crashed. He had involved Sam Garfield and Allard Roen in his investments, and for a time it seemed that Dalitz and the senior members of the syndicate might be drawn in as well. But after a complicated affair which led to perjury charges against a friend of Roen, one Roy Cohn, the syndicate escaped major damage. Roen was indicted and pleaded guilty, thus jeopardizing his position as heir apparent. He was removed from his post as general manager of the Desert Inn and given a title, "Superintendent of Construction."

But, on the other hand, the syndicate made new investments around Las Vegas and around the world. It also fought to conceal their extent. Some data leaked out. In 1964 Internal Revenue Service special agents sought to examine certain tax records pertaining to Wilbur Clark and Moe Dalitz. Attorney John Donnelley refused to provide them and the matter went to court. A delay of a year was gained, but in February, 1965, U.S. District Court ruled the records had to be produced. In making its ruling, the court reported several "findings of fact" about syndicate business activity.

The court disclosed that Clark owned one-half of Martinolich Construction Company until 1955, at which time he became owner of it all. Between 1952 and 1955 the company borrowed $450,000, without interest, from Refrigerated Transport Company. Refrigerated Transport, at the time, was owned by Anthony Martinolich—co-owner of Martinolich Construction—Martinolich's son, and Donnelley.

Martinolich and his wife also owned 60 per cent of the Martinolich Shipbuilding Company which, from time to time, loaned as much as $300,000 to Martinolich Construction.

In 1960 Martinolich Shipbuilding Company was dissolved, but the stockholders retained a ship's charter which Clark "and others" used to export slot machines to Germany in the name of Refrigerated Transport Company.

The plot gets thicker and thicker, as do most syndicate business ventures. The court noted that Dalitz had an interest in the Colonial House Motel in Las Vegas. In 1954, at a cost of approximately $200,000, Martinolich Construction was employed to build an addition to Colonial House. To get the money, Dalitz borrowed the amount from Refrigerated Transport.

Other confusing details were supplied by the court which concluded its findings with this fact:

> That when Martinolich Shipbuilding Co. was liquidated and dissolved, Martinolich received four $100,000 notes from the purchaser, National Steel and Shipbuilding Company; that the first note was paid, the second discounted by Martinolich at 15 per cent, and the third and fourth notes were assigned to Dalitz for $100,000, a 50 per cent discount; that Dalitz subsequently sold one of the notes for $97,000 and the other for approximately $93,400.

The court added a comment which well might be applied to many other syndicate deals:

> These intriguing bits of information of intricate and confusing financial transactions, a sort of "Tinker to Evers to Chance" financial baseball in which the taxpayers played an important role, do not, of themselves, prove wrongdoing by the taxpayers, but the transactions ought to be fully disclosed in order that the special agents may discharge their responsibility to the Government in determining the correctness of taxpayers' returns. . . .

The investigation continues and may bring into the open more details of "intricate and confusing financial transactions." While the details must, of necessity, wait on the investigation, it seems possible that an announcement late in 1964 that Clark had officially ended his long association with the Desert Inn is one result of the probe. In any case, Dalitz had become such a "local" man in Las Vegas, it can be assumed he no longer needed Clark to "front" for him in that capacity. Clark died in 1965. Wire-service stories called him a "hotel man."

The income-tax investigation referred to by the court was part of the "coordinated drive" on organized crime launched by Robert F. Kennedy when he became Attorney General. The campaign, while falling far short of its goal, achieved more in a short time than had ever been accomplished in the past. But before Kennedy resigned in 1964, the anti-crime drive had become almost an anti-Mafia crusade. Even J. Edgar Hoover informed the F.B.I. that there was a Mafia after all. For decades he had ignored it, but when Joseph Valachi gave it a new name, La Cosa Nostra, Hoover was able to not only admit its existence but claim his organization had known about it as far back as 1961.

Behind the scenes, other investigators were working, but on the surface, at least, attention concentrated on the Mafia. Writers attempting to put Las Vegas into perspective, explained away the Desert Inn-Stardust complex by claiming the Mafia boys from Chicago really pulled the strings. Stories circulated and found their way into confidential files from coast to coast, about how the "Wops" were "moving in." There were even tales of Chicago hoods literally chasing Kleinman and Dalitz about the casino. Some of the tales could be traced to a former publicity agent of the Desert Inn—raising the possibility he was still on the payroll.

For the Cleveland Syndicate, which hid behind the shadow of the Mayfield Road Mob for years, could not but welcome the emphasis on La Cosa Nostra. Let the public and the politicians assume Dalitz and Kleinman were nobodies—it was as nice as in Prohibition days when someone finally identified S. M. Bennett as Moe Davis. Especially was it nice at a time when tax records were being demanded and rumors were flying that government microphones were now concealed in casino counting rooms. If the investigators believed Dalitz was but a front for the Capone Mob—whatever that was—maybe they would investigate the Capone Mob instead of Dalitz.

So while the search for La Cosa Nostra raged about the country, the syndicate concentrated on one of its newest ventures, Garden Farms, Inc., and let the world assume its real interest was in raising tomatoes for Desert Inn patrons. And against that background this scene develops:

A caller at the Desert Inn executive suite blunders into a room full of clerks, stenographers, and accountants. He goes by a door still bearing, in 1965, the name Wilbur Clark, to the office of Moe Dalitz. There a prim, elderly woman says Mr. Dalitz doesn't give interviews. He broke his rule with that Mr. Turner of the *Wall Street Journal*—she meant the New York *Times*—and look what happened. After the way Mr. Turner twisted things, he isn't about to trust anyone else.

Besides, Mr. Dalitz isn't in today. He is in Miami. Seeing Mr. Tucker, perhaps? No, Mr. Tucker is in Las Vegas. Well, where can he be found? He has gone out to the farm to see how the tomatoes are coming along.

Downstairs in the casino, above the muted crash of the slot machines and hum from the tables, a feminine voice calls again and again, "Mr. Bernard Rothkopf, telephone; Mr. Bernard Rothkopf, telephone."

Let the scene change . . . to Cleveland . . . to the Theatrical Restaurant, where a short, shiny-bald Mushy Wexler pauses at a table to greet a visitor. The Theatrical burned in 1960, and Mushy rebuilt it at a cost of $1 million plus. The money wasn't wasted. It is a beautiful place and the food is the very best—so much so, according to Cleveland Safety Director John McCormick, that Mushy is considered quite respectable these days. Any man who can provide food like that just has to be considered respectable.

Mushy fits his new role. After all, Gameboy Miller is dead now and Bessie Miller has retired. He smiles, mentions the string of thirty race horses he keeps on Leslie Combs' farm down in the Bluegrass, and tells of improvements planned at Miles Park Race Track in Louisville. While there is nothing on the record to say so, Mushy is the new owner of the track. His only regret, he says, is he couldn't buy Churchill Downs. If only he had accepted an offer by "Mr. McBride," meaning Mickey, to set him up as a newspaper owner in Kentucky, perhaps he could buy the Downs.

As Mushy talks, sharp-faced men come and go among the fat, solid citizens. The syndicate seems to be catering to black hats and black raincoats these days. And, of course, the inevitable diamond ring. The Theatrical Restaurant, no matter how respectable, is still the social headquarters of the syndicate in 1965. . . .

Again the scene changes . . . to North Miami Beach . . . to a tiny shop on 163 Street. The shop sells bagels and coffee. It is a syndicate message center. A visitor tests the service by asking for the number of Solly Hart, the old-timer from Cleveland who roomed with Morris Komissarow before Morris went swimming in Lake Erie. The telephone number comes with the bagels—WI 9-1576—as, outside the window, the good citizens of America drive by in a steady stream.

Hart answers the telephone. His voice is gruff, but, sure, he's interested in a deal. Meet him at 8 P.M. at Jake Lansky's new place—you know, the Plantation Club on the Causeway. . . .

The glare of the desert replaces that of the seashore and the scene is now Grace Ranch on Wrightston Road outside Tucson. Entrance is on the left, across from a school. A sign at the entrance offers two-bedroom apartments and a four-bedroom main house for lease. The long, curving driveway is flanked with neglected cabbage palms—imported at what expense?—and native saguaros.

Also neglected is the oval track where Peter Licavoli once exercised the horses he bought from James Brink. The old landing strip is overgrown with sage brush. A Mrs. Childs, caretaker, says the place "was beautiful when the owner lived here." But the owner has returned to the suburbs of Detroit. You can lease his house, including the secret panel that leads through the wall of the master bedroom to secret doors in the walls of other bedrooms for a mere $250 a month, plus utilities. The apartments, which once housed a small army of hoods, are available for $100 a month.

Deep silence hangs over the desert. The stark mountains in the distance loom big and close, but Mrs. Childs tells you they are a day's horseback ride away. E. R. Lowe died here. Licavoli, by his own admission, made over $600,000 in real estate deals here. His brand remains, but he has gone. . . .

Return to Florida, to a subdivision known as Golden Isles in a town called Hallandale. It is next to Hollywood. There is one entrance to the subdivision, and a police substation has been erected in its center. Cars entering and leaving can be checked. Meyer Lansky wants it that way.

Meyer lives at 612 Hibiscus Lane. His home is a low, ranch-type building with a semicircular drive in front and a canal opening on the Inter-Coastal Waterway at the back.

A visitor presses a button. Chimes sound inside. There is a noise at a window on the right. The head of a blond woman appears. She refuses to open the door—afraid, she says, of robbers. She tells the visitor to slip his card under the door. The door fits too tightly; the card won't slip.

Mrs. Lansky, who was Thelma Schwartz before she became the much older Meyer's second wife, opens the door on a chain. With one hand she takes the card, with the other she clutches the front of a golden wrapper that matches her hair. She promises to pass on the message to Mr. Lansky, who is a much misunderstood man, she makes clear. You mention Sam Tucker, and she smiles. "Sam is a sweet man."

Finally she apologizes for her lack of hospitality. But Meyer has been harassed by the F.B.I., by reporters. Then too, the danger of robbers is very real. And Meyer is sixty-two, in poor health. He mustn't be disturbed. . . .

Tall mountains overlooking the Ohio shade the next scene. In a joint on the outskirts of Ironton, Ohio, near Chesapeake, a visitor is served a huge dinner of golden fried chicken—an amazing platter of chicken, french fries, salad, coffee—costing $1.03.

There is entertainment to go with it. A pimpled girl about eighteen is complaining to Ducky Corn, the man who made the syndicate's Chesapeake operation possible. Seems she has been arrested upriver in a joint. Ducky is short, dark, and stocky. The glasses with heavy frames seem out of place on his coarse face.

For some reason he doesn't talk to the girl directly, but uses a fleshy madam and several men to get answers to his questions. Everyone wants him to "fix the law." When the picture is clear, he goes out and gets into a 1965 white Cadillac. The waitress is smiling as she refills your coffee cup. "Everything okay, honey?" she asks. . . .

Go once more to Florida, to the exclusive little town of Bay Harbors. Note the two cars in the garage that extends the house in the shape of an "L". The door opens quickly as you sound the bell. You wonder if Mrs. Kleinman also has an electronic control, but, no, it is a little girl standing there. She smiles and shakes the long dark curls about her shoulders.

You are not at the door of the house after all, but, instead, at the outer wall enclosing a patio. A young woman appears at an inner door on the other side—the door to the main house. You return the little girl's smile and ask to see Mr. Kleinman. The girl half turns—"He wants grandfather," she calls.

From behind the woman comes the sound of voices—the voices of women and then deeper tones, cutting in, taking charge. "I'll see him."

The girl smiles again, hesitates, then runs across the patio. She disappears into the house with the woman. A man comes out.

Morris Kleinman looks like a cross between David Ben-Gurion and a tropical Santa Claus. Snow-white hair stands out from his head in every direction. He is clad in a baggy gym suit. "Been sweating," he said briefly. "In a hurry too. I'm late for an appointment with my doctor."

You try to tell him what you want. He misunderstands. "A reporter, is that it? You want money?" He is reaching for his wallet, but remembers the gym suit and his hand pauses in midair. You tell him you don't want money but information. He smiles. The smile is as sweet as his granddaughter.

"Look, it's Christmas. My family has come down for a visit. Call me after the first of the year." He takes your card, writes his name and telephone number on the back of it.

As you recross the patio to the outer wall, the sounds begin again in the house. A woman laughs. A blare of music follows you through the door. Christmas music. . . . "Joy to the World . . ." And, briefly, you feel a bit embarrassed. . . .

As you start toward your rented car, you recall another scene . . . a crowded little office at police headquarters in Cleveland. A command officer sits behind a cluttered desk, his face impassive as you talk. He is younger than Kleinman, but not by much. When at last he speaks, there is age in his voice and a weary cynicism in his words.

If you want to write "about niggers and communists taking over Cleveland," he will open his files to help. Those recent riots along Mayfield Road were communist-inspired. No question of that. But if you want to write about gangsters, about the old Mayfield Road Mob, about the Cleveland Syndicate—the answer is NO. You will get NO help—repeat—NO help from the Cleveland Police Department.

Why not?

Because men like Kleinman, Tucker, Dalitz, Rothkopf, and Polizzi may be gone from Cleveland, but they have brothers, sons, daughters, nephews, and cousins left. They also have friends. It boils down, says the officer, to this:

"We gotta live with those people. They're respectable now."

The memory fades as does the music. Across the street, water sparkles in Biscayne Bay. From this distance it looks clean.

INDEX

364.1
M563

63103

DATE DUE

APR 10 '68	APR 17 '68		
OCT 1 '69	OCT 10 '69		
DEC 17 '69	DEC 16 '69		
MAR 5 '70	MAR 4 '70		
MAR 18 '70	MAR 18 '70		
FEB 22 '77	FEB 11 '77		
APR 22 '77	MAY 5 '77		
DEC 8 '80	NOV 18 '80		

GAYLORD PRINTED IN U.S.A.

Lake Huron
ONTA
MICHIGAN
Port Stanle
Lake St. Clair
Rouge River
DETROIT
WINDSOR
Rondeau
LAKE
Lasalle
Ecorse
Grosse Ile
Amherstburg
Leamington
Point Pelee
Sister Islands
TOLEDO
Pelee Islands
CANADA
UNITED STATES
Fairpo
Bass Islands
Harbor View
Raisin River
CLEVELAND
Chagrin Falls
Lorain
Sandusky
Huron
Solon
Rocky River
Cuyahoga River
Chagr River
OHIO